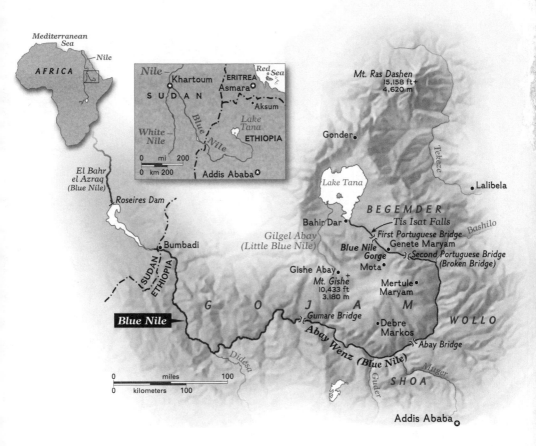

Mediterranean Sea

Nile

AFRICA

El Bahr el Azraq (Blue Nile)

Roseires Dam

Bumbadi

SUDAN
ETHIOPIA

Blue Nile

GOJAM

Didesa

0 miles 100
0 kilometers 100

Nile

Khartoum   ERITREA
            Asmara

SUDAN   Aksum

White
Nile   Blue   Lake
        Nile   Tana
                ETHIOPIA

0 mi 200
0 km 200   Addis Ababa

Red Sea

Mt. Ras Dashen
15,158 ft+
4,620 m

Gonder

Lalibela

Lake Tana

BEGEMDER

Bahir Dar   Tis Isat Falls
             First Portuguese Bridge
Gilgel Abay
(Little Blue Nile)   Genete Maryam
Blue Nile
Gorge   Second Portuguese Bridge
Mota   (Broken Bridge)

Gishe Abay
Mt. Gishe
10,433 ft
3,180 m

Tekeze

Bashilo

Mertule
Maryam

W O L L O

Gumare Bridge
Debre
Markos
Abay Wenz (Blue Nile)   Abay Bridge

Guder   Muger

SHOA

Addis Ababa

BLUE NILE

ETHIOPIA'S RIVER OF MAGIC AND MYSTERY

BLUE NILE

ETHIOPIA'S RIVER OF MAGIC AND MYSTERY

Virginia Morell

ADVENTURE PRESS

NATIONAL GEOGRAPHIC
WASHINGTON, D. C.

Library of Congress Cataloging-in-Publication Data

Morell, Virginia.
    Blue Nile : Ethiopia's river of magic and mystery / Virginia Morell.
        p. cm.
    Includes bibliographical references.
    ISBN 0-7922-7951-4
    1. Blue Nile River (Ethiopia and Sudan)--Description and travel. 2.
Ethiopia--Description and travel. 3. Morell, Virginia--Journeys--Ethiopia. I. Title.

    DT390.B5 M67 2001
    962.6'4--dc21

                                                    2001030245

Printed and bound by R. R. Donnelley & Sons, Crawfordsville, Indiana

Interior design by Melissa Farris and Suez Kehl Corrado

For my parents and Michael

and

In memory of

Preston and Dorothy Morell

and

Conrad Hirsh

one

~~~

A COLD WIND SWEPT OVER THE BROAD, GREEN FLANK OF Ethiopia's Mount Gishe, and Marigeta Birhane Tsige, an elderly clergyman in the Ethiopian Orthodox Church, stopped to pull his white robe tighter around his chest. He leaned on his wooden staff, eyed the grassy summit—another hundred feet away—took a deep breath, and pressed on. "It's not so easy anymore," he said. "Maybe I'm getting old." He shot me a twinkling glance from beneath his white turban, daring me to disagree. When I did, he tilted back his head and laughed. "Oh no, I am old," he insisted. "But I've learned a great deal in my time." No one in our entourage of guides, inter-preters, and tagalong, ragged children protested. I'd come to Mount Gishe with Marigeta (Holy Instructor) Birhane precisely because of his knowledge. He was keeper and tutor of the legends and lore sur-rounding one of Ethiopia's most holy places: the springs that give rise to the Blue Nile, or the Abay Wenz (meaning "great river") as the river is called here.

From our vantage point atop Gishe's 10,433-foot summit, we could look at the source of this great African river: limpid pools hidden behind a thicket of trees and shrubs in an alpine meadow. Beyond the springs, the river begins as a small stream, the Gilgel Abay (or Little Blue Nile). Like many another alpine stream, the Gilgel Abay cuts a deep, narrow channel through its meadow, spilling brightly over rocks and bubbling beside banks edged with wildflowers. There was nothing to suggest that this rivulet—one I had stepped across that morning with no more concern than crossing a city gutter—would grow into a river that has carved one of the deepest and widest canyons in the world, the Blue Nile Gorge, and that carries the water and silt that bring life to Egypt's dry sands, 2,750 miles away.

The many villagers below us on the meadow beside the springs probably did not know or care about either of these geographical facts. They'd come here, Marigeta Birhane explained, simply to obtain the springs' holy water. Wrapped in robes of white-and-green cotton, the supplicants had stacked every type of container, from blue plastic jerry cans and weathered gourds to old glass bottles and battered canteens, near the springs, and were waiting patiently for the priests to fill and bless each one. Some were seeking cures for ailments, others the Nile's protection. Later, a priest would annoint the "patients" as our interpreter, Ermes Kifle, called them—a daily baptism that leaves the meadow so damp and moist that a microhabitat of dark green algae slicks the ground.

"Yes, yes. They seek the power of the Abay," Marigeta Birhane explained. In exchange for a promised future sacrifice of a sheep or young heifer, the river's spirit might be enticed to cure a thousand ills, to bless a farmer with a bountiful crop or a barren woman with a child or to break an evil spell. Nonbelievers, or those who might try to use the Nile's power for devilish purposes, would be rained on with a plague of ants or have a serpent wrap them in its coils.

The Abay, he continued, may surface first here on the side of Mount Gishe, but its true font, its absolute source lies beneath the mountain. "The mountain floats on a lake," he said, sweeping his hand sideways to illustrate. "And from that lake flows the Abay. It starts like this." Leaning forward, he extended his left palm, and with the forefinger of his right hand traced a spiral like the shell of a nautilus.

In his youth, Marigeta Birhane had traveled far and wide in Ethiopia, singing for his dinner, as student-priests are expected to do, and studying with the learned men of his church. He'd followed the Little Blue Nile to the shores of Lake Tana, and crossed the lake to Tis Isat Falls ("smoke of the fire"), where the Blue Nile proper begins its journey, and he knew how different this river was from others. Other Ethiopian water courses ran in more-or-less straight lines from source to mouth. But the Abay wound like a mainspring through the land. "It flows in every direction—north, east, south, and west—making the sign of the cross," he said. "And it circles around Ethiopia, so it's like a herder boy sent out to protect the cows." He pulled back a moment. "You know," he said, "the Italians bombed us here [in 1935]. But they never defeated us. Why? They had the power of their bombs, but we had a greater power: We had the Abay."

I'D TAUGHT SCHOOL IN ETHIOPIA FOR TWO YEARS IN THE MID-1970S, and left only when the country fell into the clutches of a cruel Communist regime. I was young and thought the Communists would last a year or two, after which I would go back and resume my life of adventure in this exotic African kingdom. Twenty-five years passed. Ethiopia suffered through its Red Terror, when a military regime killed thousands of innocent people, droughts, famines, and wars. The Communists were at long last overthrown, and the country was now trying democracy. The kingdom I had known—the Empire of Haile Selassie, King of Kings and Lion of Judah—was a thing of the past, my years there something I seldom discussed.

People fall in love with countries for various reasons. It might be the way the light falls on the fields of Provence, or the sight of the impossible, unearthly whiteness of the Antarctic, or the sound of a gaucho whistling to his dog on the chilly Patagonian pampas. It might even be the blare from a New York cabbie's horn echoing down the city's glass-and-steel canyons. For me, it was the people of Ethiopia. They are strikingly handsome with large eyes, high cheekbones, even white teeth, and a proud, self-assured demeanor that only increases their attractiveness. Genetically, they are a mix of Arab and African, and that same rich, sensuous blend permeates their cultures. They are at once aloof and warm, open and secretive. They veil themselves with discrete behaviors and social graces, often talking through shawls or robes pulled across their mouths to keep their voices low, their laughter soft. Thievery and outright lying are abhorred, while dissembling and artifice are regarded as desirable skills. Secrets, intrigues, plots, and counterplots riddle every social circle, and you soon learn to not necessarily believe everything you are told. Amharic, the language of the Amhara people, particularly lends itself to such verbal subterfuge. Puns are easily devised, since the meaning of many words hinges on a single consonant or vowel. Change one sound and the meaning of the word and sentence change as well. Consequently, one of the most admired literary forms is the "insult poem," a couplet or series of couplets designed to insult your enemy, but so cleverly phrased that he or she does not at first recognize the injury. The Amharas call such witticisms *semna werk*, or wax-and-gold, referring to the lost-wax method of producing gold jewelry. When you removed the wax—that is, the words' literal meaning—you would find the gold, the hard, cutting truth. Not all semna werk poems carry insults, though. Some are about the vagaries of love or the twists of fate. Others are deeply religious.

Amharic remains Ethiopia's official language, although the Amhara people comprise only twenty-five percent of the country's sixty million people. The other forty-five million are a diverse group. Roughly speaking there are the Tigreans, whose northern border abuts Eritrea and who are closely related to the Amhara; the Somali people, whose homes are in the deserts of the east and southeast, touching the borders of Somalia and Kenya; the Omotic and Nilotic peoples in the lowlands of the southwest along the border with Sudan; and the Oromo-Borena peoples, who inhabit a broad swathe of the country from the southern deserts to the western and northern highlands.

From 1973 to 1975, I lived among the Amhara in the central province of Shoa. Like the Tigreams, the Amhara trace their roots to the ancient Axumite Empire, a powerful kingdom that had traded with Rome and once extended across the Red Sea to Yemen. Legend holds that the Queen of Sheba traveled from here to Jerusalem to meet King Solomon. He tricked her into sleeping with him and from their union a boy was born, Menelik, the first king of Ethiopia. Later, in the third century, according to tradition, two shipwrecked Syrian boys converted Emperor Ezanas to Christianity, making Ethiopia the first country to accept the new religion.

In part that long history gives the Ethiopians their appealing self-confidence, which also stems from the fact that Ethiopia has never been colonized. It was the sole African country to escape this fate. Between 1935 and 1941, Italian forces had occupied Ethiopia, but that was not the same as falling beneath the soul-grinding heel of a colonist's boot, and Ethiopians did not regard white people as their superiors. Some Ethiopians might bow to you, but that is only in recognition of your social standing—and even as they bow, they might be cutting a "secret" fart. The wheel of fortune never ceases turning and one day, perhaps tomorrow, you might be bowing to them.

And then there is the Ethiopian countryside. Many people today think of Ethiopia as a land of barren deserts and starving people—and certainly parts of the country did and still do suffer from terrible droughts and famines. But other areas, particularly the highlands of the central provinces, are grandly beautiful and green. The high plateaus are ringed by soaring, weathered peaks, which fall away to desert lands, making the country feel as if it were an island—one so remote in time and space that on occasion I felt as if I'd been transported by a time machine.

In the seventies, traveling about the country wasn't easy, either, which further heightened its appeal for me. There was a single railroad, a handful of graded dirt roads, even fewer paved ones. Most Ethiopians traveled on foot, the luckier ones by horse or mule, along earthen trails. It didn't take long after leaving the capital city, Addis Ababa, to be off the beaten path and into the unknown.

I traveled to as many parts of Ethiopia as my teaching schedule allowed in those two years. I trekked to the summit of its highest peak, the 15,158-foot Mount Ras Dashen, rafted the crocodile-filled waters of the Awash River, and journeyed through the Rift Valley to the desert shores of Lake Turkana. I visited the key historical sites, including the ruins of the ancient Axumite Kingdom, where the heirs of the Queen of Sheba once held sway, the 15th-century fairy-tale castles at Gonder, and the rock-hewn churches of Lalibela. Once I'd even joined a small party of paleontologists on a day trip to the Blue Nile Gorge to search for fossil shells. Most of my trips had been short, weekend affairs, occasionally a longer two-week foray. Then in the spring of 1999, my editor at NATIONAL GEOGRAPHIC magazine, Oliver Payne, invited me to join an expedition led by Nevada Weir—a two-month journey into one of Ethiopia's most isolated and distant realms.

The Blue Nile? Of course I wanted to go.

First, however, one question needed answering.

When I lived in Ethiopia, the Blue Nile Gorge was considered one of the most dangerous regions in the country. It had had that reputation for years, even centuries, because of the numerous gangs of bandits—or the *shifta,* as the Ethiopians refer to them. Shifta hid in the caves along the gorge's wild shores; they either held you up demanding large sums of money or killed you—or both. During my first year in the country, a young American had attempted to hike the length of the gorge and was never seen again. No one knew what happened to him, but everyone thought the same thing: the shifta had waylaid him.

What kind of protection were we going to be given against these brigands? Oliver didn't know the answer; I'd have to contact Nevada directly.

I'd never met Nevada. She wasn't a NATIONAL GEOGRAPHIC staff photographer, but she was well-known for her globe-spanning travels and photos from Asia, particularly Vietnam. I rang her that afternoon and she filled me in on her expedition's details.

From the moment we began talking, I liked Nevada. There was a pleasant warmth in her voice, and she laughed easily. She had not traveled to Ethiopia or any African country for that matter, and she was excited at venturing into this new world. She'd heard about the shifta, too, but didn't think they presented a problem. Nor, she added, did Conrad Hirsh, her main contact in the country. He was arranging the trip's logistics, and had already scouted a good portion of the Blue Nile Gorge. He would also be the head guide on the river portion of our expedition.

Conrad Hirsh! This was almost too good to be true. Conrad was a dear and close friend, I told Nevada, and I was elated to hear that he was to be our guide. I'd met him when I was teaching at the university in Addis Ababa, but Conrad had already lived in Ethiopia for a good decade before that. He arrived as a Peace Corps volunteer, returned briefly to the States, but couldn't live without Ethiopia. A brilliant mathematician, he gave up a promising career in academia to teach math to the students at Haile Selassie I University (now Addis Ababa University) and to live in the country he loved. He spoke and wrote Amharic like a native, and even had a passable knowledge of Ge'ez, the Ethiopian equivalent of Latin. Later, he'd left the university to work as a guide, leading pioneering white-water rafting expeditions on Ethiopian and other African rivers. Slightly built, but strong and sinewy with an academic's gentle manner, he was now in his sixties and a legendary figure. Few people knew the country as well as he did or were as comfortable in its remoter regions. If Conrad was confident that the shifta were no longer a problem on the Blue Nile, then I would not worry either.

Nevada laid out the general plan. She'd put together a small team, including me, Conrad and his Ethiopian assistants, a businessman and old traveling companion, Kelly Shannon, and two boatmen from the Mountain Travel Sobek adventure company. National Geographic Television also planned to send a videographer, Mick Davie. Nevada was looking for a physician or paramedic trained in emergency medicine, too. Once the team was assembled, we would meet in Addis Ababa in early September, then fly to the town of Bahir Dar on the shores of Lake Tana, where the Blue Nile proper begins its 560 mile journey to the Sudan. September marks the end of Ethiopia's rainy season when some 360 inches of water pour from the skies. The river in the upper part of the gorge would be at its highest level and consequently impossible to raft. Instead, we would hike past that section. Nevada estimated that we would need about a week to traverse these first 25 miles. Our trail would end at the river's edge, where we would be met by a support team with the rafts and supplies for the next month. She wasn't certain how many weeks we would spend on the river; she wanted us to have the time to meet Ethiopians and stay in their villages if we could. Eventually, we would reach the Ethiopian-Sudanese border where we would leave the river behind at the small town of Bumbadi.

"We're trying to do this in one continuous, unbroken journey," Nevada explained. "Other people have rafted various sections of the Blue Nile, but no one has followed the river from Ethiopia to the Sudan without breaking up the trip, or doing different sections at different times of year. It's a little bit of a concocted trip," she added, acknowledging that in the late 20th century it was tough to find any part of the world where you weren't following in someone else's footsteps.

And how had she come up with the idea?

"Oh, that's really Kelly's doing," she said. "He's mostly retired and loves to travel. And he likes cooking up 'dream' trips."

They were both residents of Santa Fe, New Mexico, she continued, and often met in the Downtown Subscription Café for coffee. One day he'd brought along his Atlas, opened it on their table, and turned to a map of Ethiopia.

"Have you ever thought about the Blue Nile?" Kelly asked, tracing its winding journey through Ethiopia. "Why don't we explore it?"

I had yet to talk to Kelly, but based on that question alone, I knew I would like him.

Only three months remained before we left for Ethiopia. I would have to buy some gear, primarily insect repellent and sunblock, since both bugs and sunlight were likely to be intense that close to the equator. And I wanted to read as much as I could about the Blue Nile Gorge and the explorers who had ventured there before us. For starters, I rummaged through our own African book collection and found one about the Nile that NATIONAL GEOGRAPHIC had published in 1966. Most of it was devoted to the White Nile, the longer of the two rivers. But there was a photograph—one—of the Blue Nile. I turned to it and stopped.

The picture was hazy, as if the photographer had shot it through a blue mist. It was an aerial view and showed a series of high, rounded hills rising above the river. There were no towns, no villages, no people. Just a big river snaking through the land and disappearing into an empty frontier. There was one narrow, two-lane road. It was in the foreground, and it wound down through hot-looking, green hills to a bridge, then charged up the other side, rushing to get across and away from that lonely river and gorge.

I showed the photo to my husband, Michael McRae. He's also a writer and was in the midst of planning his own expedition to a seldom-visited region of Tibet. He was used to traveling in isolated countries but fell silent as he looked at the picture. We were both thinking the same thing.

"It's really out there, isn't it?," he finally said. "I didn't realize…"

"Yeah. I didn't really realize it either, until I looked at this. But it's okay," I said, "I mean, I'll be okay. Conrad's leading the trip and he knows the country so well. And I trust him."

Michael nodded. He knew and trusted Conrad, too.

"You're right. If anyone can get you in and out of there, Conrad can. You're lucky to have him."

In fact, everything about the trip seemed lucky. I longed to travel in Ethiopia again. Conrad's presence meant that it would be a safe and well-informed trip. Plus it would give us time to renew our friendship and to talk about the changes that had come to Ethiopia. The Blue Nile expedition felt like pure serendipity, something that was meant to happen, and I gave myself up to it without a second thought.

t w o

≋

"**B**OY, I DON'T KNOW HOW TO REACT TO THIS...," RICHARD Bangs
wrote me a few days later in an e-mail message, after I'd sent
him one about the Blue Nile expedition. Rich was a good friend and the
most logical person to contact about the upcoming adventure. In the
1970s, he and several of his friends had journeyed to Ethiopia to start
an international white-water rafting company they'd dubbed Sobek after
the Egyptian crocodile god. I'd met him in Addis Ababa (and through
him, Conrad) just as he and his partners were tackling all of Ethiopia's
biggest rivers, the Omo, Baro, Awash, Tekeze, and of course the Blue Nile.
He and a small team had run a 150-mile stretch of that river in 1974,
and another group of his friends had rafted the upper part of the gorge
below the Tis Isat Falls a year later. That had been a bad trip. Bangs had
returned to the States to attend graduate school, and so was not present
when one of his closest friends, Lewis Greenwald, drowned. Lew had
been like a brother to Rich, and his death nearly ended Bangs's romance
with river adventures. I was still living in Ethiopia when Lew died. I'd

not known him as well as his wife, Karen, a pretty woman with auburn hair who was haunted by her husband's death. She asked me once if I thought "bones have life after death," and later hiked to the river's edge where the team had buried Lew to recover his body. He was Jewish and she wanted him laid to rest in a Jewish cemetery.

The Blue Nile was not Rich's favorite river, but like me he was enamored of Ethiopia and I thought he'd be pleased by my assignment. He wasn't.

Rich knew about Nevada's expedition. He was especially worried, as I had been, about the shifta. "Virtually every expedition that has gone below the Shafartak Bridge [one of the two highway bridges crossing the river] in the last 30 years has been attacked, and there have been several deaths." And the section of the river he had rafted in 1974 was "underwhelming to be generous…no wildlife, no culture, brutally excessive heat, no rapids, monotonous scenery…and we were attacked as well (not with rifle fire, but with rocks)…and, everything is supposedly worse from Shafartak down to the Sudanese border. [N]onetheless," his message ended, "the allure of the name Blue Nile is huge, and Conrad is a very careful guy…so, let me know if I can help in any way, and let me know what you decide."

Rich's words put me in a tailspin. This was not what I expected and I telephoned him immediately. Did he really think it was that dangerous?

"I'm not sure. It's difficult for me not to associate that river with death and dying, and I don't want to lose another friend," he said. "And the section that I ran was boring, that's the best I can say about it." He wasn't sure of Nevada's skills as an expedition leader, either, despite the glowing letter of recommendation he had written on her behalf. Rich knew he was giving me many mixed signals.

"Conrad has been there more recently than I have. What is he telling you?"

I'd also sent Conrad an e-mail, one full of enthusiasm about the adventure we were about to share. He was leading a river trip in Madagascar, however, and I had not yet received a reply.

"Well, I'd go with whatever Conrad says," Rich said. "He plays it safe and he knows everything that can go wrong with that river. He's the best guide you can have down there."

Rich did his best to end our conversation on an upbeat note, but he'd never fully forgiven the Blue Nile for taking away Lew, and even his hearty good-bye carried an edge of worry and concern.

Rich suggested that I call another old river-rafting friend from our Ethiopian days, Jim Slade. Jim had rowed that one section of the Blue Nile with Rich in 1974, and he'd been on the expedition that cost Lew his life. He might have a different opinion.

Jim now lives on a small ranch on the eastern slope of the Sierra Nevada Mountains with his lively wife, Barbara Bean. He was one of the founding members of Sobek, and like Rich had rafted rivers all over the world, pioneering runs down everything from Chile's Bio Bio to Zimbabwe's Zambezi. He knew rivers and river canyons probably better than anyone else, and he'd explored two stretches of the Blue Nile. What did he think about this expedition?

"Ahhh, you'll probably be fine. I'd go," Jim said. Jim has a slightly nasal, what-me-worry way of speaking, and it was easy to picture him swinging in a hammock, swatting at the flies with one hand, while holding his cell phone with the other.

"Yeah, the gorge is remote and that's why bad people go there," he said, referring to the shifta. "But even the villagers are a little bit testy. Some of them shot down a helicopter in the seventies. It was when WHO [the World Health Organization] was trying to wipe out smallpox. They sent in a vaccination team on a helicopter, and somewhere near the Blue

Nile, the locals shot it down. No one was killed, fortunately. The WHO team asked the people why they'd done it, and they said that they'd heard the [smallpox] shots would turn them into Muslims. You know, the highland Ethiopian Christians worry about that kind of thing."

Jim's temperament was different from Richard's. Both men had lost friends to river and climbing accidents and to sudden bouts of malaria, but Jim seemed to let these misfortunes slide stoically off his back. Yes, he'd loved Lew, and yes he could tell me exactly how Lew had died. The words came across steady and matter-of-fact, just the way, I imagined, Jim counseled his clients when they faced a big stretch of rapids or when a sudden storm blew up.

As far as I knew, Jim had never claimed any special extrasensory powers, but his tale started with his memory of a dream.

"It was the second day of our trip," Jim recalled. "We'd run into some pretty rough water the day before, Class V and VI rapids. Some of them were big enough that we'd portaged the boats. That night I had a dream. It was very vivid and the first thing I did that morning before leaving my tent was to write it in my journal." He read me the entry.

"Dreamed my brother died and that Lewis was my brother... Hoped it was not an ill-omen or presentiment of things to come on this trip."

"It was the first time I'd ever dreamed of anyone dying and I wrote it down just because it was so bizarre. It unnerved me a little bit, because I've had other dreams, vivid ones, and they always come true."

Jim read the passage to the others at the breakfast campfire, a group that included Lew and Conrad. Everyone agreed it was indeed strange, but saw no sense in halting their trip because of it. Besides, there was really no other way out of the steep-walled gorge than continuing down the river.

They broke camp, packed their two rafts, and pushed out onto the Blue Nile again. It was January, the water far below its September levels, and they faced another rough stretch of rapids. One torrent pushed the raft that Jim was on against the canyon's wall, and the boat flipped. "That was a hairy moment," Jim recalled. "Lew and Conrad were with me, and we came through okay."

They decided to make camp early and tangle with the Nile's white water after a good night's sleep. Most of the next day was much the same, one big white-water boil after another. Early in the afternoon, around two o'clock, they heard another rapid up ahead and stopped to scout it.

"It was pretty turbulent," Jim said, "and the canyon was real narrow. At one point, the river divided around an island, and it looked like our best chance was going down the right side. Our boat went first, and I was rowing. Lew was in my boat, along with Conrad, and John Yost [another Sobek founder]."

The crew in the second boat stayed on shore to watch Jim's run. He guided his raft down the chosen channel, but the river split again and swept the boat into a small pool that sloshed against the canyon wall. They weren't in any danger. The eddy, a pool of generally calm water, gave them a chance to look around and decide what to do next. Jim chose to row out of the pool and back into the rapids, but couldn't break away from the eddy or the canyon wall.

"So we decided that we'd all stand up and push the boat down the wall," Jim said. "We were making good progress until we came to this point where the wall stuck out about three inches, and we couldn't push past that point. The wall stopped us, and meanwhile, the current from the river was surging against the side of the raft. It started lifting the boat up the wall, so we all high-sided," jumping to the gunwales away from the wall to lower the raft.

It didn't work and the team realized that the boat was going to flip, just as it had the previous day. Inevitably, the current would lift the boat to a vertical position until it tipped over.

"We weren't that far from shore. Conrad actually was able to step onto it; he didn't even get his feet wet. Then John jumped and landed in about two feet of water. Lew was third."

By now the boat was at an acute angle, and it was clear that Lew's leap would land him in deep water. Meanwhile, on shore, Gary Mercado, a member of the second boat had managed to grab one of the stricken raft's lines. "He's built like an ox," said Jim, "and he was hanging onto our boat with everything he had to keep it from escaping" down river.

Lew jumped, going over the side where the line that Gary was holding was trailing in the river. The water closed over his head, and when he surfaced, fear etched his face. He managed to cry out that his life jacket was caught on the rope. The raft began to tip over, and Jim went with it, falling into the river and coming up just in front of the boat.

"There was a little rapid with a four-to-five foot drop that I had to swim, so I had no idea what was going on behind me. I didn't hear Lew's cry for help. I had no idea that he had been caught."

About a hundred yards beyond the rapid, Jim swam to a tiny gravel bar on the river's left bank. His team mates were all on the right shore. He spotted the raft coming toward him, upside down. It had apparently been caught for awhile in a whirlpool. Thinking this was a great opportunity to play the hero, Jim swam out to the boat, grabbed a line and threw one arm over the raft, and pulled it back with him to the same gravel bar on the left shore.

"It took all my strength to keep the raft from cruising into the next set of rapids, which were just around the bend," Jim continued. "I tied it to a rock, and a few minutes later I looked up, and here was John swimming across the Blue Nile. I thought that was pretty brave; I thought he must be coming to help me. But when he got there, he said in a panic, 'Lewis is missing. Have you seen him?' "

They searched under the capsized boat, but found no trace of their friend.

Only later did Jim learn that Gary had been unable to hold the boat long enough for Lew to free himself. The force of the Blue Nile had torn the rope—and their friend—from his hands. Lew had been dragged through the rapid while still attached to the line, and then disappeared.

"We had no idea if he was dead or alive," Jim said. "But when you're caught like that with your life jacket it's generally a bad scene. So many things can happen, none of them good. We hoped that somehow he'd beaten the odds, that he'd made it to shore."

The team regrouped, and while some portaged the second raft around the rapids, others went downstream, calling and shouting out Lew's name. There was no answer.

"We didn't find him until the next day," said Jim. "He was floating in a little eddy. He still had his life jacket on, but it was pulled up over his shoulders and head. He probably drowned when he was dragged over those little falls, and then his body was somehow freed.

"We cried then. There wasn't one of us who didn't think of Lew as their best friend in the world."

The team had no idea how many more days it would take them to reach their take-out point. So they buried Lew not far from where they'd found him, in a little hollow next to the Blue Nile. They covered his body with stones, built a small fire, and held a simple ceremony.

"We said our good-byes," Jim said. "And then we finished up the trip."

Unbeknownst to their little party, a shepherd boy watched the funeral proceedings from afar. A year later, when Lew's wife, Karen, came seeking her husband's grave, the boy was able to guide her to the exact spot.

"It was one of those fluke accidents, that's all you can say about it," Jim concluded. "I haven't had any dreams or premonitions about your expedition, if that gives you any peace of mind." He chuckled softly.

In a funny way, it did. So far, no one with a sixth sense was having bizarre dreams about us. I understood Rich's worries, but saw no reason to change my plans. I'd stay the course.

A few days later, a message arrived from Conrad. It sounded just like him: clear, straightforward, and succinct. Before leaving for Madagascar, he explained, he had checked with security authorities along much of the Blue Nile, and all the reports he received indicated the region was quiet. There were neither shifta nor military rebels about. That could change, but we would change with it, adjusting our itinerary as need be. He hoped I would join them on the Blue Nile.

I sent back a short reply: "Thanks for the encouraging message. I'll see you in Addis in September."

I sent Rich a message, too: "Conrad thinks the trip's okay. Thanks for your worries, but I'm going to the Blue Nile."

three

~~~

MOST ARDENT TRAVELERS ARE ALSO LOVERS OF MAPS. I find it as easy to get lost in a map's winding trails of red, blue, and green as in a good novel. When living in Addis Ababa, I often spent hours tracing routes through Ethiopia that I longed to travel. To the far north soared peaks and plateaus with strange, enticing names: the Simiens, Amba Mekdela, and Amba Gishan. The last was a tall and narrow sandstone mesa that shot skyward from the earth as if propelled by subterranean giants. Amba (the Amharic word for "mesa") Gishan had such precipitously sheer rock walls that Emperors of old used it as a prison. Every male relative who had the slightest claim to the throne was thrown into a cell on the mesa top, ensuring that they wouldn't engage in any political conspiracies. Only when the ruling emperor died was the next would-be king freed from his silver leg irons, and led down the mountain fortress's sole and closely guarded trail to assume the crown.

East of Addis, lay the fabled walled city of Harer, where sultans once ruled, and the empty wastelands of the Afar Desert, where as late as

1974 they still did. Northwest of the capital city rolled the green hills and valleys of Gojam, a mountainous land, rich in cattle, sheep, and horses. The people of Gojam apparently felt they had much to be thankful for or to protect, since their region was renowned for its many churches, priests, monks, and nuns—as well as its sorcerers and wizards. It was a land of plenty but also of black magic, and every Ethiopian who ventured here took care to protect himself from the evil eye.

Our expedition was slated to start in the heart of this spiritual-magical realm, at its capital city of Bahir Dar on the southernmost shores of Lake Tana. I spread open a map of Ethiopia on my desk. There was the lake, lying like a blue tear among crumpled, khaki-colored mountains. At the lake's nadir, the mapmaker had drawn a firm, blue line. "Abay Wenz" was printed next to the line, while the words "Blue Nile" were written in smaller type and bracketed. The river flowed east from the lake, made a hard curve to the south for more than a hundred miles, then looped to the west, before finally heading due north into Sudan. On my map, the Blue Nile was full of twists and turns, and had so many thin, blue tributaries and subtributaries feeding into it that, in places, it could have been used for an anatomy lesson: This is the artery; these are the veins; and these, the capillaries.

Tracing the river's route, I realized with surprise that something along its nearly 600-mile journey to Sudan was missing: dams. How had a river the size and energy of the Blue Nile avoided this fate? Nearly every other comparable river in the world was damned or had its waters diverted for irrigation long ago. Yet aside from a small conduit below Tis Isat Falls, which channels some of the river through a hydroelectric station, the Blue Nile remains uninterrupted until it crosses the Ethiopian-Sudanese border. Only at Roseires Dam, some 60 miles into

Sudan, is the river's steady surge finally halted, its waters corralled in a long, lazy reservoir. It seemed strange that Ethiopia, a desperately poor country, had not appealed for assistance to harness more of the river's power. Dams, of course, are mixed blessings. Because I live in the Pacific Northwest, a region that has seen the severe environmental damage dams can cause, I thought that the Ethiopians may have made a wise decision not to build a large one on the Blue Nile.

The absence of dams, of course, was what made our journey possible. After millions of years, the Blue Nile, at least in Ethiopia, remained a big, rangy river churning unbridled through the land. That was rare and something to be savored. But I couldn't stop thinking about what all this untapped water could have meant to the Ethiopians. Would not a dam and irrigation canal have saved some of the millions who died in the dreadful 1985 drought?

Turning back to my map, I followed the Blue Nile's lazy meanders from Roseires Dam through the hot Sudanese plains to its confluence with the White Nile at Khartoum, a distance of about 300 miles. The two join forces there, becoming the Nile and pushing on to the Mediterranean Sea another 1,857 miles away.

Unlike its wild sister, the White Nile has long been tamed. A dam stops its flow at Owen's Falls in Uganda, and a man-made canal for steamers and ships cuts through the swampy Sudd. Farther north, Egypt's huge Aswan Dam contains the Nile proper in Lake Nasser, and a recently completed 40-mile canal diverts the river's water into the Sinai Desert. Despite these impoundments, the White Nile has often been regarded by explorers and writers as the more glamorous of the two Niles. It is the longer river, stretching nearly 2,000 miles from its source in Uganda to Khartoum, while the Blue flows for about half that distance. And then there is the mystery and romance surrounding the discovery of the White Nile's headwaters. Like the best explorers' tales, it is a tale of endurance and rivalry, of intrigue and passion.

The source of the Nile had baffled ancient geographers since the heyday of the Egyptian kingdoms. Few things were as dependable as the rise and fall of the river. Yet where the river began, and why it flooded its banks in September, the hottest and driest month on the Egyptian delta, was a puzzle. No one realized, of course, that the upper Nile consisted of two rivers and that each had its source. Consequently, the first explorers thought they could find the Nile's font simply by traveling upstream as the Greek historian Herodotus did in 460 B.C. His is the first recorded effort to track the river's course, and he journeyed as far as the first cataract at Aswan. Another attempt was made by the Persian King Cambyses II, who once led a full army into the desert, but returned after losing most of his men—and without having found the spring.

Four hundred years after Herodotus, the Roman emperor Nero dispatched two centurions into Sudan. They followed the White Nile's flow until they found their way blocked by a vast, green swamp, the Sudd. There, they turned back. Other travelers eventually reached Khartoum, where they brought back reports of the river's great divide, how it split into two large streams, one the color of milk, the other slightly blue, a discovery which solved part of the problem. A few other ancient traders and explorers managed to venture even farther south, finally returning with sufficient information to allow the geographer and astronomer Ptolemy to draft a map in the second century A.D. He showed the Nile's course extending in a long, nearly straight line to Khartoum, where the Blue and White Niles met. From there, he drew the White Nile extending even farther into the heart of Africa, where it emerged from a large lake fed by the springs of a mountain range, the *Lunae Montes*, or Mountains of the Moon.

It was an apt name for a region few had seen and few believed to be real. For all practical purposes, the Nile's source might as well have been on the moon. The search was regarded as so futile that anyone bent on a seemingly impossible task was said to be "seeking the fount of the Nile" (*quaerer fontest Nili*).

More than 1,700 years would pass before the mystery was solved—and Ptolemy's map largely verified. By then, in the mid-1800s, the source of the White Nile had become "the greatest geographical secret after the discovery of America," according to Harry Johnston, a British explorer. To solve it, Britain's Royal Geographical Society gave a grant in 1856 to Richard Burton, a dashing, gypsy-eyed soldier, who had already gained fame by becoming the first European to enter in disguise Ethiopia's forbidden Muslim city of Harer. Burton asked a friend and fellow soldier, John Hanning Speke, to accompany him on his Nile exploration, and by various twists of fate, it was Speke alone who two years later stood on the shores of Lake Victoria (Nyanza). After gazing across the lake's waters, which were so immense that he could not see the far shore, Speke later wrote, "I no longer felt any doubt that the lake at my feet gave birth to that interesting river, the source of which has been the subject of so much speculation, and the object of so many explorers." Speke may have been convinced, but Burton, who thought that neighboring Lake Tanganyika was the more likely source, disagreed and the two men quarreled. In 1860 Speke led his own expedition back to Lake Victoria to confirm his initial hunch. He and Burton were bitter enemies by then, and when Speke returned to England in 1864, they agreed to a public debate about the source of the White Nile.

Speke was a quiet man, given to keeping his own counsel, and he apparently did not confide in anyone about how he regarded the debate. There was little doubt that the articulate Burton would be a formidable foe. He could be as savage with his tongue as he was with his rapier, and many thought that Speke was doomed from the outset. No one will ever know how the "Nile Duel," as some wags termed the debate, would have turned out. On the afternoon of their meet, Speke died from a self-inflicted gunshot wound while hunting. Some speculated that he killed himself rather than endure the public humiliation of being carved up by Burton. But close family members who found Speke dying insisted that it was nothing but a slip of his gun.

Twelve more years would pass before the journalist-explorer Henry Morton Stanley managed to circumnavigate Lake Victoria and prove that debate or no debate, Speke had been right. Here was the vast inland sea that Ptolemy had sketched from rumor nearly 2,000 years before, and close by the neighboring Mountains of the Moon, whose springs fed the lake. The puzzle of the source of the White Nile was at last solved.

FINDING THE WHITE NILE'S HEADWATERS DID NOT ANSWER THE BIGGER question ancient geographers asked: What caused the Nile in Egypt to rise and flood the desert with such dependable regularity?

The answer to this question, I discovered as I devoured historical and geographical accounts, lay with the Blue Nile. It might be the shorter river, but it carries a much greater volume of water. Modern hydrologists estimate that some 85 percent of the water and silt that flows into Egypt comes from the Blue Nile.

Intriguingly, the Ethiopians knew this long ago, several centuries at least before Europeans "solved" the mystery. But the knowledge of the Ethiopians—as well as the country itself—was lost to the world for nearly a millennium as surrounding nations turned to Islam, leaving the early Christian kingdom increasingly isolated in its mountain fortress. From the seventh to nearly the 16th centuries, the Ethiopian people slept, "forgetful of the world, by whom they were forgotten," wrote the great historian Edward Gibbon in *The History of the Decline and Fall of the Roman Empire.*

Thus, while the story of the discovery of the White Nile is one of drama and intrigue, that of the Blue is one of revelation, a drawing back of a veil that had fallen over not only the river but a kingdom and a people. The veil began to lift in the 16th century when Emperor Lebna Dengel sent a delegation to Portugal beseeching his fellow Christians for assistance against an Islamic jihad. The Portuguese helped repel the attackers, then set about trying to convert these Orthodox (and to the Portuguese vaguely pagan) Christians to Catholicism. They did not succeed, and were finally tossed out by another emperor, who then paid port officials along the Red Sea coast to keep out any Europeans who might try to venture into the Ethiopian kingdom.

Before this falling out, at least two Jesuit priests visited the source of the Blue Nile on Mount Gishe. Theirs was not a journey of deprivation or hardship. With local Agaw guides, worshipers of a spirit in the Nile's waters, to show them the way, they simply walked through a pretty mountain meadow to the springs. Father Pedro Páez, a Spanish Jesuit, was the first European to lay eyes on them. He was traveling with the Ethiopian king and his army, and took a day off to "discover" the source of the Blue Nile. "On the 21st of April, in the year 1618...I ascended the place and observed everything with great attention," Páez later wrote. "I discovered first two round fountains, each about four palms in diameter, and saw, with the greatest delight, what neither Cyrus, the king of the Persians, nor Cambyses, nor Alexander the Great, nor the famous Julius Caesar, could ever discover. The two openings of these fountains have no issue in the plain at the top of the mountain, but flow from the foot of it. The second fountain lies about a stone-cast west from the first...."

A more vivid description comes from another Jesuit priest, Father Jerome Lobo, who visited the font 11 years later in 1629 and had the good fortune of witnessing the "idolatrous" behavior of the Agaw (who were nominally Orthodox Christians) at their sacred spring.

"Once a year, their priest calls them together [on the summit of Mount Gishe]," Lobo wrote, "and having sacrificed a cow, throws the head into one of the springs of the Nile; after which ceremony every one sacrifices a cow or more.... The bones of these cows have already form'd two mountains of considerable height, which afford a sufficient proof that these nations have always paid their adorations to this famous river." The Agaw feasted on the sacrificed cows' meat, Lobo continued, and then the priest, after smearing cow grease and tallow on his body, climbed to the top of a pile of straw. One can only imagine the Jesuit's shock when the straw was lit. The Orthodox priest, however, was not the least bit perturbed. With flames leaping around him, he "harangu[ed] the standers-by," and finally emerged from the conflagration unscathed, an act that only confirmed the Agaw in their "ignorance and superstition," Lobo wrote with disgust.

Lobo could not convince the Agaw that their priest was merely a magician. But he did his best when he returned to Lisbon in 1639 to explain to Europeans why the Nile rose and fell as it did in Egypt. Other writers, he noted, had relied on "imaginary systems" such as strong northern winds and melting snows to explicate what was really very simple. It was the rain in Ethiopia, buckets of it that fell every year from May to October in the high mountains above the Blue Nile. Every tributary swelled with the seasonal rains as did the Blue Nile, and every stream carried with it some of Ethiopia's mountain soil. Fattened with this rain and silt, but channeled in its moatlike gorge, the Blue Nile rushed into Khartoum each June with such force that it temporarily held back the waters of the White Nile. From there, of course, it raced on to Egypt, spilling Ethiopia's waters, silts, and gravels over the banks, giving them life once again.

The Ethiopians knew that it was their river, their land that gave sustenance to Egypt. And at least by the 11th century, the Egyptians knew the truth as well. When droughts devastated their country, the Egyptians sent gift-bearing delegations to the Ethiopian emperor begging him to restore the river. For their part, the Ethiopian emperors weren't above using the Blue Nile as a weapon. They threatened to cut off the river when the Egyptians annoyed them, and several laid plans to build a canal from the Blue Nile to the Red Sea to turn Egypt into a desert. "The Nile would be sufficient to punish you," wrote an angry Emperor Tekla Haimonot I in 1707 to the Egyptian caliph, "since God hath put into our power his fountain, his outlet and his increase, and that we can dispose of the same to do you harm."

The Ethiopians never did alter the course of the Blue Nile. In 1999, nearly 300 years after Tekla Haimonot's threat, it flowed as freely as ever.

No account of the exploration of the Blue Nile would be complete without a mention of James Bruce. A colorful Scot with bright red hair and an outsized ego, Bruce was yet another seeker of the fountains of the Nile. He arrived in Ethiopia in 1769 and, knowing something about courtly behaviors, soon became friends with the young emperor, his vizier, and the queen mother. Ethiopia was then embroiled in several small, petty wars, and Bruce's plans of discovery were delayed for several months. Finally in November 1770, he made the journey to the meadow with the two springs. He and a Greek traveling companion lifted their drinking cups with water from the font and toasted King George III, assorted princes, Catherine the Great, and a pretty maiden Bruce hoped to wed on his return to Scotland. It's not clear if Bruce knew at that moment that the Jesuits had been there 150 years before him, or if he had simply chosen not to believe their reports. In his book, *Travels to Discover the Source of the Nile*, he derided Páez and Lobo as charlatans and always insisted that he was the first European to venture there. Historians say that he was not.

The Ethiopian emperor Tekle Haimonot II may not have understood precisely what the springs meant to Bruce—what honors he hoped to earn at home by reporting their discovery—but he could readily see that this odd, bulky foreigner had a great passion for them. So he gave the source of the Blue Nile to Bruce. "Tell Fasil [one of the King's officers] I do give the village of Gish [*sic*] and those fountains he is so fond of to Yagoube [Bruce's Ethiopian name] and his posterity for ever, never to appear under another name in the *deftar* [register] and never to be taken from him or exchanged."

It was a great gift that King Tekle Haimonot II had bestowed on Bruce. But had it lasted "for ever," as the King instructed? Did anyone today at Gishe know of Bruce's claim? Did the Agaw still worship a spirit in the springs? And did they still have a mountain of cow bones nearby and a priest willing—or deranged enough—to stand covered with grease in the midst of a hot fire?

Our expedition, as outlined by Nevada, did not begin at the Blue Nile springs. We were to start our trek at the place modern hydrologists consider the beginning of the river: the gorge below Tis Isat Falls. That

was fine. But at the end of this journey, I would set out on another—
to the place that Ethopians believe is the source of the Blue Nile, where
they say their river begins.

four

≈

NEVADA LIKED THE IDEA OF VISITING THE BLUE NILE'S springs, too, and we agreed to travel there together after we left the river. She and I had been in regular contact by phone and e-mail, discussing various aspects of the expedition. She had yet to find a paramedic but had some promising leads. She would have to wait until August, however, to make a decision because she would be leading a photographic trek in Nepal for most of July and unreachable.

"I'll get back just in time to repack my bags and fly to Addis," she laughed.

My schedule wasn't much better. I was finishing a book while simultaneously researching an article about endangered frogs. For that story, I was heading to Panama in July and Texas in August. Our fractured schedules didn't seem to worry either of us, maybe because we had both grown used to living with a suitcase half-packed, ready to board a plane to somewhere else. And then, we also had e-mail.

"I've practically organized this whole expedition via e-mail," Nevada commented at one point—in an e-mail message.

I used e-mail, too, to contact Conrad again. He was due home from Madagascar in early July. Home for Conrad was Nairobi, where he shared a sprawling house and garden with the famed elephant researcher Cynthia Moss, his partner of many years. It was easy to understand their attraction. Once when visiting their home, Conrad asked if I would like to join him on a birding tour. It was already late afternoon, and I wondered where we could drive to before night fell on Kenya's beautiful birds. "Oh," Conrad said, giving me a slight half-smile. "We'll just look at the birds here. In the garden. You may be surprised." And I was.

In an hour's exploration of their thickly hedged garden, we spotted fire finches, cordon bleus, superb starlings, and several species of metallic-hued sunbirds that hovered around a hibiscus bush, dipping their long beaks into its pink blossoms. Conrad pointed to the sky above the forest behind their home, where a kettle of kites was climbing skyward, and then, as we stepped into the woods, nodded his head toward the lower branches of one tree. An iridescent turaco peeped back at us. Shy birds, the turaco fled into the thicker bush. "Now that was fine," said Conrad. "I don't see them very often." I'd only seen one or two before, in Kenya, and felt that Conrad had known there was a fair chance we'd see this beauty. A quiet man, this was his way of speaking: showing other people the natural treasures of his world.

Perhaps there was good birding to be done at the source of the Blue Nile, I suggested in my message. Nevada and I wanted to visit the springs, and hoped that he would join us.

Conrad's answer arrived a few days later. He was still full of the river trip he'd just led in Madagascar, the splendid birds and lemurs he'd seen. He liked the idea of visiting the Blue Nile's source, but didn't think it would be possible, since he was leading a trip on Ethiopia's Omo River right after our expedition. He thought we could easily find a local guide for our trek because there weren't many tourists about and people were eager for work. He was looking forward to seeing me in September.

Then, we all fell silent. No phone calls, no e-mails while we traveled our separate ways. I returned from Panama in late July. Nevada arrived home in early August. And that was when I first heard the news: Conrad was ill, gravely so. Sometime shortly after our discussion about visiting the source, he had developed puzzling and distressing symptoms: dizzy spells, difficulty walking, fuzzy eyesight. The physicians in Nairobi diagnosed a malignant brain tumor. He was now in London receiving radiation treatments and fighting for his life. He would not be guiding us on the Blue Nile.

The news took my breath away. It seemed impossible, as it always does, that someone so vigorous, so full of life, and in love with life, could be suffering like this. I wrote him at once, telling him of my sorrow and my hopes for his good health. I promised to fly to Kenya after the Blue Nile to see him. I didn't expect a reply.

But the tumor hadn't stopped Conrad. He wrote back the next day, saying the treatments were going well and that he looked forward to my visit; he insisted that I stay at their home. In the meantime, he was still working on "one more major issue" for our Blue Nile expedition. "Always leave the toughest [one] for last," he joked. "ANd [sic] it seems like the project is well on track." He was greatly disappointed that he would not be joining us and that he would miss the camaraderie of the other boatmen.

"WHEN I HEARD THat MIKE BORCIK WAS coming to guide," Conrad continued, "I was happy for the project but sad for myself to miss working with him sagain [sic]. enjoyed his company very much on the omo trip wwe [sic] did 2 yrs ago. keep in touch. best to Michael. Love, Conrad"

The tumor's evil effects pervaded Conrad's message. His typing was askew, a mixed stream of uppercase and lowercase letters; spacing, spelling, and punctuation gone wrong. I pictured him trying to focus on the screen while typing with one hand, the other useless at his side. Yet despite his physical disabilities and the trauma of his treatments, he continued to do all he could "to make the trip happen," as he told Nevada in another message.

I didn't ask Conrad about the tumor, but its symptoms were all too reminiscent of one that had killed a close friend's brother. He had lived six months.

And I thought again of Richard Bangs's worries about the Blue Nile. The river had nothing to do with Conrad's illness, I told myself. But at night in my dreams the Blue Nile rose black and dark and menacing, a river of death and dying.

WE REGROUPED.

Alerting James Ellsworth, the director of Mountain Travel Sobek, about his condition as soon as the tumor was diagnosed, Conrad suggested that the second boatman on our trip, Michael Speaks, be moved into his original position as land and river guide, and Ellsworth agreed. Ellsworth then asked Michael Borcik, another professional river guide in the Mountain Travel Sobek stable to take on Speaks's previous job. Conrad also arranged for two local tour operators Maurizio (Mau) Melloni and Yohannes Assefa, to manage the equipment and logistics of our expedition.

Nevada's search for a paramedic had been successful, too. A woman from Michigan in her early forties, Kate Dernocoeur, would be joining us.

There were eight of us now: myself; Nevada; her friend, Kelly; Mick, the NATIONAL GEOGRAPHIC videographer; Kate, the paramedic; and the three boatmen, Michael Speaks, Mike Borcik, and Bruce Kirkby. Conrad's chief Ethiopian assistant, Zelalem Abera Woldegiorgis, would also join us as a guide, cook, and most important, as interpreter.

In this Internet age, we met each other through short e-mail messages. Kate, I learned, was an Emergency Medical Society educator and a mother of a 13-year-old daughter. This was her first "big" overseas adventure since becoming a mom. She had not been on a rafting expedition or to Africa before, but she had once been a member of the Vail Mountain Rescue team and had "worked the streets of Denver" for six years as a paramedic. She didn't expand on this, but she didn't have to. It's not necessary to travel to the Amazon Basin or raft the Nile to have experiences that make you tough, good-hearted, and resilient.

Mick hailed from Australia. He was 25 and a sufficiently talented cameraman that he had already landed a contract job with National Geographic Television. A few years before, he had traveled the length of Africa from the Cape to Cairo with his video camera, and it was that footage that opened the door for him at National Geographic. His last assignment was in war-torn Bosnia, and although he didn't say so specifically, Mick needed a break from the horrors he had seen.

Bruce was in his early thirties and lived in Calgary. He was an outdoor enthusiast, and had worked for several white-water rafting companies. He had also led his own expedition to Saudi Arabia's Empty Quarter, following in the footsteps of the famed explorer, Wilfred Thesiger, whom he'd met in London. Nevada knew Bruce and vouched for his good nature and easy-going manner. He would be working as the rookie boatman as well as Mick's video assistant—which oddly made him, despite all his experience, the low man on our expedition's totem pole. This would be his first trip to Africa.

Mike Borcik was off rowing the Colorado River in the Grand Canyon, and consequently out of touch. Conrad's comments, however, made him sound like someone worth getting to know. Mike had also been in Ethiopia at least once according to Conrad, and that relieved me. Ethiopians have some very particular customs and traditions, and while they may forgive a foreigner for not knowing them and therefore behaving badly, I didn't like the idea of affronting them. With Conrad as our guide, I knew this would not have been a problem. Perhaps Mike Borcik would now fill that role, counseling the team on such simple things as not belching and farting during meals (or in public if at all possible) and being generous toward the poor people we would inevitably encounter. Ethiopia does not have a social-welfare system. Instead, wealthy people—which we were going to be seen as—are expected to give alms to the sick, blind, lame, and indigent. It does not have to be a huge sum, just a coin or two, but such generosity would raise our status enormously and establish us as good Christians, a label not to be taken lightly in this strongly Orthodox country.

Conrad's assistant, Zelalem, might also guide us in Ethiopian manners and mores. Zelalem's English was good, I learned from Jim Slade, and he was "a nice guy, a little on the quiet side." He'd been Conrad's right-hand man for several years, had rafted the Omo, Takeze, and Awash Rivers with him, and led clients to the summit of Ras Dashen. Zelalem wasn't part of the e-mail circuit, so for the time being he remained largely a name, although I was predisposed to like him since Conrad employed him.

Michael Speaks, the head guide, was in his early forties and had also been in Ethiopia before. He had been a member of Richard Bangs's 1996 expedition on the Tekeze River in the northern part of the country, and had rafted the upper canyon of the Blue Nile as well, the stretch past which we were hiking. I learned more about him in late August, when Speaks sent an e-mail to the entire team to introduce himself. He had given it a somewhat military title, "Mike_Speaks_Communique." The message that followed was rather stiff and awkward, suggesting that he was not comfortable with the written word.

"Greetings," Speaks began. "Here is a communique designed to establish a link from me to all members of the Blue Nile Expedition. As it stand's [*sic*] we are a team of 8 plus at least two Ethiopians…. As the logistics start falling into place, an expedition prospectus can be formulated, which in short could be simply stated as an attempt to capture a glimpse of this region through Nevada's cameras and the skill of our writer, all of which will be profiled by Mick's digital video cameras. My main goal will be to help organize in a way that will carry us safely down this remote river at potentially high water volumes."

I paused at the curiously possessive phrase "our writer," unsure of how to react. Why hadn't he used my name? Probably it was a simple oversight, or maybe he didn't have it readily at hand. I didn't want to feel annoyed, but I was, and then decided something this small surely wasn't worth worrying about.

Speaks's message continued, laying out the details of our journey. We faced about 470 miles of travel on the Blue Nile, plus a 20 to 30 mile hike on the upper section that was too dangerous to raft at this time of year. Mike Borcik would meet us at the river with the boats and rafting equipment. We would have to make good time, covering the hike in 5 days, and the river journey in 22. He hoped we would pack light for our trek, and if anyone had any questions, we should contact him.

"OK I am looking forward to seeing everyone in Addis or Bahir Dar or at the river put in," he concluded.

Overall, the message puzzled me because Speaks did not refer to this as a NATIONAL GEOGRAPHIC expedition or to Nevada's key role as the expedition organizer. Also, the schedule he had laid out was very tight without any room for the exploratory hikes to villages that Nevada and Conrad had talked about. Most worrisome, the collaborative spirit Conrad had brought to the enterprise was sadly missing. Had things changed because Speaks had been appointed head guide at the last minute and felt a need to assert his position?

Speaks's message also left me wondering about the relationship between Nevada and Mountain Travel Sobek. Weren't they simply the outfitter for her expedition? The messages and materials they were sending to the members of the Blue Nile suggested that the expedition was "theirs," an exploratory river trip their guides were leading. Over the summer, Mountain Travel Sobek had sent out regular postings about the expedition, information about what we should pack and what inoculations we should have. One of these also contained a "Trip Itinerary," which laid out in chirpy travelese our "adventure vacation," and set aside times for seeing the sights of Addis, such as the city's big open-air market. The itinerary made me uneasy, suggesting as it did that the expedition was really part of a holiday tour package.

Nevada also had found the itinerary and its vacation-brochure tone annoying, and had asked Ellsworth to stop sending us this kind of material.

"Are we supposed to be on some sort of a tour bus when we get to Addis?" I asked. "Because if we are, I'm going to have to pass on that part of the trip. That's not my idea of traveling."

"No, no, no, Ginny, it's not going to be like that," Nevada assured me.

Nevada was pleased that Michael Speaks had stepped in for Conrad, and that Mike Borcik was coming. Both men had experience in Ethiopia, she noted, and at this late date, we were lucky to get anyone at all, let alone guides of their caliber. She had not met either man, but she was certain they could do the job.

All that was certainly true, and I hung up feeling that we were fortunate that the trip had not been canceled. Yet, part of me couldn't stop mulling over Speaks's message, and I read it again. No, there wasn't any question at all: Speaks saw himself as the person calling the shots. He felt he was in charge, and if Nevada had a role, it was solely as the photographer.

As for me, I wasn't petty enough to be really piqued by that phrase "our writer." Or was I?

I DIDN'T WANT TO START THE TRIP DOUBTING THE INTENTIONS OF OUR trip guide. I asked Richard what he knew about Conrad's replacement.

"Well, he's the consummate outdoors man," Rich said. "Between trips, he lives in a cabin in Alaska without electricity. He always kept a cool head on our trip. He doesn't have the most analytical mind; he's not a deep thinker or an intellectual. But nobody can beat him when it comes to the outdoors."

Had I read Tracy Johnston's book, Shooting the Boh, Rich then asked. "It's about an exploratory river trip Speaks led in New Guinea about ten years ago. He's the hero of her book. You might take a look at that."

I found a copy and read it in almost one sitting. Johnston was a clever and funny writer, and she'd been on a river expedition where everything went wrong. The only right thing about it was that Speaks had been in charge. He'd led a party of several self-absorbed European models, one timid lawyer, two staunch conservationists, and other river guides through a hellish canyon of stinging plants, stinging bees, sudden downpours, foot rot, and rapids so huge and powerful they'd spent days carrying their rafts around them. There weren't enough tents or sleeping bags or food, and the trip lasted at least a week longer than scheduled. They survived because of Speaks. Of course, he'd also gotten the girl.

Johnston admired Speaks. He was a leader and skillful boatman, and at times, he'd made her laugh.

It was hard, I knew, for anyone to step into Conrad's shoes. Speaks had had little time to prepare or think about our trip; until now, that had been Conrad's job. In his communique, Speaks had emphasized wanting to get us down the river safely. Undoubtedly, that was his primary concern. And judging from Johnston's book, he would.

I SPENT TWO DAYS PACKING FOR THE TWO MONTHS I PLANNED TO SPEND in Ethiopia. Conrad and Maurizio were supplying much of the heavy equipment, such as the rafts, tents, all the food and cooking gear. One of Mountain Travel Sobek's packages included a checklist of things team members needed to bring, and I ran down it, adding to and deleting items. It was a tricky journey to pack for. In the mountains, where we were going to be hiking, we were apt to be cold and wet, since we were starting our trek at the end of the rainy season. That meant rain was a real possibility. Ethiopia's mountains are high and close to the equator. When the sun did shine, we were going to be hot and in need of shade. I made a pile of hiking gear: boots, rain jacket and pants, umbrella (for rain and shade), sun hat and sunglasses, a big tube of sunscreen with the highest SPF rating I could find (45), two pairs of trekking pants, two long-sleeved shirts, three T-shirts, a warm fleece top, some underwear, and lots of socks. I stuck in a pair of lightweight long johns, too, just for those cold mountain nights.

My river pile wasn't that different, although I added a pair of runner's shorts and a swimsuit, since they were on the Mountain Travel list. We might swim in some of the Blue Nile's side streams. The shorts, a nice pair colored brick-red and made of a high-tech, quick-drying fabric, were more doubtful. Shorts aren't worn by Ethiopian women, particularly in the conservative highlands where a woman is expected to keep her upper thighs covered. Maybe I would wear them on the raft, I thought, although I didn't like the idea of getting sunburned. I stuck them in the very bottom of my bag.

I put in a couple of skirts for our days in Addis, and some additional T-shirts and blouses. These would be like the old "Sunday-going-to-church" clothes, clothing to be kept clean and spotless—and a treat to be opened at the end of our journey.

There were other items: a fiber-filled sleeping bag, shoes and sandals for the river journey, water bottles, toiletries, a personal first-aid kit (including tubes of insect repellent and pills to ward off malaria) and, for my writing life, a stack of yellow waterproof notebooks, as well as regular steno-style notebooks, and a couple dozen pens. I tossed in some extra Bic pens, remembering how Ethiopian school children loved these as gifts. I added a lightweight pair of binoculars, a tiny point-and-shoot-style camera and a Canon Elan with a couple of lenses, some Swiss chocolate bars for the mountain trek, two bottles of wine to share on the river, and granola bars for emergencies.

Somehow, I crammed everything into a huge red duffel bag that my husband had purchased for his recent Tibetan foray. My camera gear and binoculars, along with items I didn't want to break or lose—the wine, chocolate, and antimalaria pills—went into a special day-pack designed for photographers. I planned to carry this and my laptop computer on the plane. My computer wasn't coming with me on the trek or river trip. But I could use it on the plane and at my hotel before and after the Blue Nile.

I finished packing late in the afternoon of September 9, and piled my bags near the front door. My plane was the first one out the next morning from our local airport. I would fly to San Francisco first, then Chicago, where I'd catch a long flight to Frankfurt. I would have to wait there a few hours, then board a Lufthansa jet for the final leg to Addis Ababa. Altogether, I had about 20 hours of flying to look forward to, and I sighed at the thought. Long flights are the worst part of traveling. I was going to be cramped and uncomfortable, and suddenly I longed for a walk. Michael had been writing in his upstairs office, and I called up to him.

"I think I'm done; why don't you come down?"

Writers tend to live quietly, or at least we do. If you're going to make your living by turning out words, we've found, you have to be disciplined. That's not a new discovery, but it is reality. Most days find us in our offices by 9:00 a.m. after an early-morning workout. We eat lunch together, then head upstairs for another session of writing. If we aren't finished by 5:00 or 6:00 p.m., our dog, Quincie, makes sure that we are. A collie-huskie mix, she lies outside our office doors, sighing and moaning loudly until we give in.

Quincie was sitting with me now, and she began wagging her tail as soon as I called to Michael. She knew all the signs of departure, from the big duffel bags to the harried packing, and hated them all. While I folded clothes and sorted through my gear, she laid next to the bags, looking off in the distance, hoping that somehow I would find a way to pack her, too.

We live in a little town on the edge of a forest, and we headed off now for one of our favorite walks. The first cool hint of autumn was in the air, and we talked about how good it felt. Summers here are hot and by September we always begin longing for their end. And then, fall is a beautiful time of year, the days bright and crisp, the trees red and gold. I would miss our autumn. I would miss our walks.

Quincie ran ahead of us, as she always does, sometimes leaving the trail to splash in a stream or plunging downhill to chase a squirrel. Michael and I walked side-by-side, not saying much. He had his story to think about, and I was preoccupied with my packing list (did I really have everything I needed?), so it was nice when he reached over and took my hand. We gave each other a smile, and I leaned against him. We often traveled apart, but usually for no more than a month. Two months would be hard, especially for him. I'd be off having adventures; he'd be home, where the same old daily routine wears thin very quickly when one is alone.

"I wish I were going," Michael said, when we came home and loaded my bags into the car for our early morning run to the airport.

"So do I," I said.

Then a thought struck me. There was one other thing I did need to pack. I ran upstairs, rifled through a stack of photos and pulled out the one I had to have with me: the three of us on a cross-country ski outing. We're hugging Quincie and laughing, and the late afternoon light lies golden on the trees and the snow. I love that picture, and I'd almost forgotten to bring it with me. I stuck it in a plastic bag, then put the bag inside my document pouch. Michael and Quincie were going with me on the Blue Nile.

five

~~~

I USED THE LONG FLIGHT TO ETHIOPIA TO READ ANOTHER BOOK, *Lake Tana & The Blue Nile* by Major Robert E. Cheesman, the British consul for Northwest Ethiopia from 1925 to 1934. Cheesman was a member of the imperial service, and as expected of those who toiled for Britain's empire, a man of many talents: solider and surveyor, naturalist, explorer, and fair linguist. He'd served in India, Iraq, and Saudi Arabia, mapped stretches of the last country's coast and deserts (for which he was given the Order of the British Empire), and in all three countries assiduously collected specimens of their plants, animals, and minerals, which he duly presented to the British Museum. Arabia was his passion, and he'd hoped to join the first British expedition into its unknown Empty Quarter. Instead, he was posted to Ethiopia. Any disappointment he felt vanished after he studied the country's maps. The latest ones, he wrote with some astonishment, "showed the course of the Blue Nile as a series of dotted lines," indicating that the river remained unmapped. "It seemed almost unbelievable that such a famous river, and one on which Egypt had depended for its prosperity through-out the ages, could have been so long neglected."

Since James Bruce's self-proclaimed discovery of the source in 1771, few explorers had bothered with the Blue Nile. In 1820, when Egypt was under the rule of the Ottoman Turks, a French explorer and jack-of-all-trades, Frederic Cailliaud, managed to tag along on a Turkish-Egyptian invasion of Sudan. Although the force was small, consisting of only 4,000 soldiers, it swept up the Nile to Khartoum, meeting little resistance along the way, and capturing one town and settlement after another. They then turned their weapons on the peoples of the Blue Nile, killing those who resisted and seizing others for slaves all the way from Khartoum to Fazughli, close to the Ethiopian border. The invaders rested here, dreaming of the wealth they would reap from Fazughli's legendary gold mines. The mines, however, were a disappointment, the fabulous nuggets they supposedly held, a myth. Cailliaud had imagined returning a wealthy man, but found instead that the local people merely panned for gold along the shores of the Blue Nile and its tributaries, and stored the dust and flakes they gleaned in the quills of geese feathers. Gold quills bought them salt, spices, and cloth.

Ismail Ali, the rapacious commander of the invading force, had captured 30,000 slaves on his campaign. He may have hoped to acquire more in Ethiopia, since Ethiopian women were highly prized ("the Venuses of that country," Sir Samuel Baker called them), but stopped at the border. Beyond loomed Ethiopia's mountain massif, a daunting sight to a man from the lowlands, even one as ruthless as Ismail. The river, too, took a fearsome turn, disappearing into a dark, impassable gorge. Ismail turned back, and Cailliaud went with him. He had roughly surveyed the river, and from his notes mapmakers were able to sketch the course of the Blue Nile from Khartoum to the Ethiopian border. Beyond that, the river remained unknown to Westerners.

Another 80-odd years elapsed. Then, W.N. McMillan, a wealthy American big-game hunter, decided to tackle the Blue Nile. Keen to prove that the river in Ethiopia was navigable, and could be used to ship goods to and from Sudan, he mounted an expedition in 1902. Egypt and Sudan were both now under British control and Britain was eager to build up its colonies through trade and settlement. Already, goods and passengers were being shipped along the entire length of the White Nile via railways and steamers, while another rail line connected the river to Port Said on the Red Sea coast.

By now, too, all of Africa—except Ethiopia—had been partitioned among the great European powers. Italy had attempted to conquer Ethiopia, but suffered a massive and bloody defeat at Adwa in 1896 at the hands of Emperor Menelik II. That surprise victory (no other African nation had crushed a European army) led the British and French to include Menelik when drawing up the final maps of East Africa. As crafty at negotiations as he was on the battlefield, the emperor nearly doubled the size of his country, adding vast stretches of the deserts to the south and east, and by subjugating the lowland peoples of the southwest, nearly to the White Nile.

Menelik hoped the additional lands would protect Ethiopia's mountainous heartland from the hungry foreigners. Britain and France had other ideas: they wanted the country opened up for trade via new railroads. And Britain wanted a firm commitment that Ethiopia would not tamper with the Blue Nile in any way; there were to be no dams, canals, or water catchments built along its course without British and Egyptian approval. Not trusting the British and French any more than the Italians, the emperor warily agreed to both demands.

It was in this atmosphere of suspicion and distrust that McMillan came calling. He needed the emperor's permission to put his boats on the Blue Nile. Menelik had seen and crossed the Blue Nile many times, since like all of Ethiopia's kings he had traveled in great caravans from one end of his domain to the other, and he knew what the river canyon was like. There could be little harm in letting a *ferenji* (white foreigner) try something as foolish as this.

With permits in hand, McMillan spared no expense, and set about launching a two-pronged attack on the river. From Khartoum, he dispatched a Norwegian explorer, Burchard H. Jessen, up the Blue Nile on a small, 40-foot steam launch. McMillan and another party were to journey the opposite direction down the river on three steel boats. These were transported in sections from Ethiopia's coast via camel and mule caravans to a spot near the mouth of the Muger River, one of the Blue Nile's larger tributaries, about 250 miles from Lake Tana. The two teams would meet at the Ethiopian-Sudanese border.

Jessen hired a couple of Sudanese assistants, and with a mixture of luck and derring-do, managed to get his launch up the Blue Nile and through the largest cataracts at Roseires (the dam had not yet been built). They could not, however, make it beyond another rapid at Famaka, and stopped some distance from the border.

McMillan's team had even worse luck. His navigation of the Blue Nile lasted less than one day. "For the first few miles," Jessen reported, "everything went well, but then a bad cataract, curving into an S shape around rocky points was encountered, and there the Expedition came to grief." One boat flipped, and a second one, bearing the team's food and ammunition, sank. "There was nothing left for them to eat but one chicken and some flour," Jessen wrote sympathetically, "and as…there were no villages near, they were rather in hard straits." The party camped as best it could next to the river and sent a messenger for help. But the Blue Nile wasn't through with them. In the middle of the night, a crocodile lunged from its depths and seized one of their Somali helpers. Somehow, the poor man managed to escape, although his hand was crushed and his head badly lacerated.

McMillan retreated to Europe to regroup. He was "nothing daunted" by these first failures, noted Jessen, and he was determined to try again with better boats—after McMillan had Jessen scout the river.

On his second 1905 attempt, Jessen began where he'd left off at Famaka. He was joined this time by an American chemist, H.L. Scott, and a large retinue consisting of 32 men, most of them Sudanese, 1 camel, 3 mules and 65 donkeys. Jessen gives no background about himself in his account of either expedition. He is simply an employee of Mr. McMillan's, whom he holds in high regard. McMillan, one hopes, had the same esteem for Jessen, who despite numerous hardships, seldom loses his temper or sense of humor, and always has an eye for the beauty of the country he is passing through, pausing to write of its dramatic vistas or the sweet-scented lilies that carpeted the river's banks.

Jessen's orders from McMillan were to follow the shoreline of the Blue Nile, and for about the first 50 miles he managed to do so, taking a trail that led through hilly, wooded country. It was April, before the rainy season began, and the water in the river so clear that Jessen once spotted a crocodile floating in midstream, its legs and tail perfectly visible beneath the surface. He shot at it, but missed.

Farther upstream, the river became crooked and filled with jagged rocks; there were several small rapids, and then a large, dangerous one that ran for three long miles. Jessen began to doubt the wisdom of putting any boat on the river, but continued to press ahead. He was now into the dark gorge, and the range of mountains that had stopped Ismail. There was no longer a trail to follow. Jessen kept to the Blue Nile's shoreline by hacking out a path, or hopping from rock to rock. He sent his caravan ahead, over the mountains, and at times was forced to join them on these overland marches. "The mountains...began to close in on the river," he wrote, "and where we could get a glimpse ahead the outlook for quick progress looked very black. Nothing but rocks and high hills and mountains."

Jessen and his men trudged through the forest and up and down the mountains, trying to find a way back to the river. When they did, it wasn't long before another boulder-strewn mountain rose up before them, right from the Blue Nile's banks, and once again they were forced to carve a trail. If the shoreline route was bad, that on the river looked even worse. Jessen wrote of seeing cataract after cataract, most of them "dangerous for navigation at any time of the year."

There were "frightful" climbs that took a toll on the animals. In a single day, Jessen's camel and 4 donkeys collapsed and died from sheer exhaustion. As the days passed, 20 more donkeys died from fatigue and sickness or by losing their footing and plunging to their deaths. Jessen, Scott, and their men were suffering, too. Mosquitoes, moths, and stinging insects plagued them by night, while ants and biting flies attacked them by day. Their clothing was in tatters; their boots, in shreds. Scott was half delirious with fever and dysentery, and they had barely enough to eat, although occasionally Jessen shot an antelope or hippo. Along the river, they met parties of Oromo people panning for gold (most of which they would surrender as tribute to the emperor), and sometimes were able to trade calico and beads for Oromo grain and chickens. Other times, on their overland mountain treks, they encountered villages of the Nilotic Gumuz people and bought what food they could.

The Gumuz however, were skittish, and Jessen was never certain of the reception his party would receive. There was a good reason for their wariness. Over the centuries, they had been regularly raided for slaves. If it wasn't Arabs from Egypt bursting in from the lowlands to capture their men, women, and children, then it was a force of Ethiopians on horseback coming down from the highlands to do the same. The Egyptian raids had ceased largely since Egypt and Sudan had become a British protectorate. But the Ethiopians continued the practice, although Emperor Menelik made half-hearted promises to the European diplomats who pressed him on the issue that he would bring it to an end. The Ethiopian economy was then a slave economy, and the noble classes in the mountains had thousands and even tens of thousands of slaves at their disposal, most of them seized in the lowlands along the Ethiopian-Sudanese border.

In his book, Jessen refers to the Gumuz as "Shangallas," using the Ethiopian name for them, which translates literally to "black negroes." The golden-skinned highlanders used the term derogatorily, but Jessen seemed to think this was the Gumuzs' name for themselves. He tells of several Shangalla villages asking for his protection from a marauding band of Ethiopians, but Jessen was not equipped for such a task and had to leave them to their fate. Once some Shangallas found one of Jessen's men—a Sudanese—alone on the trail. He was ill with fever and had asked to be allowed to come along at his own pace. Perhaps he looked like an Arab slave-raider, and the Shangalla used him to settle old scores. When the Sudanese did not appear at camp, Jessen sent a search party back to find him. They did, "but he had been murdered by the Shangallas, and his body horribly mutilated." They speared him twice, slit his throat, cut off his genitals as a trophy, then used a chunk of flesh from his upper arm for fish bait. Jessen's men found one of the Shangallas fishing with this morsel, but "the murderer" escaped. There was little to be done about the man's death. Jessen briefly considered burning some Shangalla villages in retaliation, then thought about reporting the murder to the Ethiopians, although he hesitated since the punitive expedition they would send would undoubtedly turn into an all-out slave raid.

There was no way to suitably avenge the man's death. Perhaps it was for that reason that Jessen paused in his narrative to record what little he knew about this man from Sudan—a sort of hats-off salute to his fallen comrade. His name, Jessen wrote, was Samain Ali; he was born in Tadasi, Sudan; his religion was Mohammedan; his mother's name was Howa; the name of his father was unknown; he was about 20 years old. "He left with us nothing but a blanket and a few pieces of cotton clothing." Across the way from where Samain Ali had been killed, a small island divided the flow of the Blue Nile, and Jessen named it "Murder Island."

The expedition struggled on. Jessen found it increasingly difficult to follow McMillan's orders and stick to the riverbank. More often, he and his caravan struggled up and over the mountains, and looked down on the Blue Nile in its twisting gorge below. At one point, after climbing a trail so vertical the team had to unload the donkeys and carry all the gear to the top, Jessen was rewarded with a fine view of the Blue Nile Valley. It "lay open to the view for a distance of some six to eight miles," he wrote, "and through the field glasses I could plainly see every detail of its surroundings." The details were sobering. "No wonder," he continued, "the natives said it was impossible to go along its banks, and that no man had ever done so. The river itself is continuous cataracts, crooked and full of rocks, while the banks were nothing but piles of jagged sharp boulders, beyond which the hills rose up steep and forbidding looking, with apparently no footing anywhere."

Jessen had anticipated meeting a second team with boats that McMillan planned to send to where the Guder River poured into the Blue Nile. They would venture onto the river if Jessen gave them the go-ahead. He was now only four days from that meeting place, but knew what answer he would give: It would be madness to put a boat on the Blue Nile.

Increasingly, it seemed to be madness to be in the vicinity of the Blue Nile at all. At dawn the next morning, 14 Ethiopian soldiers, all armed and mounted on mules, came riding into his camp. They were from the village of Ras (Duke) Mangesha, they announced, and had orders to bring Jessen to the duke who was then living at Bure, a mountain some 60 miles away. Jessen showed them the emperor's pass, but none of the men—"a rough looking lot of rogues"—could read. Jessen's suggestion that the emperor would be angry if they arrested Jessen didn't impress them either. In feudal fashion, their loyalty was to their Ras, and they assured Jessen that it would take only one word from Mangesha to turn the whole population against him. The Ras, after all, ruled this region as his private fiefdom, collecting a steady stream of taxes and tribute in the form of gold, ivory, and slaves. Everyone, including *ferenjocch* (white foreigners) must stop and give their due to the Ras. Jessen submitted.

It took Jessen a hard two-day ride to reach Mangesha's stockade, where behind four high wooden gates, several mud huts surrounded a large, towerlike structure built of wood and bamboo. The tower comprised the Ras's living and reception quarters. Blue-painted wooden columns framed the dark interior, where the Ras was reclining, sphinxlike, on a low dais draped with Turkish rugs. An attendant dressed in flowing white robes escorted Jessen to the Ras's presence, then dropped to his knees, kissed the Ras's hand, and prostrated himself on the floor. Jessen couldn't bring himself to perform such a display. He simply reached out and shook the Ras's hand—and was relieved to see that he had not caused any offense.

The explorer studied the duke intently, noting that he had "a fine head and face, a straight cut strong mouth, a rather broad nose—but his eyes were his strong point. They were large, deep set, under heavy eyebrows, and of gray color. His expression was stern and commanding, and one could see at a glance that he was used to having his orders obeyed. Still, when he smiled, he looked like a kind old gentleman who had seen his best days and subdued all strong passions." The Ras seemed less interested in Jessen and inquired through an interpreter why he had come and what he wanted. Jessen replied that the Ras's men had ordered him to do so. Instantly, Mangesha was on his feet, angrily addressing Jessen's escort, who again fell prostrate on the floor. The duke then turned to Jessen, apologized, and explained that it had all been a misunderstanding. Or had it? Jessen wasn't sure. At least he was treated as a guest now and not a prisoner, and the Ras was kind enough to feed him and give him four mules for his trip back to his caravan.

The expedition marched on and in a week's time reached the Guder River, where since there was no sign of any Europeans or boats, Jessen decided to press on to Addis Ababa and journey's end. There he found a very ill Mr. McMillan, who had once again canceled the river portion of the expedition. Jessen thought it a wise decision. He had spent four months trekking along the Blue Nile and had come to one conclusion: The Ethiopians were right: The Blue Nile would not provide a trading link between the Ethiopian highlands and the Egyptian-Sudanese lowlands.

McMILLAN'S FAILURE WAS CHEESMAN'S OPENING. SINCE JESSEN'S explorations, two other adventurers had traveled into Ethiopia's Blue Nile region, but they left behind only brief descriptions of the geography. Thus, one-quarter of the way into the 20th century, the course of the Blue Nile was still unresolved, "offering what might be considered the only bit of pioneering exploration left in Africa," Cheesman noted.

Cheesman seized the opportunity and at his very first meeting with Ras Hailu, the governor of Gojam province, asked for permission to explore the river. Ras Hailu had welcomed Cheesman as the representative of the British government in splendid style at his palace. Thousands of armed men dressed in white stood in attendance, while Ethiopian buglers blew their trumpets and Gumuz musicians from the distant reaches of the Blue Nile blasted eerie notes on their long, bamboo horns. The two men exchanged gifts: honey, chickens, eggs, beeswax candles, a sheep, and young bull from the Ras; coffee, brandy, whisky, preserved fruits from the consul. The Ras sat on his throne, while Consul Cheesman perched on a straight-backed chair to his right. They discussed the business of Cheesman's appointment, and then the consul asked Ras Hailu if he would support the proposed expedition. The Ras answered like an Amhara. He thought the trip ill-advised; no one could journey into the gorge and return alive; it was impossible to travel there either on foot or in a boat. If Cheesman doubted his word, he could go to the gorge and look at it himself. In the meantime, the Ras said he would telephone the appropriate authorities in Addis Ababa about the permits. He did not, however, tell Cheesman that Ethiopian government officials had already contacted him about the expedition and that the permits had been granted. Instead, he had urged his colleagues in Addis to reconsider their decision. He did not want the responsibility of losing the British consul in the Blue Nile Gorge.

Ras Hailu was one of the more powerful and forward-looking men in Ethiopia. In addition to his telephone, he had recently brought a car to his palace on the far side of the Blue Nile Gorge. In 1926, the year of Cheesman's visit, there were still no major roads leading to the river nor highway bridges across it in Ethiopia. The car was thus transported in sections and on mule back from Addis Ababa and across the Blue Nile, and then reassembled. The Ras had tracks cut for his vehicle around the outskirts of his capital, and drove around and around them while attendants on horseback galloped along on either side. Cheesman witnessed this horse motorcade—and the astonishment of the Ras's subjects who had never seen a car before and who "flung themselves face-downwards on the ground…, clawing the earth with their fingers, with mouths wide open and expressions of abject terror on their faces" at the sight.

Slowly, reluctantly Ethiopia was being drawn into the modern, European-dominated world. The country had gone through a brief, tumultuous period after the death of Emperor Menelik II in 1910. His nephew, Lij Iyasu, succeeded him, but Iyasu ruled only five years before the aristocrats turned against him when they discovered he had secretly converted to Islam, a treasonous act in this Christian state. When Cheesman arrived in the country, Empress Zawditu, Menelik's daughter, sat on the throne, but the real power was wielded by her distant cousin, the regent and prince, Ras Tafari Mekonnen. He was already de facto emperor and when he fully assumed the throne in 1933, he would take the name of Haile Selassie I.

Ethiopia was still the sole island of independence in an otherwise colonial sea, and Ras Tafari Mekonnen was determined that Ethiopia remained free. In 1924, he had visited Italy, France, and England, making him the first Ethiopian prince to travel to Europe, and he had successfully bid for his country's membership in the young League of Nations. In exchange, he had agreed to end its slavery. He was eager to develop Ethiopia, and when the British Legation in Addis proposed the idea of building a dam to generate hydroelectric power at Lake Tana, he listened. Much more needed to be known about the Blue Nile, of course, and so despite Ras Hailu's worries, Cheesman received his exploration permits.

Cheesman's book begins with a preface in which he relates the heart-sinking tale of losing the book's manuscript. He had spent six years writing it and had gone to London with it locked in a suitcase in his car. Someone stole the car and despite public appeals, neither it nor Cheesman's book were ever seen again. Cheesman sat down, picked up his pen, and began again.

In that anecdote alone, one senses that the Blue Nile had at last met its match.

At the outset Cheesman, a kindly man with a tidily trimmed mustache and fine creases around his eyes, thought his mapmaking quest would be fairly simple. "On the map, [the journey] seemed moderately easy," he wrote. "I was to be undeceived later, as it proved to be a venture not to be lightly undertaken, and I then understood why the secrets of the Blue Nile Valley had remained so long unrevealed."

Like Jessen, he intended to follow the course of the river, although from the opposite direction, and like Jessen he found this impossible, especially if he was to map it. "When you are deep down in the canyon of the Blue Nile," he wrote, "you can see nothing but the sky." From its depths, he could not discern the landmarks necessary for his surveying. So he kept to the upper plateaus and mountains, traveling with a small mule caravan, his personal attendant and guides, and working his way down to the river where he could, then climbing back out of the gorge to take his bearings. The British Legation had asked him to keep an eye out for possible dam sites on the river, and so in addition to the theodolite and pocket chronometer he carried for his surveying work, he also brought along a barometer to measure the river's depth.

Armed with letters from the regent and the local governors, Cheesman did not face Jessen's diplomatic difficulties. Yet Ethiopia retained the feudal air and practices that made it seem both familiar and foreign, as if one had stepped backward into the chivalric age of France. Crossing the Portuguese-built brick-and-mortar bridge below

Lake Tana's Tis Isat Falls, Cheesman passed from Gojam province into Begemder province. Although the two provinces were in Ethiopia, the officials at the bridge acted as if Cheesman were crossing into a foreign land. Each side had its own customs and passport officials, and each set of officials carefully examined Cheesman's papers. Then they held a white cotton shawl in front of him and cut the cloth, a ceremony which had endured since the 17th century reign of King Fasiladas—and which broke the power of the evil eye.

Such protective traditions had actually had a curiously adverse effect, turning the lands around the Blue Nile into a haven for shiftas, Cheesmen noted.

Government officials did not have the right to enter another province, even if they were pursuing a criminal. Thus, if bandits robbed someone in one province, they simply slipped across the river and hid in the forest, knowing full well that they could not be followed. And by the time the police in this new province were alerted to the bandits' presence, they had leisurely crossed again to the other side.

Robberies in Cheesman's day were about as common as muggings in Central Park are today. Even the British consul was not immune. On one of Cheesman's journeys, some of his men came running back to say the shifta were stealing his mules. Cheesman had three Sudanese policemen with him, and they galloped to the scene of the crime. "I rode up close to the outlaws, who were too occupied…to notice my arrival, and forgetting my Amharic shouted in English, 'What the hell are you doing?'" The bandits dropped the goods they were pilfering, and waited for their leader to explain. To Cheesman's surprise, the man apologized, explaining that they'd been instructed by their chief, the notorious outlaw Shiguti, to rob only Ethiopian not European caravans. The bandits then stepped aside to let Cheesman and his mules pass unharmed.

Cheesman's journeys took him through some of the most remote stretches of Ethiopia's terrain, most of it never seen by a European before. From the highlands of the Orthodox Christians, he marched downward to the rumpled hills of the Oromo and Shinasha people, and then farther down to the wide valleys of the Nilotic and pagan Gumuz, who'd been so heavily raided by the Ethiopians in the 20 years since Jessen's trip that they'd abandoned their villages and moved across the border to the safety of Sudan. Cheesman found only their grinding circles in the granite stones where their women had once pounded their grain above the Blue Nile. On his travels, he saw a few prides of lions, and a sacred mound where the Gumuz had buried the eye of a lion to protect them from the slave raiders, and hundreds of hippos snorting in quiet pools and countless crocodiles that slithered away into the river for safety. There were antelopes in abundance and myriad birds—egrets and herons, buffalo weavers and spur-winged geese—in the willow thickets along the river's edge. He'd made notes of their names, then turned back to the task at hand, tracing the river's journey as it twisted and narrowed and widened and narrowed again, and dropped 4,500 feet from the highland plateau through layers of sandstone and limestone and granite to the broad Sudanese plains. At the beginning of his trek, he had stood in "amazement" at the base of Tis Isat Falls, watching as the entire volume of the lake's water was funneled into the river gorge's "narrow chute." And at the Blue Nile's far end, not far from the Sudan border, he'd stood equally amazed—and disappointed—as the river he'd come to so admire dwindled to a stream he could easily toss a stone across.

It had taken Cheesman two separate journeys of several months each and spread out over three years to get this far. The river widened again as it approached the border, and here Cheesman found a vehicle track leading to Roseires. He was making good time down it with his mules when two cars came roaring along to meet him. His mules, like Ras Hailu's subjects, had never seen a vehicle, and they bolted into the forest at once.

In all, it took Cheesman eight years to complete his project. At the end of that time, he had trekked the length of the Blue Nile in Ethiopia, and mapped all but 15 miles of it, only because the smoke of grass fires in the region prevented him from getting the proper bearing. He had traced and mapped the Little Blue Nile from its source at Mount Gishe to its delta at Lake Tana. And he had circumnavigated and mapped the lake itself, becoming the first European—and possibly first person ever—to travel the lake's circumference. Cheesman looked for Ethiopians who had made this journey, but "could find none who had done so," since the lake's shore was divided among three provinces, and as before traveling from province to province was akin to venturing into a foreign land. "[M]en know the country of their own local ruler, but even a short journey beyond it is looked on as an adventure, and when they pass the boundary their attitude of mind is that of a trespasser," he wrote.

Cheesman's own mind-set was more that of a gentle guest. Dignified and curious, doughty and kind, as deeply interested in the local people and their customs as he was in the course of the river, Cheesman was the river's "first true geographer," as Alan Moorehead called him. Fittingly, the Royal Geographical Society awarded him its Patron's medal in 1936 for his mapmaking explorations.

More accurate maps would be drawn later, particularly by an American government team that investigated the gorge with helicopters in the 1960s while searching for dam sites at Ethiopia's request. But Cheesman's journeys were of the path-breaking kind, and even though we were going to be traveling on a river he deemed unnavigable, we would still be following in his footsteps.

six

~~~

MY PLANE LANDED BRIEFLY IN CAIRO AFTER CIRCLING
the pyramids. Some passengers disembarked, new ones
boarded, and then we were airborne again. It was late afternoon, and
through my window, easy to see the Nile below us as we jetted south to
Ethiopia. The river was a rich brown, dark with silt, and it made wide,
lazy curves through the desert. On both banks stretched narrow strips
of green and beyond them, startling because of all the greenery, was
immense desert. There was something about seeing the Nile, even from
these heights, that was calming and reassuring. An old river in an ancient
land, it drifted steadily along, forgetful of all that had happened on its
shores: the empires that rose and fell, the canons that once sounded
victory, the armies that fled upstream in defeat, the lonely wanderers
seeking something they could draw on a scrap of paper. The waters that
would carry me on my own journey would in a very few months be
here, too, spreading silently over the desert and giving it life, no thoughts
of their origin, no memory of my voyage. That was the way of the Nile.

We flew into a purple dusk. The sun set, spreading a golden halo across the desert, then winking out. The first stars appeared and the first town lights. For a while longer, I could still track the Nile's course because of the villages below. People were lighting their lamps and cook fires in their homes next to the river. Then I slept.

We landed a few hours later in Addis Ababa. It was about nine o'clock at night on September 11, 1999. Ethiopia has its own way of counting time and its own calendar, and for the Ethiopians on board it was two o'clock in the evening on the first day of the first month (called *Meskerem*) of the New Year of 1992. I had regained seven hours, ten days, ten months and seven years.

People were in a celebratory mood, and so was I. It had been a good flight; I was back in Ethiopia and heading on an adventure. I picked up my day pack and joined the line of people leaving the plane. Many Ethiopians were coming home to be with their families for this holiday, and as they balanced bundles and children, I heard them softly wishing each other well, "*Enkon le Adis Amet adersechu!...* Welcome to the New Year!"

Then I stepped outside into the chill night air and onto the rubberized stairway leading to the terminal. A light rain was falling, and people hurried to get back inside and out of the damp cold. It was a good five-minute walk down the linoleum-floored corridors to the Immigration Hall, where three officials in khaki uniforms sat in their glassed-in cubicles, waiting for our passports. I handed mine to one of the men, took a deep breath, and said softly in my rusty Amharic, "*Tenaystellegn...* Hello, May God give you health."

The man raised an eyebrow, smiled slightly at my salutation, and stamped my passport. I could do it, I thought, I could still manage a little of my Amharic.

Beyond the immigration officers lay the cavernous baggage room. People were racing each other to grab carts, but for no apparent reason. There seemed to be plenty. I wheeled one toward the baggage ramp, then looked around for Kate Dernocoeur, our team's paramedic. We'd met briefly in Frankfurt before boarding this flight, but she'd had a seat toward the rear of the aircraft while mine was closer to the front. Kate was a little taller than me and her hair was a mass of soft-brown curls; it would be fairly easy to spot her in a crowd of predominantly black-haired people. I kept one eye on the ramp for my bags and another on the door leading to immigration. A few minutes later, Kate pushed through, smiling broadly as she spotted me.

"That was easy," she said.

"Very," I agreed. "We'll get our bags and be out of here in no time."

We each had large duffles and had just wrestled these onto our carts when we heard our names being called. A man in a safari jacket came sauntering our way, an impish grin on his face, and a cigarette in his hand.

"I'm Maurizio—Mau," he announced. "I'll get you through this," he said, nodding at the customs officials. Somewhere in his thirties, with sandy hair and light green eyes, Mau, an Ethiopian citizen of Italian descent, was our expedition's in-country manager and a good friend of Conrad's, he explained, as he waved us through the customs line, speaking now in English to us, then in Amharic to the officials. "There's no problem here," he said, pointing to our hugely stuffed bags, and giving the officers an Italian shrug. They didn't look convinced, but no one stopped us, and we were out the door.

The chill of the night air hit us again, and I pulled on my sweater, while Kate looked for a jacket.

"This is Africa," she said, puzzled. "I didn't expect it to be cold."

"No one does," said Mau, his English tinged with a sprightly accent. "But, you know, Addis is high—a little less than 3,000 meters. What's that? About 8,000 feet? And it's still really winter here; just coming on to spring. And it's the New Year's Day! So Happy Ethiopian New Year to you."

Mau's movements were as quick as his speech, and in short order, he had us, our bags, and Ermes Kifle, an Ethiopian assistant, bundled into his car and heading down the road to Addis. I tried to keep an eye out for familiar landmarks, but it was hard to see very much in the dark and the rain. There were large, Western-styled buildings along the road leading from the airport, tin-covered bus stops, where clusters of people wrapped in white robes huddled from the rain, then little shops with assorted goods stacked on the shelves and lit by a single, bare light bulb. In an open area, groups of young boys stood in knots around big fires, where they laughed and danced in their shorts in the rain.

"Those are Meskerem fires, New Year's fires," said Mau. "You know, everybody has to light a fire tonight; that's the tradition."

He turned down a cobblestone road, then pulled up in front of an iron gate and beeped his horn. Someone on the other side drew the gate open, and we drove inside and parked.

"OK. It's like this," Mau continued. "We'll meet most everybody from the trip here, have some dinner, then get you to your hotel. OK?"

Mau's cell phone rang. He looked annoyed, but answered it cheerily in Italian, and waved us into the restaurant. He'd managed to light another cigarette, too. The restaurant was Italian-Ethiopian and smelled of fragrant sauces, fresh-baked breads, pizza, and wine. Several tables had been pushed together along one wall, where two American-looking men were seated. Mau called out to them.

"Mike! Bruce! Here we are. I found them."

The two men rose and shook our hands. Big smiles all around, and quick introductions: Michael Speaks and Bruce Kirkby. Bruce was tall and strapping, a Canadian logger's build, I thought, and had his blond hair pulled back in a long ponytail. He had a quick, easy smile that lingered; it was easy to see why Nevada liked him. Mike was shorter, under six feet, and had a Lyle Lovett cast to his jaw. His hair was mouse-brown and his narrow blue eyes were framed by a pair of aviator-style glasses. Around his neck and shoulders hung a red-fringed Arab scarf.

Mike seemed distracted, and nervously opened and closed his right hand. He was tense, uneasy, and didn't settle back to laugh and talk as Bruce and Kate were doing.

"Now where are Nevada and Mick?" he queried Mau. Speaks spoke with a southern drawl, and he drew out the "where" as if it had multiple syllables. "We need to have the group together."

"Well, I told them the time. They'll be here," Mau replied, giving his shrug.

I wasn't sure what to do. I wasn't the least bit hungry, having just had a large meal on the plane, and was beginning to feel that utter exhaustion that hits you after a long flight. I wanted to meet Nevada, and thought to myself, just stay awake long enough to say hello, then you can get to your hotel.

"I don't mean to be rude," I said, "but I'm going to have to rest my eyes for a minute." I leaned back in my chair, then came to with a start. Mau was whooping, chairs were being slid back, there was another hearty round of hellos. It was Nevada and the videographer, Mick Davie. They'd been out filming the Meskerem scenes, and were bursting with stories and visions of the celebrations they'd seen.

They moved around the table, exchanging names, shaking hands, giving us all a shot of their energy.

"Hello, Nevada," I said, holding out my hand. "I'm Virginia." For a moment she looked flummoxed, then smiled and laughed.

"I thought you had blond hair," she said. "I mean I thought you were Kate!"

I laughed, too. "No, I've never been a blonde, always a brunette."

Nevada was a blonde with a good salting of gray, and she had blue eyes, and a manner of looking at you that was warm and reassuring— a photographer's gaze. She was a little taller than I, and had a nice way of tilting back her head when she laughed. A pair of gold hoops and tiny silver earrings gave her an exotic, traveled air, and the rings on her fingers—a large turquoise stone on her index finger, a silver chevron on her thumb—drew your eyes to her hands. They were thin and fine-boned, and looked like an artist's.

Then I was shaking hands with Mick, who greeted me with a broad Australian, "Hello." Mick was short, and had a model's chiseled good-looks, wavy blond hair, and wide blue eyes. He had been racing around the streets of Addis, shooting film of the evening's festivities, and could hardly bring himself to sit down. He wanted to be back out there in the night where the action was.

We would meet the other members of our team, Mike Borcik and Kelly Shannon, in about ten days at the Blue Nile after we'd completed the trek.

With Nevada and Mick corralled, Mike Speaks relaxed and set out the next day's agenda, while everyone except me ordered dinner. Mau and Nevada had arranged a flyover of the Blue Nile Gorge, which would give us a chance to see how rough the white-water portion of the river was going to be. We'd do that early the next morning. There was a place on the plane for me and Mick, but not one unfortunately for Kate. After that, we'd meet for lunch and then repack our bags. We could leave whatever we didn't need at Mau's home. And we'd be flying to Bahir Dar on the shores of Lake Tana the following morning—early.

I jotted down the schedule, then raised my hand. "As much as I want to stay here with everybody, I've got to get some sleep if I'm going to make that 6:45 flight tomorrow morning." People nodded sympathetically, and Mau volunteered to drive me to the Hilton, where he'd booked our rooms.

The Hilton—it had been Ethiopia's best hotel when I lived here. It has beautiful gardens and a pool in the shape of a cross, where I'd gone swimming occasionally with friends. Sometimes I went with other American or foreign friends just to get away from the pressures of living in Addis Ababa. You could get a hamburger there, and milk that tasted like American milk and real ice cream. And no one would shout "ferenji" at you. That was the one aspect of Ethiopia that had made me weary—the xenophobia. You were a ferenji, a foreigner here, always.

The Hilton is a multistoried building, with the narrow upright shape of one of Ethiopia's distinctive plateaus the emperors of old had used for prisons. Once Emperor Tewodros locked up a few missionaries, some diplomats, and the British consul for several years on one. I thought of that as I rode the elevator up to my room and fell onto my bed. Here I was back in Ethiopia and in one of the best ferenjocch hotels in town that maybe, only coincidentally, looked something like Amba Magdala where Tewodros had housed his foreign guests. Or maybe beneath the gilt and marble and crisp white sheets, you'd find one of those wry Amhara jokes. Yes, the ferenjocch are all safely here, locked away on top of Amba Hilton. We have the key.

I SLEPT FITFULLY AT FIRST AND TRIED VARIOUS RELAXATION techniques and deep-breathing to squelch my mind's treadmill: too many thoughts about the upcoming trip, and about being back in Ethiopia and my previous life here. The Ethiopians are a fatalistic people—not in the sense that everything is foreordained, but rather that each of us has a destiny, *eddileh,* as they call it. My friend, Rahel Fikre Selassie, a great-granddaughter of the Emperor Haile Selassie, often points out moments of eddileh, as if something had to happen in a particular way; there was no other possibility. This is not to be lamented, rather she utters her exclamations—"You see it was your destiny!"—as if making a great and wondrous discovery. It is almost like noticing a miracle, a rainbow in one's life, where destiny has stepped in to hand you something rare and unexpected. Rahel had many times of destiny in her life. She had to flee the military government that deposed her great-grandfather in 1974, but then found people and relatives who spirited her and her brothers and sisters to safety in America—that was destiny. It was destiny that made it possible for her to return years later to Ethiopia to host a special Orthodox prayer service, the *fetate,* for a beloved grandmother, and destiny that kept her other grandmother safe in a palace that the revolutionary soldiers occupied. It was even destiny that she and I had become friends. As for this trip of mine, it was, of course, my destiny.

My sleepy mind kept circling around one memory from my previous life: a trip I made with two women friends, one Ethiopian, one American, to visit a monk outside the city of Debre Markos. He had the reputation of a soothsayer, and Elfranesh, who hailed from Debre Markos, had made him her special advisor. She was a senior student at the university, and whenever she went home, she made the short pilgrimage to his monk's cell. He lived near one of the large, round countryside churches, in a small crib—a hole, really, that had been dug into the side of a hill and faced and roofed with corrugated tin. We hiked up the hill and waited in line to see him. The monk was elderly, wizened, and losing his sight from cataracts. He lay inside the crib on a mat stuffed with straw and covered with a rough cowhide. A white turban covered his hair, and an elaborate brass cross hung from a heavy metal chain on his neck. Elfranesh leaned inside to kiss his cross, and then introduced us. We bowed and thanked him for agreeing to meet us, two foreign women. He smiled and studied us through his milky eyes. He asked us to bend close, raised his cross and showered us with a litany of blessings, then asked a few questions. How long had we been in his country and what were we doing here? Elfranesh translated our answers, and then he said he would dream about us and tell us our fortunes the next day.

I'm not a superstitious person. I've covered science subjects nearly all of my writing life. But I've never forgotten the monk's prediction. "Your heart," he said to me, "is here in Ethiopia with the Ethiopian people and children. You will always be here. You won't leave and you will help the children."

Of course, I had left. But a big chunk of my heart had remained behind. By some fluke, I was back now. Was it eddileh, my destiny, stepping in? And how would I help the children?

I'D SET MY ALARM CLOCK AND ALSO ASKED THE HOTEL STAFF TO give me a wake-up call, and both went off almost simultaneously. It was 5:45 in the morning. I pulled open a curtain and looked out over Addis Ababa. This close to the equator, every day is split nearly evenly between daylight and darkness. The sun wouldn't rise for another 15 minutes, but its rays were already turning the horizon a soft pink. Addis Ababa sits on several low hills just below the Entoto Mountains, and the Hilton Hotel has a perch halfway up one of the hills. It faces a wide, six-lane boulevard that is divided by an overgrown parkway. On the opposite side of the boulevard is the Jubilee Palace (now the National Palace) where Haile Selassie reigned. From my window, I could see the treetops surrounding the palace, and the roofs of various concrete buildings that mark the business section of the city, and the Hilton's own gardens directly below. The city's streetlights were still on, and a smoky haze from the New Year's fires hung in the air. The first taxis of the day were already sputtering up the hill to the Hilton.

I dressed quickly, grabbed my day pack and notebook, and went downstairs. Mau and Mike were already there, and Nevada, Mick, and Bruce soon joined us. We exchanged quick good-mornings, then followed Mau to his Land Cruiser.

"We can get some coffee at the airport," Mau said, cheerfully. "That will help everybody wake up."

Nevada and the others had been in Addis for nearly a week and were by now on Ethiopian time. It was really six o'clock in the evening for me—West Coast–U.S.A time—but I decided not to think about that. Although I'd slept badly, it was morning, I was up, and I wanted to stay awake for this flight.

We drove down the Hilton's hill, past the bolted palace gates, and to the first big intersection, Meskal (Springtime) Square, where many of the revolution's public displays had been held. In 1974, the first year of the revolution, the military government had renamed the square, Kai, or Red Square, and erected enormous, billboard-sized posters of Marx, Lenin, and Engels. Those three bearded ferenjocch had glared out over the citizens of Addis Ababa for almost 20 years. I was glad to see they were gone, and that no posters of other men with larger-than-life egos had been put in their place. The new government had reinstated the square's original name, which was much more fitting for a city named "New Flower"—Addis Ababa.

No one in our party was very talkative. It was too early, and we all needed that first cup of coffee. At the airport, everyone was moving slowly after the New Year's revels. It took Mau a little while to find a clerk from Ethiopian Airlines to ask about our charter. No, there was no problem. But yes, we would have to wait a little while. "Take a seat," the clerk said hospitably. "Make yourselves comfortable."

Mau guided us to a coffee lounge upstairs, where the staff was just making the first fresh brew of the day. We pushed a couple of tables together and sat down. As in many developing countries, time is regarded differently in Ethiopia. It moves slower; people don't always show up for appointments. I sank back in my chair: I had a feeling our flight was going to happen on Ethiopian time.

Nevada and Bruce seemed equally unperturbed. Mick was still pumped up from being in a strange, exotic country with so many wonderful things to photograph, and a little itchy to get going. Mau lit a cigarette. "It's a bad habit, I know," he said, waving the smoke away, "but, you know, I can't give it up. I've tried." He laughed and leaned his elbows on the table. Mike Speaks didn't seem particularly worried either. He pulled out a map of the Blue Nile Gorge and studied it. The waiter brought us each a tiny china cup filled to the brim with espresso-style Ethiopian coffee, then returned to pour tea into a large mug for Nevada. Personally, I was thankful for the strong coffee—I needed the jolt—and sipped it down quickly.

From the lounge, you could look down over the ticket counters and terminal entrance, and Mau jumped up from time to time to see if he could spot the Ethiopian army guard who was supposed to accompany us on our flight. We needed such a security official along, Mau explained, because Ethiopia was at war with Eritrea. Our flight—and our rafting trip—would take us into militarily sensitive areas. The guard would make sure that Nevada and Mick did not film anything the Ethiopian government did not want photographed.

"It's the border war," Mau said, taking a long drag on his cigarette. "It's heated up a little bit."

"In the States, it's been reported as a minor skirmish," added Mike, "but it's not seen that way here."

Several months before, Eritrea had invaded Ethiopia, claiming a border town and a 1,200-square-mile triangle of land as its own. Ethiopia had responded swiftly and mounted a successful counterinvasion. Neither side would yield, and despite appeals from the United Nations, the two countries were hammering each other with every weapon they could lay their hands on.

"I don't think it's really so much about the border," Mau said, voicing an opinion I would hear from many Ethiopians. "These two leaders [Meles Zenawi, the prime minister of Ethiopia and Issais Afewerk, the president of Eritrea] are cousins, you know. They fought together, side-by-side, to free Eritrea from Ethiopia, and then to free Ethiopia from the Derg, Ethiopia's military government. Now, they can't stand each other. So they're fighting."

It was like hearing about the long-ago wars in Ethiopia's Age of the Princes before Emperor Menelik I united the country and restored meaning to his title of *Negusa Negast*, King of Kings. Every province had its own Ras, who were then really like kings, and every Ras had his own army. Menelik had broken the power of the Rases, and then partly as a sign of the centralization of power, built Ethiopia's new permanent capital, Addis Ababa.

Menelik's men had fought on horseback with breech-loading rifles, spears, swords, and rhino-hide shields for protection. The Ethiopian and Eritrean soldiers were blasting at each other with a modern arsenal: AK47 assault rifles, rocket launchers, land mines, and jets laden with bombs. Both sides were in a heightened state of suspicion, and Mau made it clear that our expedition had been very lucky to receive official approval.

"In fact," he said, stubbing out his cigarette, "I'm still working on getting you the last permit—the big one. It gives you permission to raft beneath the Abay Bridge," the modern highway bridge that links Ethiopia's Shoa Province to Gojam. "That's the main highway to the north, where the war is, and it's the major supply route. The army has soldiers crawling all over that bridge."

Ethiopia's soldiers had itchy trigger fingers, too. Only the week before, the army shot down a small private plane belonging to a South African company that flew across the border from Eritrea to Ethiopia. Several foreigners, reportedly Belgians and South Africans, were aboard. All were killed.

"I think the pilot did something a little strange," Mau said. "He didn't stick to the flight plan. He disappeared over Eritrea for a while, as if he had landed somewhere."

To the Ethiopians, it appeared that the foreigners had given some form of aid, possibly weapons, to the Eritreans. They didn't ask the plane to land so they could interrogate the pilot; they launched a missile and blasted the plane from the sky.

"We want to be sure we have that permit," Mau concluded, a little twinkle in his eye. "We don't want any soldiers shooting at you. Anyway, you'll be traveling the other direction, away from the war, so it shouldn't be a big deal. The permit will come."

But if it didn't, the trip was off. There was no sense heading into a military zone in our army-gray rafts without the complete approval of the Ethiopian government.

"We'd look just like some invading force coming down the Nile," said Mike. "And I'm sure every soldier on the bridge would do his utmost to protect mother Ethiopia."

By now, we'd waited for our pilot and security guard for more than a half hour. Mike checked his watch impatiently. "Don't you think it's about time to shout at somebody?" he asked Mau. "I mean we *have* all the permissions for this flight."

There was a strident, demanding edge in Speaks's voice that surprised me, given the amount of international travel he'd done—and the country's state-of-war. Mau shrugged. "Well, yes, we have the permissions, but the pilot must be given his route, and maybe they are a little short-handed because some people came in late today. Maybe there are some hangovers. It was New Year's last night, you know."

Nevada said nothing. So far she had let Mike issue every order, and seemed content for him to take the lead. They had been in Addis for a week, making the final trip plans, so perhaps they had come to some agreement about the trip's hierarchy. We were going to have a team dinner that evening. I thought—hoped—that Nevada would speak up then and talk about her role as organizer and leader of this National Geographic expedition.

Mau went downstairs to check once again on our flight, and was suddenly bounding back up the stairs. "Let's go! Grab your stuff, the pilot's here," he called to us.

A few minutes later, we boarded the chartered Cessna and headed down the runway. We were only an hour later than planned.

The pilot, a slim, distinguished-looking man, headed a little north and then west toward the Blue Nile. In minutes we had left behind the high-rises of Addis and were over Ethiopia's central highlands, the countryside a lush green from the rains. Below us, little clusters of round, thatched homes stood grouped in tight circles, while fanned around them like the rays of a halo were the farmers' freshly planted fields. We crossed canyons and big plateaus, then spotted the Muger River, one of the Blue Nile's main tributaries, winding along a wide rocky bed. The pilot flew along the Muger, then guided our plane over another plateau and across one more large canyon with blocky, black walls of basalt and waterfalls spilling over its lip, and then into the canyon of the Blue Nile.

"This is the Abay," he announced. "Your river."

Nevada gave a thumbs-up and a big smile, then turned to her cameras. She wanted an aerial shot of the river, one that would capture the immense size and grandeur of the landscape below. Plateaus, mountains, and canyons in shades of soft pastel reds, creams, and pinks marched to the far horizon, and there in the middle, its waters a milk-chocolate hue, ran the Blue Nile.

Mike Speaks had his map at the ready. "Okay, there's the bridge," he said, pointing to a concrete structure spanning the river. "Let's hope Mau's permits do the trick."

The security guard had moved to our side of the plane. "No pictures, no pictures," he said, scowling at Nevada and Mick. We had heard enough about Ethiopian soldiers to heed his orders, and they quickly put down their cameras.

The pilot banked left and headed downstream above a section of the river known as the Black Gorge. Arne Rubin, one of the first explorers to successfully put a boat on the river, traveled from the Abay Bridge and through the Black Gorge in a kayak in 1965. He had taken out just a few miles from the Sudanese border. In his book, *Ensam med Blu Nilen*, the Swedish Rubin mentioned encountering a "huge wave" some distance into the gorge, and Speaks wanted a look at this.

"I also need to get some idea of places we might camp and find fresh drinking water," said Mike. "We'll need to find some clear streams with all that silt in the river. And if we don't find some beaches in this rocky stretch, I'm not sure what we'll do—maybe build sleeping platforms in the trees."

Below us, the river flowed through a narrow channel between steep mountains. The mountains kept it in a tight embrace, and the Blue Nile roiled along, kicking up a series of waves that Speaks called "haystacks," as if it were trying to break free. Sharp black rocks covered the shoreline and beyond them rose a thick and prickly acacia forest. It wasn't an especially inviting environment, and I wasn't surprised that there wasn't a village to be seen. Our pilot, who'd given the controls to his copilot, felt differently.

"It's uninhabited!," he exclaimed. "Not a soul down there. All that good land and it's empty. I'd like to come back and check it out; find a place to farm."

I liked his pioneering spirit and said so. "Well, you know, in our hearts every Ethiopian wants a farm," he said. "And that's open country."

"The river's well below it's high-flood line," Speaks said, pointing to a white line on the rocks. "That's good; the rapids won't be such big boils."

We flew on, studying the river and land, until Speaks announced, "Ok. This looks like Arne's big one—that's a huge cataract." He was silent for a minute, watching as the waves below foamed and fought their way downstream. "Well, it looks like death on the far right, but doable on the left, through that big wave. We'll just go right down the center of it: 'Hey diddle, diddle, right down the middle.'" Speaks smiled broadly.

Our reconnaissance flight ended at the second modern bridge over the river and about 120 miles downstream from the Abay Bridge. The pilot banked and we flew back up the river. "There's another big set of rapids right there," Speaks said. "See how they're curling back on themselves, rising up and folding over? If a wave like that is big enough, it could capsize a raft, but it looks to me like there's plenty of room to maneuver. I've seen what I need to see."

The pilot had helped Nevada and Mick open the rear door of the aircraft, and the two photographers were leaning as far out as they dared to get their shots. Nevada seemed frustrated. She wanted the plane to fly across the river at an angle, not fly parallel to it. We tried to pass along her request, and the copilot made a bit of a turn, but it didn't seem to be what Nevada wanted. She pulled back from the door and looked down at the river, shaking her head. We were almost back to the Abay Bridge, and I gathered she had not gotten the shot she needed. And we were out of time.

I turned back to the river. A steel blue Goliath heron was flying upstream, its body stretched out like a swimmer's, its wings lifting and falling in lazy arcs. On the near shore was the land of Gojam. The Blue Nile encircled it like a moat, and it was easy to see how in the past warring kings and princes had used the river like a barricade; they could retreat to their mountaintops beyond the Nile and feel as secure as if they'd pulled up a drawbridge behind them. Gojamis, the people of Gojam, were proud and independent-minded, even by Ethiopian standards. In their isolation, they regarded themselves as the keepers of the old empire's true culture; their spoken Amharic was the purest, their poets the most clever. Theirs was the land, too, of wizards and magic, and of the *buda*, people cursed with the evil eye, who took the shape of hyenas at night and went prowling for victims in the dark. We'd be among them all—saints, songsters, and sorcerers—tomorrow.

seven

~~~

OUR RECONNAISSANCE FLIGHT HAD GIVEN ME A BETTER IDEA of what we were getting into—and made it perfectly clear why the river wasn't used like the Mississippi or White Nile as a link between towns and a way to transport people and goods. It wasn't because of the great numbers or size of the rapids, but more because of the narrowness of the river. It was like a rock-filled, wet toboggan run. And this was near its high-water level. Later in the year, some months after the rains had ended, it would be far lower, and pocked with more boulders, making it even harder to travel any distance in an ordinary boat. No wonder the Ethiopians regarded the Blue Nile as a barrier rather than a conveyor.

The landscape, too, looked exceedingly harsh even from the plane. The gorge's narrow walls would hold in the heat, and its black-rock shoreline would drive the temperature to blast-furnace heights. It was likely to be humid down there, too, since the rains were only now trailing off. And all that heat and water this close to the equator meant mosquitoes, the malaria-bearing kind. For the highland Ethiopians, who are used to a cool, temperate clime and lack immunity to malaria, this was like a double-whammy. It didn't help either that the river was said to be thick with numerous examples of East Africa's crocodile, *Crocodilus niloticus*, which reportedly grew to the size of small dinosaurs and had tempers to match. No, for the highlanders, there was only one way to deal with the Blue Nile: cross it as quickly as possible and leave it behind.

Most of the river in Ethiopia, about 99 percent of it, lacks bridges even of the simplest kind. From the books I'd read, however, this proved less of a handicap to the Ethiopians than might be imagined. Bridges are expensive, difficult to engineer in such terrain, and prone to washing out. And so the local peasants long ago devised what was essentially an inflatable raft for crossing the river, the *jandi*. Using the closest materials at hand, they created these small floating barges from tanned ox hides that are stuffed with dry grass and tightly sewn shut. Father Pedro Páez saw people using jandis on his visit to the Blue Nile in 1613, and they were still in use during Cheesman's time more than 300 years later. The explorer Charles F. Rey and his wife crossed the Blue Nile on one in the 1920s.

"If goods are to be transported," Rey wrote of this journey, "they are put inside [the jandi]; if human beings, they squat on the top *à la turque* or let their legs dangle in the water; in either case swimmers pull and push the unwieldy craft, which rocks and rolls like a Channel steamer on a bad day. It looks much more alarming than it is," he added, but the passage so worried some of his porters that they decided they wanted to be carried across *inside* the float. "How they escaped suffocation I cannot imagine," Rey continued. "They certainly seemed rather sad when we extracted them from their quarters on arrival at the opposite shore." Rey thought the jandi the most "primitive form of boat in use today," yet the Ethiopians managed to safely convey everything from salt to Ras Hailu's disassembled car in or on top of them.

Ethiopians also crossed the river at its higher levels by simply swimming with their mules and livestock after first firing bullets into the water to frighten off the crocodiles, and at one crossing another traveler reported that the people held on to the tails of buffalos that had been specially trained to brave the Nile's waters. Closer to the Sudan, Cheesman saw a rough-hewn dory on the river, but it too was solely used to ferry people from one shore to the other. In the dry season, when the Blue Nile's waters dropped, there were several places where the river could actually be waded across.

There were about a half dozen of these well-known fords or ferry points, and the trails that wound down to them through the mountains and plateaus were as wide in places as country roads from the human foot and livestock traffic. The Abay Bridge—which we'd been forbidden to photograph and was heavily guarded against Eritrean attack—had been built at one of the most popular crossings, called Shafartak. The Blue Nile's Gorge was really a canyon here: eighteen miles across, and nearly a mile deep. For the rulers of Gojam, it was like having the Grand Canyon as your backyard, and they weren't necessarily keen about having the enormous gap bridged. That changed in 1933, when the recently crowned Emperor Haile Selassie I ordered a road for vehicles to be built from both sides of the canyon to the ford. He'd already had his share of troubles with the Gojami ruler Ras Hailu, the car buff, who'd been caught in a plot to restore the former deposed emperor, Lij Iyasu. That stunt landed the wily Ras in a prison cell; his freedom was gone and so now was the isolation of his province. Like it or not, the road was built and Gojam linked to central Ethiopia.

Cheesman happened to witness part of the road's construction as thousands of Ethiopian peasants labored with pick and shovel to clear rocks and shape a track that curved in long hairpin turns to the river. At first, a large pontoon connected by ropes to windlasses on either shore transported vehicles over the Blue Nile. Then, a few years after the end of World War II, the present bridge with its great central arch was built across the river. One small stretch of Ethiopia's Blue Nile had at last been drawn into the 20th century.

Yet no one in a boat or raft had succeeded in navigating the river's length. That "un-run" quality was like a dare for boating afficionados, and in the 1950s, the first explorers since McMillan's failed enterprise decided to brave the Blue Nile.

These explorers were of a decidedly different breed than those of the past. By now the airline industry was beginning to open up exotic lands to everyone. Armchair travelers who may have once been content to read about Speke and Burton and Bruce could take a little adventure holiday of his or her own. How else to explain the unlikely quartet of German and Swiss naturists—also known as nudists—who decided to tackle the Blue Nile in 1955?

Herbert Rittlinger and his wife, Aveckle, made up one of the pairs; the other couple was named Rosie Mobius, and her boyfriend, a certain Bob. In his book about their journey, *Ethiopian Adventure*, Rittlinger never does reveal Bob's last name. Indeed, Rittlinger provides only the barest of details about his boating partner: Bob is Swiss and an air force jet pilot, and the idea of journeying down the Blue Nile was his. The two couples planned to travel in three collapsible kayaks, one a tandem. Naive and slightly arrogant, they seemed not to recognize the hazards of their journey, despite numerous warnings from the Ethiopians and Europeans in Addis Ababa about "whole acres of crocodiles [in the gorge], shiftas, places teeming with snakes." "'Always wear high boots!'" they were warned. "'Take dubbin! [a snake-bite treatment]' Fever, leprosy, bilharziasis, and [a] poisonous steam [are other dangers] in the Abbai valley." The deathly steam was supposedly released when the sun heated the gorge's black basalt rocks.

There was also the unhappy account of an unnamed Austrian couple who apparently attempted to canoe the river in the 1930s. The husband launched his craft about a quarter of the way down the river at the old Second Portuguese Bridge (also called the Broken Bridge, since the center arch was destroyed by Ethiopian patriots during the Italian occupation). A mere ten yards from shore, his canoe capsized and a crocodile dragged him to his death, right before his wife's eyes. Rittlinger and his partners heard this gruesome tale on 27 separate occasions.

None of the warnings put them off. They seemed to regard every story as a kind of myth or legend, and considered their journey a lark, a jolly pleasure-outing. "Why did we do it all?" Rittlinger imagines his reader asking. "[T]he answer comes lightly and freely from my pen— because we *enjoyed* it."

Beginning at the Abay Bridge, they intended to travel as far down the Blue Nile, "Africa's last enigma," as they could. Like our team, they needed many permits from the Ethiopian government, and they had these in hand when they unloaded their boats and gear at the bridge. Then, as now, it was under heavy guard, and as they carried their kayaks to the water's edge, a sergeant came running up, and cried, "*Abai yellum*—The Blue Nile—No!" He would not let them launch their boats and, since neither he nor any of his men read Amharic, he could not understand their permits. The impasse lasted a week, but eventually the team succeeded in getting an oral command sent to the soldiers from no one less than the emperor saying that the naturists should be allowed to carry on. Rittlinger and crew had kept their kayaks packed, and they pushed onto the Blue Nile at once. It was the dry season, the water was low and clear—and blue (unlike the muddy river we'd seen on our flight).

The team encountered their "first fair-sized rapids" not long after they set out, wrote Rittlinger. "It was a pleasure to shoot across whirlpools and foam in our fast kayaks, with the clear waters of the Blue Nile coming to meet us…. In the great heat, the bubbling of the white water was delicious." The superheated air of the canyon wasn't the least bit poisonous; in fact, the foursome found it health-inducing and "went about in the accepted naturist fashion. We wore open sandals on our feet and at the most an old canoeing cap on our heads"—and nothing in between. They were alone on "an innocent, enchanting, paradisiacal dream river," and exploring "the great canyon of the Blue Nile…one of the last mysteries of the Dark Continent."

It didn't take them long to discover one of the reasons the Blue Nile had remained a mystery. The crocodiles they'd been warned about and which they'd dismissed as legend were real. And they were very large. "The first we saw—well, they were really something!" wrote Rittlinger, his usual what-me-worry attitude gone. "I would never have believed such things existed. They were not only longer, but also broader and higher than our boats." Some measured between 18 and 20 feet in length, and they lay on either side of the river, which had shrunk to a mere 30 yards at this point and was very shallow. To continue their journey, the team would have to run this toothy gantlet. They shouted and slapped the waters with their paddles, and two of the behemoths slithered into the water, disappearing beneath its surface. "They didn't leave so much as a ripple on the mirror-smooth surface of the water," Rittlinger wrote. "It was done so quietly that we believed we had suffered an hallucination. A trick of the heat. It gave us an eerie feeling."

Nevertheless with the crocodiles out of sight, the kayakers decided to paddle on—over the backs of these reptiles. And they made it.

"'You see,'" Rittlinger commented to his wife, "'they're afraid themselves. Handle them the right way and they're scared stiff.' After that, we went over hundreds of crocodiles."

The next day, they paddled over even more crocodiles, all the while "singing, shouting and whistling" to keep them at bay. Rittlinger admits that the silent crocodiles and their "glassy, staring eyes" were beginning to get on everyone's nerves. And then they encountered one that wasn't so easily scared. The crocodile shot up from beneath his wife's boat, nearly capsizing it. She whacked it on the head with her paddle, an action so futile that Rittlinger described it as comparable to "striking a dragon with a match-stick." The crocodile nevertheless retreated, and dived back into the river's depths.

Bravely—or foolishly—the team carried on. Rittlinger's account is not clear about how far or long they traveled, but the crocodiles with their "deadly eyes" were always with them and always made their "hearts beat loudly." When another one attacked, they decided to stop. This one made a beeline—once again for the boat of Rittlinger's wife. With a great crunching sound, it picked up the stern of her kayak and lifted it so high that she fell forward onto the bow. Once again, luck was with her. Aveckle did not capsize or panic and, when the crocodile dropped her boat, she began paddling furiously toward shore, even as the beast "appeared by her side again, its jaws wide open, hissing." Then for some reason, perhaps because it had not liked the taste of her metal rudder, it sank from view. She reached the sandy bank and safety, and broke down, weeping. But Aveckle collected herself and urged the group to go on. Her husband, however, had tired of watching crocodiles chase his wife, and found some local people with mules to take them and their boats back to Addis Ababa.

Later Bob of the missing surname and Rosie Mobius launched their kayaks closer to the Sudanese border, near the Dabus (or Yabus) River where there were more people and consequently fewer crocodiles, and paddled without mishap to Khartoum.

Four years later, in 1959, another explorer, Kuno Steuben, decided to test the Blue Nile's waters. In some ways, he appears to have been cut from the same quixotic cloth as Rittlinger. He, too, was German, but he was younger, in his early twenties, and had given himself up to a nomadic life—although not in the naturist's style. He was seeking an "earthly paradise" and, despite having read Rittlinger's crocodile-filled account and hearing many of the same warnings in Ethiopia from the same Cassandras who'd tried to talk Rittlinger's team out of its jaunt, believed he would find it in the Blue Nile Gorge.

Steuben met no one in Addis Ababa who shared his romantic belief. "The Blue Nile does not give its secrets willingly," one old German advised him. The German had lived in East Africa and Ethiopia most of his life, and regarded the gorge and its river exactly as the Ethiopians did: It was a place to be avoided. "It has every means with which to fight off intruders," he told the young man, "and it is guarded like the mythological Hades, from dragon-like creatures to insects, to kill you. It will always be the unexpected that will do you in...."

Steuben wasn't about to be put off, and in January 1959, after winning enough money for his trip in an Addis Ababa casino, launched himself Huckleberry Finn-style down the Blue Nile from the Abay Bridge—on a homemade raft. He'd built his 17-foot raft at the river's edge from a dozen eucalyptus logs. For carrying his provisions, he had three waterproof oil drums, and he fixed these fore and aft, and in the center. He used another long eucalyptus pole for steering, although the raft was so heavy, he could not really guide it. Instead, he gave himself and his craft up to the river (after escaping from the Abay Bridge soldiers who had detained him just as they had Rittlinger's troop).

Of all the journeys on the Blue Nile, Steuben's surely ranks as the most intrepid and romantic. He had a shotgun and fish hooks, a tent and sleeping bag, matches, flour, salt, sugar, and spices, cooking gear, three bottles of Scotch, some beer, and a small medicine chest; and with these few stores and his crude raft, he traveled farther down the river than anyone had to date. He also had a great deal of common sense, and the skills of an Eagle Scout, despite what seems the utter foolishness of his undertaking.

Like a latter-day Daniel Boone, Steuben drifted down the Blue Nile, alert and fearless, a bowie knife strapped to his waist. His raft, he learned, was tough and stable, and could bang its way against the rocks and through the rapids. He wasn't in a hurry. If he traveled five-to-ten miles a day that was plenty, since he was very capable of living off the land. He shot antelopes, game fowls, wart hogs, and monkeys for his pot, or cast a line and reeled in a fat catfish. Sundays, he slept in late and took little exploratory hikes.

Two weeks passed in this idyllic manner and even Steuben could not quite believe the perfect, dreamlike nature of his trip. "The crocodiles I found were much better than their reputation," he later wrote. "On the whole I was surprised to find everything going so easily and it seemed to be much more of a vacation trip through a national park than the 'first navigation' of a wild river in an 'evil, notorious country.'"

Perhaps it was the size of his raft that deterred the crocodiles. Once three charged him simultaneously, but two turned away, and he shot the third one as it rose up beneath his raft. Sometimes he shot them for food and, ever mindful of his wallet, salted down their valuable skins to trade when he returned to Addis. Hippos and hyenas caused him occasional headaches, too, but his biggest problem by far came from the people—the shiftas.

One night as Steuben slept on shore in his tent, thieves stole everything he had stored on his raft and in the oil drums. He lost half his ammunition supply, his liquor, clothing, many of his medicines, and extra rope. The theft momentarily depressed him, but he still had his raft, shotgun, and enough other supplies to sustain him until he reached Sudan.

Another three weeks passed. And then one morning, four young Oromo men walked into his camp. One had a muzzle-loading rifle slung over his back; all carried spears, bows and arrows, and knives. They seemed merely inquisitive at first, inspecting his white skin and aluminum pots. He gave them some fish hooks and coffee. They smiled as they squatted around his campfire, then turned sullen. Suddenly, without warning or provocation, they attacked. One threw him on the ground, while another stabbed him in the side. But Steuben grabbed his own knife and struck out wildly. "I fumed with rage not so much because I was fighting for my life, but rather because the natives had been almost visibly sure that they would succeed." He was certain they wanted what the Gumuz people had taken from Jessen's Sudanese assistant: a male trophy. Somehow, although outnumbered, Steuben stabbed one of the men, hit the second in the face with a rock, and managed to shoot the third with his shotgun. The "natives" ran into the bush, and Steuben, after grabbing his tent and few belongings, staggered onto his raft and cut it loose. He was bleeding heavily from his wound and had no thoughts except to get away. The Blue Nile could carry him where it would.

Steuben remembered little about the next several days. He had landed his raft, pitched his tent, stuffed his wound with medicine, then collapsed in a fever. Slowly it healed; slowly he resumed his journey. He found a stream with gold flakes and nuggets, and the energy to spend

An Ethiopian Orthodox priest blesses a woman with water collected from the sacred springs of Gishe Abay. Many Ethiopians regard the springs as the source of the country's greatest river, the Blue Nile, or *Abay Wenz.*

Thundering out of Lake Tana, the Blue Nile Falls—or *Tis Isat* (Smoke of the Fire)—plunge 150 feet into a narrow canyon. Our expedition started its month-long trek and rafting journey on the Blue Nile from this overlook above the falls.

Two Ethiopian farmers joined Nevada and me on our climb to the summit of 10,433-foot Mount Gishe. Below them, in the green lands of Gojam, lie the springs of the Blue Nile.

Sunset on Lake Tana finds two fishermen heading home with their catch in traditional reed boats, called *tankwas*.

Like many of the Ethiopian highland people we encountered,
Mati Eich, a woman we met in the market of Sakhala, displays her devotion
to the Ethiopian Orthodox Church with a cross and prayer beads.

Flanked by his fellow priests, Mariegeta Birhane Tsige stands on the steps of Saint Michael's Church at Gishe Abay. Mariegeta Birhane guided us to the summit of Mount Gishe, sharing his knowledge and legends of the Blue Nile along the way.

VIRGINIA MORELL

Our trail from
the Blue Nile Falls
wound through rich
farmland above
the river. The falls'
waters funnel through
a steep canyon far
below us, visible
here only as a line
of dark-green trees.

Kasawol Abate, at far
left, and several other
porters and guards
warm themselves at
a campfire along
our trail above the
Blue Nile.

Some of the highland Amhara villagers we met were afraid of us and watched us warily. Our light-colored eyes might hit them with the *budda*, an evil spirit, they feared. The young girl wears safety pins, beads, and leather amulets for protection; her chin tattoos indicate that she is married.

Zelalem Abera Woldegiorgis, our chief interpreter, greets a group of lowland Gumuz people we met on the lower reaches of the Blue Nile.

Abush, a young boy traveling along the Blue Nile, attached himself to our trekking caravan for a few days. He had been bitten by dogs, so Kate, our paramedic, patched his wounds. Abush left us at the Second Portuguese (or Broken) Bridge, braving the rope crossing above the river's surging waters. The three boats for our raft trip are visible on the far shore.

Ethiopian Orthodox Christians adorn themselves with embroidered and silver crosses to show their faith. They wear amulets to protect themselves from evil spirits, such as the *jinn*, which live in the depths of the Blue Nile. The rings of brass and silver attest that this woman is married.

Atele Asseras, the headman of the village of Abo Gedam, looks out over the valley of the Blue Nile and the land of *Genete Maryam*—Mary's Heaven. Atele Asseras nearly shot our boatman, Mike Speaks, a few years before, believing that he and his rafting companions were invading Ethiopia.

several days panning for treasure. His wound, however, festered, and he fell into a fever again. When he awoke, he was in a native's hut far from the river, on one of the high plateaus. The villagers had found and rescued him, and in time, they cured him. They offered him one of their daughters as a wife, but Steuben declined. What he really wanted was a mule and a guide, and when these were provided, Steuben started back for the Abay Bridge. He had traveled 160 miles on a raft down the Blue Nile where no white man had ever gone. And even he was somewhat incredulous at what he had achieved.

"I had never quite believed this business about 'untouched country,' because everyone who happens to travel off the beaten path sounds off about these secret, virgin territories. But now since I have found and seen one…I am convinced that more such places still exist. I might get under way soon in I don't know what strange or remote part of the world, but I wonder whether I shall ever get back to the canyon of the Blue Nile."

IF NOTHING ELSE, STEUBEN'S SOLO JOURNEY PROVED THAT THE Blue Nile could be rafted. Others soon followed, although they were not always as lucky as he had been. An Italian geologist reportedly started down the river in a kayak from the Abay Bridge in 1961; he was never seen again. The next year, a Swiss-French team of six launched below the bridge in two three-seater fiberglass canoes. They were well-equipped and prepared, and were only eight miles from their takeout point near the Sudanese border when they were attacked in the middle of the night. Two members of their expedition, Henry Kadrnka, a world-class kayaking champion, and Dr. Stanley Walter, who had been a Swiss Olympic athlete, were shot and killed as they slept. The others fled on bare feet and hid among the rocks. They each had a revolver and for a few terrifying moments had a pitched gun battle with the intruders. Then another member of their party, Freddy Weber, was wounded in the neck and collapsed. Realizing they would all be killed if they stayed where they were, the four survivors, including the injured Weber, managed to fling themselves into one of their boats and escape, shooting the rapids by night. Later, the Ethiopian government provided them a plane to fly over the murder scene. Everything had disappeared—tents, boats, and the two bodies of their friends. The incident did not amuse the emperor. He dispatched a punitive force from the Ethiopian Army, which apprehended the murderers. They were tried and convicted, then returned to the site of their crime, and hung on the spot.

Another lone kayaker, named Mr. Haas, tried to run the river between the Broken Bridge and the Abay Bridge in 1964. He lost his boat and equipment five days into his journey, and is said to have returned to Addis in nothing but his swimsuit. That did not deter two Germans, Klaus Denart and Gunther Kriegk, who launched their kayaks two days later from the same spot and traveled as far as the Didesa River, one of the Blue Nile's big tributaries.

Then in 1965, the Swede, Arne Rubin, pushed off from the Abay Bridge in his kayak, and in a record-setting nine days made it to the Sudanese border. It was Rubin's account that Mike Speaks carried on our aerial reconnaissance.

Rubin and a friend, Carl-Gustav Forsmark, tackled the upper portion of the river below Tis Isat Falls the following year. They fought their way through the white water for 15 miles before giving up and walking out.

Finally, in 1968, a British-Ethiopian expedition set out to bring the Blue Nile to its knees. Under the leadership of Captain John Blashford-Snell, a team of 70 servicemen and civilians equipped with four motorized metal, double-hulled boats, three inflatable rubber rafts, and airplane and wireless support, managed to run nearly every mile of the river, including the tumultuous portions above and below Tis Isat Falls. They did so by breaking the river into sections. One team in the metal boats journeyed from the Abay Bridge and reached the Didesa River several weeks later; a second team took one day to paddle the 20 miles of torrential white water just above Tis Isat Falls; and this same group then spent the next five days traveling from the waterfall to the Abay Bridge through extremely rough rapids, some of which they had to portage. In spite of their military training and apparatus, they lost a man to drowning when he was dragged on a rope across the river. And perhaps because of their military appearance, they were attacked by local people and fought two gun battles in the night, much as the Swiss-French team had seven years before, although on a different stretch of the river. This time no one was killed.

The British Ethiopian "Great Abbai" expedition provided the most detailed account of the river and its rapids, and most of us had a copy of Richard Snailham's book about it, *The Blue Nile Revealed*.

The success of this massive assault did not put an end to other peoples' more individualistic dreams. In 1970, two Germans, Rudiger Nehberg and Hinrich Finck, journeyed down the river from the Broken Bridge in a fiberglass boat they had designed and that had all the grace of a bathtub. They had read Steuben's book and yearned for a similar adventure. They got it. In the same area where the British expedition had been attacked, young men hurled rocks and shouted "high-pitched war cries" at them. They shot back and wounded one of their attackers, which only infuriated them more. For the next three days, the two Germans endured a fusillade of stones, hurled insults, and hostile behavior from angry men on shore. Some even dared to swim out toward the boat as if hoping to capsize it. The pair finally paddled beyond this "region of the ill-tempered people," and reached the Abay Bridge, but there lost their boat when it lodged below a sunken tree.

In 1972, four British kayakers traveled from Lake Tana to the Abay Bridge, fending off crocodiles and dodging shifta bullets, and a four-man Italian team used motorized rubber rafts to journey from the Abay Bridge to close to the Sudanese border.

Two years later, Richard Bangs, Jim Slade, and Cherry Jensen traveled nine days in oar-powered rubber rafts from the Broken Bridge to the Abay Bridge, a distance of 140 miles. They carried supplies for a young American, Scot Johnson, who planned to walk the length of the Blue Nile Gorge. Johnson was starting his trip a week before Bangs's, and the two men had agreed on specific tributaries along the way where Johnson would leave the rafters messages about his progress. For the first several days, the rafters found all of Johnson's notes. Then they rowed through the section of the gorge where the British team and two Germans had been attacked, and suddenly found themselves being similarly treated. Above them, along the canyon rim, a crowd of angry men appeared, hurling jagged chunks of rock at them and their boats. Bangs and Slade pulled hard on their oars, moving the rafts out of harm's way and into the main current. Still shaken by the encounter, they camped that night at the next tributary where they expected to see Johnson's next note. They did not find one. And despite searching several side canyons and other tributaries, they never found another message from Johnson. He was never seen again.

And then, the next year, the Blue Nile claimed Richard Bangs's close friend, Lew Greenwald. Two other Americans, Bill Hammatt and Peter Antles, were also killed during their attempt to hike from the Blue Nile's source at Mount Gishe to the Sudan. Bandits apparently attacked and murdered them; their bodies were never found. Rudiger Nehberg and three other Germans also ran into trouble with shiftas during their third attempt to raft the river. A group of men, some armed, came into their camp one morning. They were not friendly, and one suddenly lifted his rifle and shot Michael Teichmann, Nehberg's cameraman, in the back of the head. The Germans were armed, and a short battled ensued and they escaped. Police were dispatched to investigate these murders—but this time they were not sent by order of the emperor, because there was no longer an emperor.

THE LAST SERIES OF TRAGIC INCIDENTS HAPPENED IN 1975, THE second year of the Ethiopian revolution. Much of the country was in turmoil, and remote regions such as the Blue Nile Gorge were close to anarchy as small uprisings and rebellions tested the strength of the new military regime. I was still living in Ethiopia, watching as the country lurched from empire to rebellion to the uncertainty of the Derg, a committee of 120 men from the armed forces that was formed to rule the country. The revolution—the dethronement of the Emperor Haile Selassie I—had not been an instantaneous, single event, but had happened gradually almost languorously over many months as a group of noncommissioned officers chipped away at the emperor's strength, drew back, then pushed forward to lop off a little more.

Finally, on September 12, 1974, at six o'clock in the morning, two tanks clanked up the asphalt drive of Jubilee Palace, followed by a dark green Volkswagen. Three military officers walked into the emperor's chamber. As usual, he had risen before dawn and was dressed in his full military uniform, a row of ribbons and medals on his chest.

During the preceding nine months, the military had slowly stripped the 82-year-old emperor of his powers. They had imprisoned many of his closest advisors and family members, nationalized his palaces and private businesses, and denounced him and his family on the radio and television stations as thieves who had stolen millions of dollars from the state treasury. Throughout these humiliations, the emperor insisted to his family that his soldiers were loyal to him, to the crown, to Ethiopia. So he stood erect and proud before the three officers, and did not blink or tremble when one of the trio stepped forward and read a proclamation deposing him. The emperor's only response was that if this was being done for the good of the people and Ethiopia, then he would accept it. He followed the soldiers outside to the Volkswagen.

That was the only moment the emperor hesitated. "I'm supposed to go like this?" he asked with surprise. He had always been chauffeured in black limousines. "Yes," the soldiers answered. Haile Selassie offered no other protest, but bent down and climbed into the back of the car and was whisked away to the Fourth Division Headquarters.

It was done so quietly, so peacefully, I never imagined the horrors that would follow. The day the emperor was deposed, I was actually far from Addis Ababa in a town called Jima near the western border of the country. The university wasn't scheduled to open for the fall session for another week, and I'd gone with some friends on a country bus to see this distant part of Ethiopia where the hills were green with coffee plantations. We were staying in a small hotel run by a large, demonstrative Oromo woman who kept her hair wrapped in a white embroidered turban and wore a heavy gold cross at her throat.

I didn't hear the soldiers' announcement that morning on the radio, proclaiming the end of Haile Selassie's reign. I wandered into the hotel's coffee bar around 7:30 a.m. I'd been there a couple of days and usually at this hour, there were small groups of people sitting at the metal tables, sipping little cups of espresso. But it was deserted. There was a curious tenseness in the air, and the owner looked agitated. I'd thought about returning to Addis later that morning and asked her if she knew when the bus would leave.

"No, no…no bus," she said, waving her hands. She used her bulk to block the door leading outside.

"I don't understand," I began.

"Haile Selassie…*Abakah!*… finished," she said, searching for an English word to convey what had happened.

"*Mut neh?*—Is he dead?" I asked, wondering if he had died of natural causes or if the soldiers had killed him.

"*Yellum!*" Encouraged by my little Amharic, she spouted a string of sentences, which only left me more puzzled. Finally, she grabbed the emperor's picture from the wall, threw it on the floor and stepped on it, breaking the glass.

"*Abakah,*" she repeated. She wiped her hands together as if she'd just dusted off a dirty countertop.

Slowly the full meaning of her words dawned on me. The revolution was complete, the new military government had ordered everything shut down while they secured their power, and everyone was in a sense under house arrest. A small wave of uncertainty hit me, and for a few minutes, my heart raced. But there was nothing to be done. I could not leave Jima; I did not want to leave Ethiopia. Better to follow this woman's advice and stay indoors and wait. I went back to my room, got a book to read, and returned to the bar to order a cup of coffee.

I never read a word of my book. The emperor had been deposed, and I sat there at the table, waiting with my friends and the owner of our hotel for the next bit of news, waiting for the ground to shift.

I'd lived in Ethiopia for a full year when Haile Selassie was toppled. As an American, I'd never known exactly what to make of him or his institution. Even if he was a benevolent dictator, it seemed an outdated, anachronistic way of governing. I sympathized with my students, who were generally in their early twenties, like me. They'd invited me to some of their illegal student union meetings—"illegal" because the emperor or someone in his government had issued an order saying that no more than three students could gather to discuss anything at any time anywhere. But there was a massive drought and famine in the northern part of the country that was only slowly coming to light as thousands of poor, skeletal souls made their way from the hinterlands into the towns and cities. The students wanted to speak out on behalf of the peasants and donate the money the government spent on their university breakfasts to feeding their starving countrymen and women. So they had defied the order and held big meetings in the student cafeteria. They spoke in English, because it was not Amharic (the emperor's language) nor the languages of the Tigray or Oromo peoples, Tigrinya or Orominya, but a neutral language whose accents would offend no one. Much of what they said was couched in Marxist or pseudo-Marxist lingo, as if they had all been reading too much Che Guevera. It was hard to see how their calls to turn over "Ethiopia's industrial complexes" to the masses made any sense in a country where nearly 99 percent of the people were farmers. But then some of them spoke about the burdens of the peasants, the great disparity between rich, absentee landlords and poor farmers, and the dreadful, mass starvation. One young man was particularly eloquent about the suffering these poor Ethiopians faced, while their emperor chose to look the other way. "There is only one way to end this," this student had cried. "Land to the Tiller! Land to the Tiller!"

It's always been a matter of dispute whether the emperor ignored the starving masses or simply was not informed. He was elderly and, some say, slipping into senility. He never seemed to grasp the full implications of his fall, even after he had been imprisoned in the Emperor Menelik's old palace. He lived there in a basement room looking out onto the gray stone building of the Menelik Mausoleum, where several members of the royal line, including his own daughter, Princess Tsehai, lie buried. Then, on August 28, 1975, a few weeks before his 83rd birthday, he was found dead in his bed.

I was in Addis when that announcement was made. Those days, every news broadcast began with a military drum roll, followed by children singing the revolution's song, "Ethiopia Tikdem"—"Ethiopia Above All." Usually, the announcer then read off a list of names of people arrested the day before for crimes against the motherland. The prisons were swelling with these "criminals." Many had been executed; others were soon to be; and many more would languish in their foul, dark cells for years. This day's news, however, began with a brief message: The emperor had fallen sick the night before, and his military guards had searched throughout Addis for his physician. They were unable to find the doctor before the 9 p.m. curfew, and when the former emperor's servant brought Haile Selassie his breakfast the next morning, the emperor was found to be dead.

Nothing was said about a funeral or what had happened to the emperor's body. And nothing would be, until the end of the Derg government 16 years later. Haile Selassie's body was then recovered from a deep, cement-covered pit beneath Menelik's palace. Major Mengistu, the dictator who replaced Haile Selassie, had taken over the palace, and reputedly took some delight in working in an office above the emperor's grave. In 1991, after the fall of Mengistu and the Derg, the new government permitted Haile Selassie's family to exhume his remains; these were placed in a crypt in the Menelik Mausoleum. In November 2000, the family was allowed to give the emperor a more official, state burial, and his body was reburied in St. George's Cathedral in a crypt Haile Selassie had designed for himself. His wife, Empress Menen, is buried next to him in an identical crypt.

Haile Selassie's death was convenient for Mengistu and the Derg, since in 1975 many people still continued to hold the emperor in high regard despite the military's efforts to vilify him. He had managed, after all, to enlist the aid of the British to free Ethiopia from the Italians, had founded schools, universities, and hospitals, and guided his country into a leadership position in Africa, and he was loved for these things. With his death, the Derg worried less about rebellions aimed at reestablishing the empire, and it pressed ahead with its socialist plans and reforms, including freeing the peasants from their aristocratic, absentee landlords as the students had demanded. Now, only those who worked the land could own it. But it was a backhanded kind of relief, since the peasants still paid high taxes—the only difference was that the money went directly to the central government. And such reforms did not bring an end to the suffering of the people.

Over the next 16 years, they would endure the Red Terror, in which hundreds of thousands of people died, more droughts and famines that were cruelly manipulated by their leaders, and wars between Ethiopia and Somalia, and Ethiopia and Eritrea. Ethiopia won the former war, but lost the latter. And it was not long after losing that war, that the Derg government fell. The liberating army of the Ethiopian Peoples Revolutionary Democratic Front took command. Its leader was one Meles Zenawi, a former university student and member of the illegal student union. I had left Ethiopia years before Meles was elected Prime Minister of the newly democratic Ethiopia. Yet I often wondered if he had been there in the university cafeteria at the illegal meetings I had attended. Had he been the one I so vividly remember calling out "Land to the Tiller!"?

The Ethiopian wheel of fortune had turned, toppling the emperor, then the military leaders who had deposed him. In the country I returned to, a former rebellious student was Prime Minister. There were no longer any Rases in the provinces, no emperor to bring them to heel. The 3,000-year reign of the Solomonic line and its ruling Lion of Judah, the King of Kings was no more.

DURING ETHIOPIA'S YEARS OF TURMOIL, THE BLUE NILE HAD ONCE again been forgotten by the outside world. Only in the late 1990s did adventurers renew their interest in riding its waves. Mike Speaks had guided one such trip. In 1996, he and four clients thrashed their way with paddles through the white water of the upper gorge on two rubber rafts. It was a rough trip, the rapids thoroughly punishing. One wave slammed their boat against a canyon wall. It capsized and Speaks took what he called "the swim of a lifetime." The other boat also collided with the canyon, hitting its wall with such force that one of the raft's inflated tubes collapsed. And people were injured: One man suffered bruised ribs and a partially collapsed lung; another hit his head and had severe contusions and swollen eyes; a third damaged his pelvis. There was no way out except to continue down the river, so they did.

Now it was about to be our turn to face whatever the Blue Nile in the republic of Ethiopia had to offer.

eight

≈

BAHIR DAR, WHERE WE WERE TO BEGIN OUR TREK, LIES ABOUT 200 miles northwest of Addis Ababa and on the southern shore of Lake Tana. We took a commercial Ethiopian Airlines flight there the morning of our second day in the country. It was a cloudy, bumpy trip, but the clouds parted briefly over the Blue Nile Gorge giving us another view of the river slicing through the mountainous terrain. This was a section we had not yet seen. The land was higher here, rising in a series of stepped plateaus, and the countryside below us as green as emeralds from the rains. Every stream and small river we spotted on both sides of the gorge was red with silt and churned frothily toward it, ready to dump more water and soil into the Blue Nile. And there seemed to be hundreds of these shiny watercourses. Indeed, almost every Ethiopian stream and river eventually finds its way to the Nile.

I thought of Mau's comment over coffee the previous afternoon. "The Blue Nile is a big-belly river," he'd said. "You'll see when we fly—it swallows every little creek and the big ones, too. They all go to the Abay."

Mau, Kate, and I had taken a brief car-tour of Addis, driving up the six-lane Churchill Avenue, past the white City Hall building with its two wings spread to either side like an open triptych, down a hill where the devoted stood kissing the wall of St. George's Cathedral, and through the piazza, the city's main western-style shopping drag, lined with gold and silver shops. People, wearing a mix of Western and traditional Ethiopian garb, thronged the streets. Some marched along purposefully, others lingered outside a movie theater, waiting for tickets, or leaned against the buildings, simply waiting. There were knots of laughing children, chasing each other, and beggars dressed in rags, hoping to catch a rich man's eye. It was a busy, chaotic scene—not all that different from what I remembered, although the numbers of people had increased dramatically. There were some 30 million people in Ethiopia in 1974; now their numbers had nearly doubled. Addis, too, had swollen to some two and a half million souls.

We drove across the little Ras Mekonen Bridge with the Kechene stream tumbling over rocks below, and I turned to glance up a nearby cobblestone street, just making out the corner of a blue house behind a high stone wall. That had been my home for two years. I thought about stopping and knocking on the gate, but then what? The current occupants might not understand my nostalgia. The little house I'd shared with a friend, Frances Dakin, who taught geology at the university and had a pet dog she called Wusha (Amharic for "dog"), was still there—and that was enough.

Ethiopians are not generally fond of dogs, and Frances's attentiveness to her yellow-haired Wusha made her the butt of many jokes. She had lived in Ethiopia for six years before I met her, and often had walked Wusha as a puppy to the university. She had not done this in a long time, but nevertheless, many people remembered her strange behavior, and nearly every day as we headed to the campus, someone would call out: "Mrs! Mrs! Where is your dog?" Then they would erupt in laughter. Frances had also dared to ride a bicycle to school, and again, although she had not done so for some time, this had not been forgotten. "Mrs! Mrs!" came the demands, "Where is your bicycle?... Where is your dog? Mrs! Mrs!" Frances was shy, and the pointing and shouted questions always made her drop her head and giggle nervously. I tried to show no response, and walked with my eyes downcast or looked straight ahead, and said nothing.

Other people delighted in pointing out the obvious: that we were white and foreigners. "Ferenji!" they would call after us, trumpeting the news to the street at large. Sometimes, children would walk beside us, staring as if they had never seen anything quite as shocking as our white skins, and shouting, "Ferenji! Ferenji! Ferenji!" Once, in exasperation, I shouted back, *"Habesha!"* To my amazement, the word silenced my tormentors—although it wasn't a slur. It's the Amharic word for "Ethiopian" and roughly translates as "someone of mixed race." But the little fellow I'd said it to looked so crestfallen, I could never bring myself to utter it again. Besides, even if the word wasn't an insult, I'd used it that way, and I felt ashamed.

It was just something you had to accept: As a white person in Ethiopia, you were—and are—a spectacle.

And when there are five of you together in one place—well, for the Ethiopians, you're a circus. That was how our group was received when we tried to see a little of Bahir Dar. We'd been prevented from getting a good look at the town from the air, since 15 minutes before landing, the steward instructed us to shut our windows, which made the plane's narrow interior as dark as a coffin. Our steward, however, wasn't trying to turn our thoughts to the afterlife; he was protecting Ethiopia. The

Ethiopian Air Force launched most of its air strikes on Eritrea from a base near the airport, and with our windows closed we couldn't spy on these activities. We heard them, though. Not long after we disembarked, two fighter jets thundered into the sky. And once again, I thought that the Ethiopian government was either being very generous to allow our expedition to continue or was indifferent to our fate. We were in a war zone, the front lay a mere 400 miles away, and we were about to head out on what Mountain Travel Sobek characterized in its pretrip materials as an "adventure vacation." At least one of the two words was accurate.

Later, after we'd checked into the Tana Hotel on the shores of the lake, several of us piled into a Land Rover to see the local sights. Although I'd sworn at home that I wouldn't join in any of these tour-bus activities, here I was doing just that. It was hard not to: As soon as our little party met over the first night's dinner, we started to meld into a group. Mike Speaks wanted it that way. He had talked about the importance of learning each other's strengths and weaknesses and working like a team to make the expedition a success, a philosophy I agreed with at least in the abstract. But I grew up the second of four children and am cursed with the second child's rebellious, independent nature, and I knew that at some point I was apt to have trouble with the team stuff. Somehow, I'd have to carve a space for my own "Private Ethiopia"— those moments and thoughts I wanted to have to myself about being back in this country I loved.

At an elevation of slightly less than 6,000 feet, Bahir Dar is 2,000 feet lower than Addis, and its air is humid and tropical. Gardens filled with colorful bougainvillea, towering hibiscus, and sweet-scented frangipani bushes surrounded our hotel, and an abundance of birds—sunbirds, sugar-stealers, buffalo weavers, rosy finches—flitted from bloom to bloom. The town, too, was pretty with its wide boulevards and sidewalks cafes shaded with palms and flame trees. I'd visited it a couple of times before the revolution and always liked its easygoing atmosphere. Maybe because of that tropical warmth or because even Ethiopians regard the town as a resort, things move a little slower here than in Addis. It's a flat city, too, unlike the hilly capital, and people on sturdy, Chinese bicycles wove their way among the busy press of taxis, buses, and trucks.

Over the years, Bahir Dar has become a center of provincial growth, and signs of progress, primarily in the shape of new government buildings, were everywhere. We drove past several swish glass-and-stone buildings and construction sites with piles of gray stone waiting to be shaped—by hand—into building blocks.

The new symbols of progress had not yet displaced the old traditions, and we headed first to a village of papyrus-boat builders. Dense stands of papyrus grow along parts of Lake Tana's shoreline, and the local people have used the thick stalks for years to shape into their buoyant, kayak-shaped *tankwas*. The boats are far sturdier than they appear, and are used to transport everything from enormous loads of firewood to cattle to trade goods across the lake, a distance of about 40 miles. Less than 100 years ago, tankwas were also used to carry slaves captured in the valleys of the Blue Nile. The slaves were ferried over the lake to a trail that led through the mountains and desert to a port on the Red Sea—and then by dhow to the Arabian Peninsula.

The tankwa makers' village lies on the outskirts of Bahir Dar, and we drove down the palm-lined streets to a dirt road and a collection of round, thatched Ethiopian homes edged by a row of eucalyptus trees. The instant our vehicle stopped a crowd of children and adults surrounded it, all peering at us with great curiosity. Admittedly, we were pretty curious, too. That's why we were barging into their village in midday. So it was hard to say who was more rude: our uninvited, camera-toting group, or the locals, who gleefully shouted "Ferenji! Ferenji!" and seemed to encourage their children in their constant cries of "You! You! You!" and demands for money.

During my previous stay, I'd never traveled with so many ferenjocch; either I was alone with Ethiopian friends or with one or two other foreigners. Even in those instances, I was conspicuous, but I'd never experienced anything quite like the hysteria at the tankwa village. Kate, Bruce, Mick, and I stood in a little knot with kids and adults circling around us as if we were zoo animals. Nevada had gone off on her own, looking for a place away from the crowd and a good shot. I followed her example, breaking out of the circle and walking away in the opposite direction from Nevada. A couple of little boys followed me, and I tried out my beginner's Amharic, eliciting peels of laughter. Then one brave boy spoke up in English. Enunciating each syllable and rolling every r, he asked, "Mister? Where your country?"

Our language skills were obviously on a par, and I laughed in turn, before saying, "America."

My young friends sucked in their breath at this answer, and one managed to respond, "Oh. America is very good."

I smiled again. "I'm glad you like my country."

This was a more difficult sentence and left puzzled looks all around, so I suggested that they study their English some more and gave them each a pen.

The circle around Kate, Bruce, and Mick had dissipated a little by now, and we walked together to a hut where some thin, bent men were working on a tankwa. They stopped their labor and greeted us, then motioned for us to come close and watch. To make the boat, they had tied bundles of dried reeds together, then shaped the bundles into a pointed prow and bottom, and were now fastening other bundles to the sides.

Despite the initial shouts and squeals at our arrival, it was clear that the villagers were used to seeing foreigners. Probably almost every tour group that came to Bahir Dar, also came here or to another tankwa making village. Such visits were a boon to their economy: They expected money in exchange for showing us how to build a tankwa or for letting us take their picture. I didn't blame them. They were, like the majority of Ethiopians, poor. Their homes were earthen and lacked electricity and running water; their clothing was torn and patched; their few possessions—some wooden bowls and stools, an iron grill for making bread over an open fire, baskets for storing food—were simple and worn. On average, Ethiopians earn $120 U.S. a year, and dispensing a few Ethiopian *birr* to our hosts would make everyone happy (at the time one Ethiopian birr equaled eight U.S. cents). But there was a group rule: We were not to give money to anyone, lest it ruin the local culture and economy. The rule had first surfaced in the same "adventure vacation" literature Mountain Travel Sobek sent to us; Mike Speaks reiterated it over dinner, and everyone seemed determined to abide by it.

"No," Bruce, Kate, Mick, and Nevada said when our guide suggested we might want to give some money. They smiled and shrugged about the request in a nice way, but they didn't want to pay for our visit. It wasn't that they were indifferent to the villagers' poverty, they just accepted the travel wisdom and rules laid down by our outfitter.

I did not, however, and although I didn't open my wallet then, I knew I was going to at some point. I was rich, any Ethiopian could see that, and I would have to give. That was the social rule here. It was said that whenever the Emperor Haile Selassie I traveled in the countryside, an aide threw coins and bread from his limousine's windows. I was shocked and dismayed the first time I heard that story—it seemed so degrading to his people to have them scrabbling in the streets after money and food. Later, after I had traveled a good bit in the countryside, I was less judgmental of the emperor's behavior. The poor and crippled and blind were everywhere; there were no ready solutions to their plight. So when some of them were lucky enough to see the emperor, he acknowledged their luck: He gave them a gift.

I imagined that was how these villagers regarded us, as a lucky turn in their lives. It made me feel mean, not giving them the gift that went with their luck. Nevertheless, this time, I reluctantly let the rules of the group prevail.

We visited two other local sights: a street market where dark-eyed young girls put their hands over their mouths and giggled when they saw us, and then asked us to buy their beautifully coiled, cowhide-covered baskets (we wanted to, but had no room in our travel bags); and a spot along the lake shore where the fishermen launch their tankwas. Some men were out fishing, balancing their bamboo pole-paddles across their laps, while gracefully casting out their nets. It was a pretty scene with the tall green papyrus reeds edging the shore, and the soft cream-brown of the boats mirrored against the lake's silver water— and the fishermen casting and retrieving and casting again as they have for a thousand years.

Later in the afternoon, our party split up. Nevada, Mick, and Bruce went to photograph the Blue Nile Falls in the setting sun, while Kate and I went with Mike Speaks and two Ethiopian guides, Zelalem Abera Woldegiorgis and Belie Abitew, to an overlook above the lake, a trip that also gave us our first close look at the Blue Nile.

Lake Tana lies in a shallow basin bounded by mountains and rich plains of black soil, and covers about a thousand square miles. It was formed about 30 million years ago, when a volcanic flow blocked the southern end of the basin. That is where the Blue Nile begins as well, and to reach it, we drove a short distance from our hotel to a highway bridge spanning the river. The river scarcely seems like a river at this point. The lake's waters drift lazily toward the volcanic lip, only gradually picking up speed as they reach this small drop. Two fern- and reed-covered islands divide the flow, and it's only when you look past them downstream that you realize there's a break in the shoreline—and that break is the Blue Nile.

The river's rain-swollen waters were high and dark brown, and washed over the roots of the big fig trees on its muddy banks. Belie was from Bahir Dar, and that particular spot was a holy place, he told us, where people came at dawn on Sundays to make sacrifices to the Abay, the spirit of the river.

"They give Abay a chicken or a sheep for their protection or if they want something, like to get well or to have a child," said Belie. "It is holy water."

So holy that people also come to bathe in the Blue Nile as a form of baptism and to collect its waters. "Anyone coming here from Addis will take water home for themselves, their family, their friends," Belie added. "My grandmother says it can heal everything. She walks here every day from the center of town to bathe and take the water."

It was quiet now at this holy site, but on some special holidays the river's banks and the bridge are crowded with souls, slitting the throats of chickens and sheep, then tossing their gift to the Abay. We crossed the bridge and in doing so passed from Gojam province into Begemder—a journey that had in Cheesman's day required special passes and ceremonies. A short distance beyond the bridge, we left the asphalt highway and turned onto a dirt road, following the course of the river. More fig trees, acacias, and the foreign eucalyptus shaded its grassy banks, and beyond them the muddy Blue Nile swept south toward Tis Isat Falls. The road wound up a steep hill, and our driver pulled into a turnout just below the locked gates of one of Haile Selassie's old palaces (now used by the new government).

Below us the lake spread over the land and to the far horizon like an inland sea.

Its waters lap at some 37 islands, many of which harbor churches and monasteries, and some of these are very old, dating to the 13th century. Their roots go back even further since it is here in Lake Tana's basin that Ethiopia's highland history began. But it is a strange history, blending the tales of the Falasha, a lost tribe of Israel, with those of the indigenous, hippo-eating Waito, and later with the myths and legends of the Christians and Moslems. Belie pointed to a small island on the lake's eastern shore and said that there, beside a church, stands a boulder where Saint Mary, the mother of Jesus, paused to rest on her flight with the Holy Child from Palestine to Egypt. Several hundred years before her journey, a Jewish priest came to this island, too, to find a place of safekeeping for the stone tablets given to Moses on Mount Sinai. "That is the Ark of the Covenant," Belie said, "and even today it is here in Ethiopia." The Ark was held in a tent on Tana Kirkos Island for 600 years, Belie explained, before being moved to a church in Aksum— where, some say, it still resides today.

Right next to these important Christian sites are a few remaining Waito villages. The Waito were some of the region's original inhabitants. They worshiped the spirits in the trees and lake until Imam Ahmad Gragn swept through in the 16th century on an Islamic jihad, converting many of them to Islam, and killing the Christians and burning their churches, paintings, and holy books. Ahmad Gragn died in battle against a combined force of Portuguese and Ethiopians that saved Christian Ethiopia in 1543, and his grave and the grave of his horse lie just beyond the lake in the Lebo highlands.

On other islands monks are said to have escaped the Devil by leaping from a high rock wall. They did not die; an angel interceded, and the monks sprouted wings and flew to safety. Another monk behaved in such a saintly manner he was given command over all the birds and animals in the lake. He asked the crocodiles to stay away, and even today, there are no crocodiles in Lake Tana, although they are found in abundance below Tis Isat Falls. Some of the islands' holiest churches house the bones of these saints, and in others are found the skeletons and mummies of blessed kings, such as Zara Yakob, who did so much for the poor that even after he died his spirit (fully embodied) wandered along the lake shore for seven years doing good, and tyrants, like Tekla Haimanot, "the Accursed," who killed his father to seize the throne.

"If you went there to Daga Island," said Zelalem, "you would also see our king, Fasiladas. He built the castles at Gonder. But you cannot go," Zelalem added, looking sad. "The monks do not allow women."

"That's okay," I said. "That's the rule at some monasteries. I had the same problem when I tried to see some of the holy sites in Aksum."

Zelalem brightened. "You know Aksum?"

"I went there to see the obelisks and churches some years ago. I visited Lalibela, too."

At the mention of this Ethiopian town, famous for its fabulous churches carved from single blocks of stone, Zelalem beamed. "That is my home, Lalibela," he said, a note of pride his voice. "Do you know the church of Giorgis?" he asked, referring to the most beautiful of Lalibela's churches. Rising two stories from a huge pit in the ground, it is carved from the bedrock in the shape of a cross. "My grandfather was a priest there."

Zelalem was to be the chief interpreter on our trip, and his religious background meant that he knew a great deal about Orthodox beliefs, practices, and legends. A handsome young man of about 30, he had a square jaw and an Ethiopian's large eyes, although his were of a chestnut hue. He had worked with Conrad for about eight years, and was now his right-hand man, managing Conrad's camping and rafting equipment when he was away, and helping him plan and lead expeditions. Conrad was "like a father" to him, Zelalem said, and he was, of course, deeply worried about Conrad's health—but also sure that the Western physicians would cure him. "I have prayed to my special saint, Wolde Giorgis—Saint George—for this," he told me. "Conrad will become well, I think."

I was not sure how to respond. The kind of tumor Conrad had was almost always fatal. I knew he was in a desperate fight for his life. Zelalem didn't seem to realize the seriousness of Conrad's illness; or perhaps because Conrad had been in England, receiving Western treatments, Zelalem thought his recovery certain. And Zelalem's life and livelihood depended on that happening. For an Ethiopian, the expression "he is like my father" or "she is like my mother" is more literal than metaphorical, and by choosing to use this, Zelalem implied that his relationship with Conrad was not simply that of employee and employer. During some low point in Zelalem's life, Conrad must have helped him as a father would—caring for, sheltering, and guiding him. In turn, Zelalem had given him a son's loyalty, love, and respect.

Losing Conrad would devastate Zelalem's life. That was probably why no one had yet conveyed to him how deathly ill his "father" was. I wasn't about to tell him, either. So, I smiled and said that yes, we all hoped that Conrad would recover soon. One of the other boatmen, Mike Borcik, planned to stop in Nairobi to visit Conrad before joining us on the river in a week's time. For Zelalem's sake, I hoped that Borcik would bring us good news.

Zelalem was happy to learn that I had lived in Ethiopia and knew a little Amharic, and promised to teach me more.

"You have a good accent," he said, encouragingly, "and little by little it will come back."

There is an Ethiopian proverb that I had heard many times from my Amhara friends as I struggled with their language: "*Kas-be-kas inkallu begru yehedelleh*— Slowly, slowly even an egg can walk on its legs." I quoted this to him and added, "My egg doesn't even have toes yet."

"No, no, he has feet," Zelalem assured me. "He has feet!"

We laughed, and I knew I had found a friend. From Zelalem, I could learn about the stories and proverbs of the people we traveled among, as well as more about his own life. His town of Lalibela lies in the Wollo region, east of Lake Tana. During the droughts and famines of the 1970s and 1980s, it was one of the hardest hit areas. Jim Slade had told me before the trip that Zelalem was a quiet person and unlike some other Ethiopian guides that Slade had worked with, had few noteworthy experiences from the time of the revolution and troubles that followed. It was true that Zelalem was too young to remember the emperor, or the early days of the revolution or Red Terror, but he had been a teenager during the 1984 drought, and a young man when the military government, the Derg, fell. Where had he been, what had he done during those years? How had a boy from Lalibela ended up working in Addis Ababa for Conrad? Zelalem, I was sure, had a story to tell.

THAT NIGHT IN OUR HOTEL'S RESTAURANT, WE DINED ON PASTA, vegetables, and tilapia, a native African fish with a sweet white flesh.

Our meals would be much more prosaic over the coming weeks, and fresh vegetables, in particular, hard to come by. But that scarcely mattered: We were anxious to get under way and into the heartland of the Blue Nile.

When Mike Speaks gave a toast to "our epic undertaking," we cheered and clinked our glasses. There were smiles all around. Yet given the tragedies and troubles that had befallen many of our predecessors, all of us were also secretly wondering just how epic our undertaking would be.

nine

∿

WITH ITS LANGUID AIR AND BOUNTY OF FLOWERS AND BIRDS, Bahir Dar is about as close as one gets to paradise in Ethiopia. Every once in a while during our stay, a jet fighter would launch into the sky breaking the peace with its thunder, but then it was gone, and the birds resumed their singing and a breeze from the lake filled the air with the scents of jasmine, ginger, and honeysuckle. No wonder it was a popular resort with vacationing Ethiopians, who spent the day sitting under the shady mango trees in the gardens next to the lake.

If they'd known what we were up to, they would have smiled piteously and laughed when they thought we weren't looking. Ferenjocch often behaved in the most inexplicable manner, like voluntarily walking long distances through rough and perilous terrain, when they had enough money not only to buy cars but to pave the highways they drove them on. Sensible people wouldn't set off on a month's-long journey into a malarial and bandit-ridden gorge. But then, ferenjocch were very much like spoiled children, prone to doing willful things, and there was no point in trying to dissuade them. So when we left our hotel early the next morning for the drive to the beginning of the trailhead, the porters and hotel staff gave us sad little bright smiles. Here we were in the center of paradise—and we were leaving it behind—by choice!—for a land that was about as close to hell as any highland Ethiopian could imagine.

That was certainly our porters' opinions. There were 13 of them, and they were well armed with Kalashnikovs (Russian automatic rifles), long fighting sticks, called *dulas*, and knives. The head porter, Teno Amashi, was in his fifties and had a long, thin face and graying hair. He eyed us with a slightly disapproving look as we jumped from the van to greet him. He touched our extended hands limply, then he turned away to talk to Zelalem about the more pressing business: getting our gear loaded on the donkeys he and his crew had brought.

Teno and his men were dressed in knee-length shorts, patched short-sleeve shirts, and green or white cotton blankets, which they wore toga-style over their shoulders. Most of them were barefoot, although Teno wore a pair of black plastic sandals, and all of them were thin. Their arms and legs were pared down to sinewy muscle, and the thinness of their faces accentuated their eyes and flaring cheekbones. A couple of the men had wrapped white or blue turbans on their heads, and since all of them were Christians, they each wore a dark, cotton string, called a *mateb*, around their necks to distinguish them from Muslims.

Our porters—more accurately, our wranglers and guides—were Gojamis, and *ya wenz lijoch*, children of the river. They hailed from the village of Tis Abay, "Smoke of the Nile," a settlement along the shores of the upper Blue Nile, and had lived all their lives within shouting distance of the great waterfall that gave their village its name. We had driven through Tis Abay on our way to meet them, and Belie had pointed out the blue mists from the falls curling like smoke into the air beyond the eucalyptus and acacia trees.

Now, as Teno, Zelalem, and the other guides sorted our gear into donkey-size loads, our little party made its way down a grassy hillside trail to the river. The trail descended abruptly to one of the stone-and-mortar bridges Portuguese and Indian masons helped build in the 17th century. Beneath it, the river ran along in a narrow rocky gorge, like a flood of boiling chocolate. At the bridge's far end, stood a little boy, playing a wooden flute. His notes rose and fell above the sound of the river, and he gave an added little trill as we passed over the bridge from Gojam to Begemder, as if saluting our passage.

"Mr! Mr!," came the shouts from another small boy who suddenly appeared at my side. Kate and I had been walking together to the falls, and she continued on ahead, while I stopped to greet this child, who was eagerly reaching out to take my hand.

"I be your guide," he announced. His name was Taddesse and he looked to be all of ten, but he was he assured me *"gobez,"* (very strong), and he rolled up his sleeve and flexed his muscles like Mohammed Ali to prove it. He would not let me slip off the trail and fall to my death in the Nile's treacherous waters, he promised.

I laughed and hired him. Taddesse grasped my hand and with great care guided me up the rocky path to the overlook above Tis Isat. Young girls in well-worn Western-style dresses emerged from the bushes, holding up little handmade baskets and brightly woven belts for sale. I shook my head, but that did not deter them. Barefoot, they ran along like gazelles, leaping over the rocks to the top of the hill, carrying their handicrafts and beseeching me to buy something.

With every step, the roar of the waterfall grew louder, and at last Taddesse and I walked through the long, green grass to the shade of a fig tree.

There, arrayed across the horizon, were the Blue Nile Falls, a 1,500-foot sweep of water plunging 150 feet into what seemed like a bottomless chasm. All that was visible from above was the white foam of the water as it dashed and leaped against the rocks, and shot its spray skyward so that it fell like rain on the grasses and ferns, and viewing public, a good quarter of a mile away. Someone had placed a wide wooden plank on some rocks for a seat, and Taddesse reached into his back pocket and produced a sheet of white paper. He carefully smoothed this out, set it on the plank, then urged me to take a seat. I obliged him, amused at his concern about sullying my derriere—at least it would remain clean for the beginning of our trek. And it was a nice place to sit and watch the perpetual rainbow that curved like a length of silk over the thundering cataract.

Taddesse gestured at the rainbow. "Saint Mary's belt," he pronounced in his carefully rehearsed English. The Virgin had left it there during her sojourn at Lake Tana as a gift for the Ethiopian people who sheltered her and her infant. If the holy pair's hosts had been half as solicitous as Taddesse, then they had been very well looked after, indeed. My young guide stood like a retainer at my side, ready to push away any other children who might step too close to me, and kept a close eye on the nearby bushes as if they might harbor spies or dangerous beasts.

Belie, though, was part of my group and so when he came to sit on the bench, Taddesse stepped aside. A husky fellow with slightly bulging eyes and a gap between his front teeth, Belie had a heavy, plodding air about him even when he smiled, and he was full this morning of rather mournful tales about the dangers ahead. As he passed on the burden of each, he grew somewhat less morose, until he was almost chipper. I, on the other hand, began to feel increasingly dejected. First, pointing to the hillside that tumbled down to the rocks and water below, Belie admonished me to be careful on the wet grass. At least three ferenjocch had slipped and died here, while fiddling with their cameras. Their bodies were never found. He looked very grave.

"And Ethiopians?" I asked. "Have any ever fallen or jumped here?"

Belie nodded. "Yes, the forbidden lovers have jumped sometimes. And one couple, their parents said they cannot love one another. They wanted to escape, so they tried to cross the river—just there," he said, gesturing to the wide river above the falls. "But their tankwa sank and they drowned."

Even more dangerous, though, were the *jinn*, evil spirits that lurked in the river's raging waters. They lived down there in the murky depths alongside the Abay's good spirit, Belie said. Their skins were jet black and they had long, pointed claws, and in general "looked like Satan."

"The female jinn lure men into the water," said Belie. "They make you fall in love, then when the man goes to the water, they drag him down to die. Some jinn can take different shapes, like a hyena or snake, so maybe they will attack you at night, but you will never find them."

"Are there jinn in all of the Blue Nile?" I asked.

"Yes. They can be anywhere. They watch for you when you are not looking."

The jinns' behavior sounded very much like that of some of the shifta who lurked in the gorge. We had Teno's men and their Kalashnikovs to protect us against the latter, but what could one do against these evil, shape-shifting spirits?

Belie shrugged indifferently. "Some people give them a chicken, but it's not the right day for that," he said. "Other people go to a *dabtera*, a special priest. He can write some magic against them. But you have to have an appointment to see him."

It seemed we were going to have to face the jinn on our own.

Belie looked around at the young girls. "See that girl," he said, pointing to one about six or seven years old. "She has some protection in that leather box around her neck."

The little girl, dressed in a pink dress with a torn shoulder, stepped back shyly as I glanced at her. Around her neck, she wore a wooden cross faced with a bit of gold paper, and on a separate cotton string, a fat square of dark leather. One of her parents had taken her to the dabtera, perhaps when she was sick or when they feared something evil would befall her. The priest had probably written some Bible or prayer book verses on a piece of hide, added a magic drawing, then folded these up with a little piece of hyena skin and stitched it all inside the leather case.

"It can protect her against the jinn and the *buda*, the people with the evil eye," Belie said.

We didn't have protection against the buda-people either, and I briefly thought about asking the girl if she would loan us her magic, but it wouldn't have done us any good, since these sorts of amulets are prepared with a particular person in mind. No, we were just going to have to deal with these unseen spirits as best we could, and hope that we didn't encounter a buda, who were somewhat more worrisome since they were everywhere. You could be living with one or have one for a neighbor or see one just by bad luck in the market, and wouldn't even know it—until evil befell you.

"It's just someone who has a bad spirit in them, and if they look at you that bad spirit can hurt you," Belie explained. "The person doesn't want to cause that hurt."

To further protect her against the spirit world and as a symbol of her Christian faith, the little girl had a blue cross tattooed on the center of her forehead, and two small scar-slashes through each eyebrow. Gojami parents often cut their children's eyebrows in this fashion, believing it protects their eyesight and is beautiful. Almost all of my Gojami university students had their eyebrows cut, and it did not take me long to learn to spot that telltale sign—or other scarification signs that distinguished one ethnic group from another. I often thought that if it was easy for me to tell these people apart, then it was even easier for an Ethiopian to do so. And in fact they were keenly aware of which group they and others belonged to. They could spot the differences in a flash, and as a rule were very careful about keeping the lines drawn. Theirs was a richly diverse society, but not an especially well-integrated one.

Belie was studying the waterfall. It was stunning with its mass of foaming water shining under the sun and small yellow-and-blue birds darting in and out of the rainbow. Belie was looking for something else. "There are big snakes there," he said with just a hint of excitement at the worry this might cause me. "I think you call them 'pith…'" He hesitated.

"Pythons," I said.

"Yes, pythons. Very big ones. They can be six meters [18 feet] long, and they can eat anything: monkeys, large birds, children."

I would have loved to have seen such a huge snake, but didn't tell Belie. He wanted me to be shocked, and I raised my eyebrows in mock horror.

On his expeditions, Cheesman had had the good fortune of seeing a couple of pythons. One nearly brought him to grief. He came to Tis Isat Falls in May 1926, the time of year when the Blue Nile's water is at its lowest point, and the volcanic lip of the waterfall is exposed. He and his men clambered from rock to rock above the falls, then lowered themselves over the cliff to a shelf behind the cataract while hanging on to vines and tree roots. Only one of the roots wasn't a root at all, but the tail of a python. The man who grabbed it "nearly toppled over with fright…and bumped heavily into me," Cheesman wrote. The collision almost sent the British consul tumbling into Tis Isat's wet maw. The men beat the snake until it appeared dead, then threw it onto the rocks below, where it lay still. But when they climbed down to find it, the snake—like a jinn—was gone.

Other famous Blue Nile explorers, Father Jerome Lobo and James Bruce, had come to the Blue Nile Falls, too, and stood on this same hillock to watch the thundering display. Perhaps they'd had a guide like Belie, charming in a teasing sort of way, and maybe a little pleased to see a worldly ferenji feeling a tad uneasy.

I shrugged off Belie's dark worries. Tis Isat's rainbowed beauty and its friendly pack of kids were images to store in my heart. Here was the gorge's gateway, some even say the real beginning of the Blue Nile, and it seemed fitting to start our journey at a spot that had called to true lovers, seductive spirits, and bold men—and where Saint Mary had so graciously left her belt behind.

Nevada, Bruce, and Mick had been busy photographing the great cascade of the Blue Nile from as many angles as possible. There were other, smaller cataracts on the river, but nothing as grand, and they wanted to make sure they had the best shots. Then Belie's brother, Adane, came striding up. It was time to go, he said. Mike Speaks had sent him to tell us that the donkeys were loaded and Teno's men were leading them down the trail. We needed to join up.

The ever solicitous Taddesse leaped immediately to my side, offering his hand to help me from the bench. Since I was a ferenji, Taddesse seemed to think I must be feeble. It was an attitude I had run into before when hiking in the Ethiopian countryside. Peasants would gaze at you with utter consternation, unsure if they should fetch a litter or carry you on their backs. It was wrong that you—obviously a person from the upper class—should be traveling on foot. Inevitably, they would ask, "Missus! Where is your car?" Sometimes, someone would fetch a horse or mule and urge you to ride.

I gave Taddesse a few birr for all of his attentions, but especially for that thoughtful, bum-protecting sheet of paper, and let him guide me back to the Portuguese bridge. The team of basket-bearing girls followed close on my heels, and finally I gave in. From one girl in a dark green dress, I bought a small round basket, woven of red-and- green grasses with a little shell fastened on top, and stuck it in my dayback, thinking how sad and worn it would surely look by the journey's end. My one purchase seemed to please the others; at least they stopped pursuing me. Then another boy appeared, offering me a worn walking stick, made of olive wood, and I bought that, too. The trail was slick and muddy in places and the walking stick would be good to have.

I waved goodbye, and started down the trail with Belie and Bruce. Mike Speaks was waiting for everyone a little farther on. Our group had been together now for about three days, and it was clear that Speaks wasn't an Indiana Jones kind of guide, at least not in the fashion sense. He'd worn the same ripped, long sleeved T-shirt every day, and liked to say that he would wear it until it shredded from his body. For our hike, he'd tucked the shirt into a pair of old, faded shorts, slapped a visor on his head, and wrapped his fringed Pakistani scarf over the top turban-style, an outfit that made him look a little like a poor relation of Richard Burton's. Speaks had some of that Burtonesque intensity, too, and he squinted up the trail like an impatient father. Was everyone coming, he wanted to know. I said I thought so.

"Well, I want to get everybody together and down the trail. We'll have lunch downstream aways," he said. There was that same insistent tone in his voice that I'd noticed when we were waiting for the pilot for our reconnaissance flight.

Speaks's lackadaisical way of dressing obviously didn't carry over to his sense of time. He was on a schedule of some sort, so we had to be, too, although I wasn't sure what the rush was. We planned to walk only a few miles the first day, and I thought it understood that people— particularly Nevada, Mick, and me—would travel at our own speed, stopping to talk or take photographs as our work demanded. Nevada had never spoken up at any of our pretrip dinners together, giving her "this is a National Geographic expedition" speech that I had hoped she would make. And I hadn't asked her about the relationship between herself and Mike Speaks, presuming that this was how she had chosen to arrange things: He would run the logistics, so that she could concentrate on her photography. She was under a lot of pressure, since this was her first assignment for the magazine, and of course didn't need to be worrying about organizing lunch or camps or finding someone who had wandered from the trail. But I was already wondering if she hadn't taken too much for granted about where Speaks's role as head boatman left off and hers as expedition leader kicked in.

I didn't like being herded down the trail, even by someone in a dashing Arab scarf, and picked up my pace to get away from him. Belie came, too, and Bruce followed not far behind.

It was a fine day for a hike. It was just past mid-morning, the sky was blue with a few puffy clouds, the air was warm and moist—and I was walking beside the Blue Nile. For a short distance beyond the Portuguese Bridge, the river cuts through a lava channel so deep and narrow it looks more like a trough or chute than a riverbed. In the dry season, the river is only seven feet across here, and local legend tells of a warrior who, right at this very spot, leaped across the Nile, killed an enemy, and then leaped back. Even with the river at its low point that was no mean feat, and the king raised the warrior to a noble for his bravery. But on this day, no one was about to try to win a Blue Nile-jumping prize. The river was swollen to a width of at least 50 feet, and churned through the black basalt, carrying detritus, branches, and small trees down the chute, around a bend and off to Sudan with all the speed, force, and commotion of a locomotive. "This is the fight of Water against Stone," said one old man Belie and I met on the trail. "Now the Abay is winning, but soon he'll grow tired and take a rest, while the rock will shine and grow hard in the sun."

The Abay's battle with the rock was an epic one and had been raging, geologists say, for some 30 million years, when the black basalt poured out of fissures in the Earth and flooded the Ethiopian Highlands with a blanket of hot lava more than a mile deep. Such a mass of rock would fill the Grand Canyon from bottom to rim, yet it had all oozed from the Earth over a one-million-year period—a mere blink of the eye in geological time.

Beneath the basalt lie layers of sandstone and limestone, the ancient sediments of a sea that once spread across Somalia and Ethiopia to Sudan some 200 million years ago. Millennia will pass before the Blue Nile cuts down to these softer layers and wins its war against the lava. In the meantime, like a jailer's firm hand, the basalt holds the river in check, bending it in a wide curve around the central highlands.

Other volcanic eruptions formed the high and blocky Choke Mountains on the Gojam side of the river, and the hills and plateaus on the Begemder side, where we were hiking. It was an easy trail to follow. Black and earthen, it had been beaten into the land by tens of thousands of farmers' bare feet, and wound its way over rocks and through groves of spindly trees close to the riverbank. It was also a busy trail, with a steady stream of people walking both up and down river.

Those on the upstream trip were generally headed for the shopping stalls and big-city lights of Bahir Dar, while those going downstream had finished their trading and had their purchased items—small paper sacks of salt and sugar or jars of cooking oil—packed away in bundles of homespun cotton cloth. They were going home to their farms and villages on the plateaus and mountains above the Blue Nile, a journey that might take them four or five hours or more. Theirs was not a leisurely walk; they marched along at a brisk pace, a look of concentration on their faces that was only momentarily interrupted when they caught a glimpse of Bruce and me. For an instant, they looked like startled deer and stared in disbelief at us and our white skins. Most of them had rarely, if ever, seen ferenjocch, and certainly not white foreigners hiking in the countryside. But we were staring, too. Like our guides, these highland Ethiopians were largely Amharas, and they were a good-looking people with finely sculpted features and large eyes. Many of the women were dressed in belted and embroidered white cotton dresses that swished around their bare ankles. They wore silver or wooden crosses at their necks, and longer necklaces of half-moon and triangular silver charms to protect them from the bad effects of the crescent moon and evil eye. The men were dressed much like our guides in knee-length, green shorts, old suit jackets, and homespun *shemmas*, the ubiquitous white robes, and had white or green turbans wrapped around their heads. Several that we passed had such distinctive, Biblical features—long, oval heads, hooked, aquiline noses—that they looked as if they'd marched straight from the pages of the Old Testament. But they'd found an arms dealer somewhere along the way, since most of them also carried automatic weapons—Kalashnikovs and G3s—as well as their fighting sticks.

Some groups paused to talk with us, curious about who we were and where we were headed, and one couple accompanied us to our lunch spot, the husband peppering Belie with questions, while his pretty wife listened but never lifted her eyes from the trail. For all she knew, I might be hostess to a buda. It was safer not to look directly at my brownish green eyes.

It had not taken long to catch up with the donkeys. Several of the loads had shifted, and Teno's men stopped from time to time to adjust these. Lunch gave them another opportunity to rearrange the baggage. Zelalem had led the way with Teno, and they were waiting for us in an orchardlike grove of trees. Kate was not far behind; then Nevada arrived with her usual smile, giving everyone a lift, and Mick came in with Mike Speaks. We were all a little unsure of the camp routine, yet, and waited while Zelalem laid out loaves of bread, jams, and honey on a blue tarp for us. A little rain started to fall, so we didn't linger, but quickly ate, then each grabbed an orange and granola bar for a later snack. Teno wanted his donkeys out in front, so his men pushed them on to the trail, whacking at their backsides with their sticks, and they trotted down the path with our gear sashaying and jangling along like big jars of nickels.

In some places, the trail followed so close to the river's edge that, with the water at flood stage, the main path at times vanished beneath its muddy flow. We jumped across its dirty water, or stepped gingerly from tree root to tree root. The local people were not nearly so fastidious, and simply sloshed through with their wide, bare feet. A group of women bearing massive loads of wood on their back pushed past us. The poor ladies were bent nearly double from the weight, and Bruce looked at me sympathetically.

"I wouldn't put that much on a donkey's back," he said.

"Nor would I," I agreed. It was an all-too common sight in many parts of Africa, I added, telling him about the old saying of how donkeys were somewhat higher here on the social scale than women.

Bruce, Mick, and Mike Speaks were all carrying day packs, and Bruce and Mick had video camera gear, too. And while Nevada, Kate, and I were also carrying small packs, those of our male friends were bigger and heavier. From an Ethiopian's point of view, our group must have looked as odd and "wrong" as these women with their loads appeared to us. It was easy to imagine these countryfolk wondering how our male companions could protect us since they were burdened with their heavy packs. A man needed to be free, my Ethiopian friends always explained, to fend off would-be thieves and fierce animals.

Fortunately, we had the well-armed Teno and crew along, too. They were part of their village's militia, Zelalem had explained to me over lunch, and the government requires such militiamen to bear their weapons at all times. One, Kes Yeshambel Berhanu, was also a priest (*kes* is Amharic for "priest") and, alongside his Kalashnikov, wore a large brass cross on a metal chain. His was a curious mix of talents, but apparently only to us. Almost every villager we passed recognized our well-armed priest and stopped to seek his blessing and to kiss his cross. This was protection of an altogether different sort, and as other riflemen strode down the trail, we were glad of the bristly yet holy image our team projected.

A woman with a shawl pulled over her head walked beside me for a ways, asking Belie many questions. She clucked her tongue when he told her about our intended journey. "Be sure you give some bread to the Abay," she cautioned me. "There are bad jinn in the water that might reach up and grab you."

I thanked her for the warning and glanced over at the river. It rushed along angrily just a few feet away, its waves slapping long, dirty fingers against every rock in its path. It was easy to imagine one finger rising up to drag you in, and I gladly tossed the river the last of my granola bar—and hoped that the spirits liked it as much as they did bread.

Every step we took seemed to lead us farther down a path where the spirits and Old and New Testament gods and saints communed. Not long after placating the Abay, I stepped aside to let a large worried group of travelers pass. Four men wrapped in soiled white robes carried a wooden litter on their shoulders. On it lay a child bundled in homespun rags and blankets, and beside the child walked his mother, lamenting and praying with every step.

"He has a fever, *weba*, malaria, " Zelalem said. "They have walked since morning. They'll go to the clinic in Bahir Dar."

The magic and potions of the local priests had failed, and now the family was reduced to this last, desperate act, akin to raising Lazarus—although, the kid looked so far-gone, I doubted he would ever get off his litter.

I had caught up with Zelalem and Teno and the jostling string of donkeys, and walked the last half mile with them to our camp. It was mid-afternoon, and Zelalem had chosen a site in a grassy meadow edged with acacia trees to pitch our tents. Not far from it, a clear stream spilled over the trail, and after setting up camp, we walked in pairs to swim and bathe. Behind our camp rose a high, tree-covered bluff, while in front, the Blue Nile roared along in its dark gorge. A pair of emerald green turacos flew up into the trees at sunset, and as I watched them through my binoculars, I spotted little groups of people. They were huddled under the shrubs and trees, and were studying us. Most of them seemed to be children, but I saw a few turbans, too—men, and probably men with weapons. I waved and they ducked down.

It was a little unsettling to be watched like this, especially knowing the stories about other attacks. But I'd noticed Zelalem and the other guides casting glances up at these people, too, and then going on about their work. The local people were very likely only curious, and understandably so. It wasn't often that a large caravan with six ferenjocch stopped in your neighborhood—it was like a reality show unfolding right in their front yards, and they had to watch. When I'd lived in Ethiopia, I found that no matter where you camped, the local people would find you. Once, some friends and I spread our sleeping bags on a tarp on the empty mud flats of Lake Stephanie in the southernmost part of the country. Not a soul was in sight, but when we awoke, two men with feathers in their hair and rifles at their sides were sitting beside us, waiting for us to rise and entertain them. We gave them tea with two big tablespoons of sugar, and after they drank the syrupy brew and nodded their thanks, they picked up their rifles and walked away into the desert.

The local people above our camp weren't brave enough to come down from their bluff, and they disappeared as twilight descended. Our porters made a big fire and sat around it with their guns pointing over their shoulders. They would take turns standing guard through the night. We had a simple dinner of pasta, then warmed ourselves by the fire, while Speaks talked a little about the rest of the hike.

"We'll need to cover about six-to-eight miles a day, which is do-able," he said. "And we have one big river crossing, one of the Nile's tributaries, on the day after tomorrow. We'll stop there, check it out, and then decide when to cross it. We're just going along here one day at a time."

I watched Nevada while Speaks talked. Like the rest of us, she listened to him as if he was the leader, and never questioned anything he said. So be it, I decided. She had turned that role over to him, and although I found myself bridling at the tone of his voice, I would keep quiet. It was easier that way. I didn't want any confrontations; I wanted to enjoy the Blue Nile, its country and its people. I'd stick with the Ethiopians, who had stories to tell.

None of us stayed up late. I had a little residual jet lag, wrote up my notes, and fell happily into my sleeping bag. I listened awhile to the sounds of the night. The soft voices of our guides at the fire; the crackling noise as another log was tossed on the flames; and the steady rushing of the Blue Nile. For the next month, I thought, that would be the sound I would fall asleep and wake to: the waters of the Nile on their way to Sudan.

ten

W E WERE CAMPED ABOUT 800 MILES NORTH OF THE EQUATOR, so that our days were almost evenly divided between 12 hours of daylight and 12 hours of night. The first hint of dawn came at close to six o'clock, when the forest around us erupted with the bright calls and songs of tropical birds. I quickly dressed and crawled out of my tent.

Mick was up, too, packing his video camera into its carrying case, and he nodded my way. "A bright and breezy morning to you," he called out. Mick had a ready supply of these colorful Aussie expressions, and I gave him a smile and greeting back.

Photographers are always up before the morning's light, and Nevada soon came walking into camp. She'd been down by the river, looking for a dawn shot.

"How'd you do?," I asked.

"Well, it wasn't quite what I wanted, but I got a few things," she replied. "Isn't it just great being here?"

"Absolutely. It still feels rather unreal. But what a pretty spot."

I looked up at the bluff behind camp. A small crowd had gathered to study us once again, and I waved, then walked to the campfire for coffee and a bowl of cereal.

Zelalem and another of our guides, Yergale Tilahun, were tending the fire and coffee, while Mike Speaks stood nearby talking with Bruce. I'd only spoken with Yergale a little bit the day before. A short fellow in his early twenties, he had a round face with the plastic features of an actor. Greeting you, he would arch his eyebrows, turn up the edges of his mouth in a wide grin, then reach out to clasp your hand. If something shocked him, he would pop out his eyes, purse his lips, and grab his heart. His laughs were big; his gestures, broad and theatrical. The instant he saw me approach the fire, he was on his feet to welcome me. And with a great show of courtesy and an effusive string of greetings, he gallantly poured my coffee.

I laughed and thanked him, but also noticed that Zelalem did not smile at any of Yergale's antics. There was some petty competition going on between them, I guessed.

It never takes long for schemes, intrigues, and plots to develop among any group of people. Already, after one day of hiking, small alliances and partnerships were forming in our little party. We were polite to one another, but looking, too, to make our own minisupport networks within the larger group. So far, Yergale had spent most of his time with Nevada and Mick, and they liked him and his dramatic ways. His English was a bit more facile than Zelalem's, and he was funny. Maurizio had hired Yergale for us, but only for the trekking part of the journey. Yet Nevada and Mick were talking about having him join us for the entire trip—a request that jeopardized Zelalem's role. And now Yergale was trying to ingratiate himself with me.

Yergale was humorous, that was true, but there was also something about him I didn't entirely trust—perhaps, he was a little too clever and knew it. If we were forced to choose one over the other, I'd stick with Zelalem.

One of our other local guides, Belie, was not trekking with us anymore. Apparently, he had been hired only for our time around Bahir Dar, and had already started for home. His quiet and likable brother, Adane, however, stayed behind. Slowly, we were also getting to know our wranglers, who were somewhat more relaxed around us this morning. Mick had shot some digital video footage of them washing their faces and working around the camp, and had then played it back for them on his camera's screen, which made them laugh. Now, they greeted us with smiles and bows, some also pulling back the hoods of their robes, as if doffing a cap. Even Teno's sour, disapproving look had softened.

Two of our wranglers were brothers, Kasawol and Adunya Abate. They looked to be in their early thirties, and knew a little English, having gone as far as the sixth grade in their village school. Kasawol had a slightly aggrieved way of looking at you, as if certain he was about to be wronged, while Adunya had a sunny disposition, and liked to laugh. Kasawol wasn't shy about trying out his English, and called to me as I walked toward my tent, "Sister! Good?"

"Yes," I called back. "I'm good—*tiru negn*."

It was a perfect phrase for the start of this day, our second along the Blue Nile.

A MILE FROM CAMP, THE TRAIL LED AWAY FROM THE RIVER AND UP a steep, cultivated hill. Ethiopia's spring comes at the end of the rains, and over the next few days, we walked through a land that was vibrant with its flush of new green grasses, yellow daisies, freshly sprouted fields of teff—a kind of millet—and corn. Bowers of star jasmine, tumbling through the branches of acacia trees and euphorbias, scented the air, and red-and-black bishop birds shot skyward like sparkling firecrackers.

The trail wound past clusters of round thatch-roofed homes and fields of teff edged with low stone walls and clumps of wildflowers. Mountains shaped like huge ocean liners towered above both sides of the gorge, and every flat bit of land was quilted with a patchwork of fields that shimmered green and gold in the sun. In many fields small groups of men, women, and children squatted on their haunches, weeding each row by hand. Some stared as we passed; others rose and made three or four quick bows in greeting. One farmer stopped his team of oxen, walked away from his plow to the edge of his field, and cracked his whip into the air. He then cupped his hand around his mouth and whooped the news of our arrival to his neighbors down the valley. Others felt compelled to rush up to shake our hands and offer us thick slabs of *injera* (bread) or invite us to their homes for coffee.

"*Tenaystellegn!*—May God give you health!" we learned from our guides to call out. "*Endemen adderachehu!*—Good morning to you!"

But some still trembled in fear at our approach. A teenage woman, carrying a large clay water jug on her back, simply dissolved into tears.

"She's not seen a white person before," said Zelalem. He reached out and took her gently by the hand, then spoke softly to her, assuring her of our good intentions—and explaining that our skin condition was not a communicable disease. She looked down and away, and her tears stopped.

I liked walking close to the front of our long caravan with Teno and Zelalem. Teno had spent much of his life climbing through these mountains, and had a mountaineer's steady, easy gait. He carried a black umbrella in the crook of his arm, popping it open at midday to shelter himself from the sun. But if I was hiking with him, he would insist that I take his umbrella.

"He wants you to have it," Zelalem would say. "It is better for you."

So I walked along behind them with the umbrella open over my head, feeling like a modern version of the 19th-century explorer Mary Kingsley, who traipsed across West Africa in full Victorian garb, carefully shaded by her black umbrella.

Other times, I joined Nevada and Mick, who were busy with their photography. Mick liked filming anything that made our journey look arduous, like mucking through a muddy trail after it rained or struggling to set up our tents in the wind. He would run ahead with his camera on his shoulder, calling out, "Wait! Wait!" Then turn, focus on us, and shout instructions at us, like a director. Nevada was just the opposite. She would study a scene for a minute, then raise her camera to her eye and click away. People were her forte, and she often lingered along the trail to clasp the hands of farmers we met, and only start shooting after they returned to their work. Our porters especially loved having her take their pictures. Sometimes, she used a flash, which at first elicited cries of surprise. The two brothers, Kasawol and Adunya, sat side-by-side in their white robes for her one morning. At every click and flash, their bodies jolted backward as if they were being shot by a machine gun. Nevada lowered her camera to reassure them, but they weren't frightened.

"They say, 'Take as many as you want,'" Yergale translated. So Nevada raised her camera again, and the two brothers continued to jerk with every click.

Sometimes, I walked with Kasawol and Kes Yeshanbul, our warrior-priest. He was, I guessed, in his late forties, and had a kind, avuncular expression. He liked to walk with his Kalashnikov balanced horizontally across both shoulders. While hiking, he kept his big brass cross tucked away beneath his white robe. But in the mornings, he hung it on the outside so that all our porters and guides could come forward to bow and kiss the cross. With a nod of his head, he would point out for me the churches that we passed, saying, "*Bet Christian* [Christian House]." These were invariably located on narrow ridges, high in the mountains and far from us. They were centuries old, and round and whitewashed, and usually covered with a tin roof, which made them shine in the sun so that they caught your eye. Sometimes we passed a pile of rocks, like a small quarry along the trail. "*Bet Christian*," the priest would say, jerking his head toward the rocks. That puzzled me, but Zelalem explained that somewhere up the valley or on a distant peak was another church or monastery which couldn't be seen. People knew the church was there, though, and so the faithful could drop a rock together with a prayer at these sacred spots.

In the early afternoon, Kasawol came up the trail to find me. We greeted each other in Amharic, and walked along silently for a ways. Then he turned to me, his eyes glistening with hurt and injury.

"Sister," he said in English, and his chin quivered. "Zelalem and Yergale not good. They are false-talking. We [have] no food. Yergale, he give nothing to eat. Sister! Help us." He patted his lean stomach.

False-talking and nothing to eat! These were serious charges, and I wondered why he'd chosen to tell them to me. I knew the porters were studying all of us, sizing us up along with our own pecking order. Of most importance to them was who had the money. They had very likely written off Speaks since he wasn't dressed much better than they were. Nevada and I not only had nice clothes and good boots, but gold and silver earrings and bracelets, not to mention our cameras and binoculars; we looked to be people of substance and clout. We could talk to the other ferenjocch about these injustices.

"*Asnalo*—I'm sorry," I said. "I'll look into this. Don't worry." First, though, I needed to find out what he meant, and if his allegations were true.

Kasawol nodded sorrowfully, then walked on ahead.

I spotted Zelalem and talked to him about Kasawol's complaints, although I didn't say he'd been accused of lying. Zelalem knew all about the problem; something indeed had gone wrong. Somehow there was neither food nor money to buy food for our wranglers. Maybe Yergale hadn't been given sufficient funds, or had used them for something else—it wasn't clear. But the men had had to ask the villagers near our first night's camp for dinner. "It wasn't good that you ferenjocch ate and they had nothing," Zelalem said.

Of course it wasn't good. At our next rest stop, I passed Kasawol's story of woe on to Nevada and Mike Speaks. We never did understand what had happened to the funds for our guides' food, but they never went begging for dinner again.

OUR TREKKING DAYS GENERALLY BEGAN SUNNY AND WARM, AND GREW steadily hotter as we climbed higher above the gorge, and up and down the steep hills. The Blue Nile became but a distant roar, a black crack in an otherwise green landscape. Occasionally, we found an overlook that gave us a better look at the river, which raged between the black canyon walls like a bad-tempered beast.

At one overlook, Mike Speaks showed us the section of river that had given him and his clients a fright. "I was definitely in the washing machine down there," he said. "See how sheer the canyon walls are. Even at lower water levels, the river is like we saw it at the base of Tis Isat, all boiling and roiling." His team had hoped to portage their rafts or use ropes to line them through this rough set of rapids, but there were no riverbanks. "The only solution was to get in the boats and go, and hope for the best."

That's when their boats flipped and several people were injured.

"It was a brutal day—which is why we're hiking this stretch," he concluded. He gave a big smile, and raised his arm in the air as if pulling on a train whistle.

"Whoo-whoo! Whoo!"

That was Speaks's way of telling us to get a move on.

We hiked about seven miles a day, not many in linear miles, but we weren't walking a straight line. It was more like climbing up and down the pitched pleats of a giant's accordion. The mountain ranges did not run parallel to the river; rather they hit at right angles. And since we were trying to follow the river's course, we were forced to climb up and over every mountain that knifed its way to the water's edge. Small streams and some big rivers ran through the canyons between the mountain ranges. Most of these were fairly easy to wade across, but one, the Wudjow River (or Encata, depending on the map), would be a challenge.

Speaks had brought up the crossing several times. "We'll stop there. Take a look at the river, and then decide when to cross it," he said. He figured we would reach the Wudjow sometime on the afternoon of our third day.

That day started off in the usual way with lots of sunshine, but after lunch dark thunderclouds built up over the mountains. Soon we were hiking in a drenching deluge. The same weather pattern had hit us the day before, just as we reached the spot that Zelalem and Teno had chosen for our camp. For a good half hour we sat against some rocks, huddling under our umbrellas as dime-size raindrops pelted us and the wind howled.

"I thought the rainy season was over," Bruce commented, as water poured over his umbrella like a miniature version of Tis Isat.

"Well, maybe it's tailing off," Speaks had replied. "Anyway, it's a good thing. It means the Abay will stay high. There'll be enough volume to carry us to Sudan."

The rain made the air cool and moist, and when it stopped, the green fields and mountains glistened like the emeralds of Oz.

When the rains swept over us the next afternoon, we were about a mile from the Wudjow.

"Well, we'll stop and set up camp close to the river," said Speaks. "Cross it tomorrow in the morning."

Like most of the rivers that spill into the Blue Nile, the Wudjow starts high in the mountains. It runs over the hills and plateaus of the Begemder region, then drops into a V-shaped canyon and shoots downward in a series of small falls and cascades until it merges with the Nile. We reached the Wudjow about a mile from this confluence, following the trail down a steep hillside to a grassy terrace above the river's gravel bed.

The Wudjow was about a hundred feet wide at the ford, and as red and muddy as the Blue Nile. Its waters coursed along at a good clip, and looked to be very deep. Teno and several of his men had reached the river before us, and he and a couple of the other wranglers were already on the other side.

Speaks stopped when he spotted Teno on the far shore. He looked momentarily confused, then angry.

"Shit!" he said. Then he stomped over to the rest of the donkey team, who were getting ready to lead more of the animals across. Some of our Ethiopian guides had stripped down to their underwear or to nothing at all in preparation of their crossing, and politely dropped a hand in front of themselves when Nevada, Kate, and I appeared.

Speaks started shouting. "What the hell is he doing over there?" he demanded of Zelalem and Yergale. "I told everybody to wait at the river's edge. No one was to cross until I gave the order. Tell him to get back over here."

Zelalem and Yergale looked at each other, then at Teno, who was signaling for his men to join him. They called Speaks's order to him. But Teno shook his head and shouted something back.

"He says we must cross now," Zelalem translated. "The river is rising because of that rain. We must go now. Maybe tomorrow it is worse."

Speaks shook his head. "This was not my order."

"Yes, but Teno says it is better that we go now," Zelalem repeated patiently.

Yergale nodded. "Teno knows this river. We should cross now."

In the few minutes we had been standing at the river shore, the water had risen a good three inches and was spreading out across the dry cobblestones that lined its banks.

Speaks, however, would not relent until he watched the men take a donkey across. That would slow things down, but no one wanted to continue the argument. Adane and two other guides marched one of the donkeys to the river's edge, then plunged into the current. Adane stayed at the donkey's head, leading and cajoling, until they reached the other side. Then he swam back, taking strong strokes through the peaked red swells that rose up as the Wudjow's volume increased. It had apparently rained buckets in the mountains, and that water was now headed our way, like a flash flood.

Teno shouted again and shook his stick at us.

"He wants us to come quickly," said Yergale.

Speaks still looked angry, and held his jaw clenched, but finally gave in. There was no way of knowing what the morning would bring;

and if the river could be crossed now, the men kept saying, then we should go.

"Okay," he said. "But I want three men crossing over with every ferenji."

Kate went first, tying her skirt up to her waist. Two guides grabbed her arms and another one supported her from behind. She stepped carefully, using a stick for support, and in a few minutes had safely reached the other side. At the deepest point, a little more than halfway across, the water had reached just below her waist.

Kasawol and Adunya then took me across; three men to assist one ferenji weren't really necessary, although the current was swifter than I'd expected and it only required a couple of steps to reach a depth that was thigh-high. I kept my boots on, and it was easy to find my footing—until about two-thirds of the way over, when the water suddenly rose above my waist, and lifted me up and off my feet.

"*Ayezoch! Ayezoch!,*" Kasawol and Adunya shouted, tightening their grips on my arms. "Don't worry; you're okay!"

We plunged forward, fighting the water and a small set of rapids, then stumbled onto the rocky shore. Kasawol and Adunya did not wait, but immediately recrossed the river to fetch Nevada, while Bruce pushed through the current on his own. Most of the donkeys and guides had made it to safety, too. Teno stood near me, watching intently as the two brothers brought Nevada and then Zelalem over. The water by now had risen several more inches, and Yergale, who had come over with some of the other guides suddenly called out in alarm, "Look!" He pointed to the water that was lapping at several of our bags and supplies. Only a few minutes before, they had been far from the river's edge, but now they were about to be swept downstream.

"It's getting too high," Yergale shouted, as we rescued our bags.

Mick, Mike Speaks, and Adane were still on the wrong side of the river, and readying to cross it. Mick had stayed until the last minute, wanting to film everyone else, and now he had to pack up his camera.

"Don't come!," Yergale called to them. "It is too high, too dangerous."

Speaks shouted something back, but we couldn't hear him. They continued to arrange their gear, and the river continued to rise.

Mick slung his tripod over his shoulder, and Adane grabbed the camera bag. The trio then locked arms and stepped into the water. In an instant it was over their waists, and rising toward their chests. Halfway across, they all simultaneously gritted their teeth and began kicking as the river swept them off their feet and downstream.

"Oh no!" shouted Nevada and Kate.

People were crying and shouting, and several guides rushed to the river, hoping they could somehow reach the three men. But they swept past, with Mick and Mike kicking furiously and Adane facedown in the river, off balance from the camera bag. Somehow, he managed to twist his head up for a breath, then another, and in the next instant, they reached shallow water and a boulder. Saved.

"Well, I thought I was on my way to revisiting some of those old rapids on the Blue Nile," said Mike Speaks, after he staggered ashore. "Hoo-whee!"

Mick looked pale, and Teno, Kasawol, and Adunya ran to hug him and kiss his cheeks. Then he sat down to catch his breath, while Adane rested nearby.

Teno walked down the riverbank and I followed, thinking I might try to let him know in my limited Amharic that we could all see he had made the right decision. I didn't have a chance to get a word out. He whipped around the moment he saw me, and let fly a volley of angry words. He shouted and his eyes flashed and he pointed at the river and shook his head. I understood only a word here or there, but the overall meaning was clear. We should have crossed as soon as we had reached the ford; we'd nearly lost some men because of the delay.

Teno had every right to be angry. He knew the country, the trail, the rivers; we did not. I wanted to tell him, if I could have found the words, that I didn't know why his advice wasn't followed, or why Mike Speaks didn't turn to him for more assistance. Maybe it was like asking for directions—something that women can do, so the joke goes, but men cannot because the gene for asking for help at gas stations isn't found on the Y chromosome.

I muttered, "*Asnalo*—I'm sorry," and then, spotting Zelalem, asked him to offer a bigger apology.

Teno shrugged and tossed his robe over his shoulder and stalked away, huffy and surly again.

Behind us, Kasawol and Adunya had opened a bag and taken out three loaves of bread. They broke them into pieces, said a prayer, and tossed the bread to the river. They were still naked, and stood on a black boulder, gripping the rock with their brown toes while giving their gift to the Nile.

"They thank the spirits for letting us cross and not taking our lives," said Zelalem.

The other men stood by, watching closely as the bread fell into the rapids and was whirled away to the Abay.

Mike Speaks seemed oblivious to it all: Teno's anger, the spirit ceremony. He was busy adjusting his pack, and had his eye on the next stretch of trail. I wanted to like him, and did when he sang a silly song or tried to lighten our spirits with an old television jingle from the 1950s. But there was also an unpleasant stubbornness about him that sometimes made him unapproachable. He had told us over lunch that an old girlfriend of his had once tried to get him to buy some new shirts to replace his ragged ones. He shed the girlfriend rather than his shirts.

"People are always trying to get me to change," he had drawled. "But I don't change. I never have and I never will."

I looked up the trail. Teno was far ahead, making his way through the stubble of a cornfield. I picked up my pace and fell in quietly behind him.

A FEW HOURS LATER WE REACHED OUR THIRD CAMP. AS ON THE previous days, we camped on the outskirts of a small village, and were soon surrounded by a small, admiring crowd. The farther we got from Bahir Dar, the shyer and more polite the people became. No one shouted "ferenji" or "you! you! you!" or asked for anything. They merely wanted to watch the circus that had pulled into town.

We were a good show. We had bright yellow dome-shaped tents with fancy black poles, and like magicians pulled all kinds of miraculous things from our bags. We had medicines, too, and Kate kindly held a small clinic each morning, treating people for bad cuts and burns, stomach- and headaches.

In this village there were about 20 homes, all separated from each other by dirt paths, and each sheltered behind low, stone walls. One family invited Nevada and me to visit. We walked through a wooden gate and into the earthen compound, where chickens scrabbled for grain. Three women—a mother, daughter, and daughter-in-law—stood at the doorway of their home, eyeing us carefully. Two rows of blue tattoo marks ran from one ear, around their chins and up the other side like necklaces—a sign that they were married. They wore embroidered dresses, silver crosses, and amulets to protect them against the buda, and copper bracelets and earrings. Nevada had on several beautiful gold earrings, and the women drew close to look at these. They also wanted to look at our hair and skin. The daughter reached forward shyly to hold my hand, then carefully turned my arm over to study the underside. My veins were blue and visible, and had to be shocking to someone who had never seen such white skin before.

"I must look like I'm made of glass," I said to Nevada. "They can see right through me."

The daughter gave a little cry of surprise, and ran her finger gently along my arm. All right, so we weren't just magicians in the circus; we were the freaks, too. They smiled at us—but I had a feeling these were smiles of sympathy. "Poor you…to have such dreadful skin!"

We had pitched our tents below the village on a green, open field. Below our camp, the land sloped down to the Blue Nile Gorge, and on the far side, rose back up again in the high, stepped mountains of Gojam.

That night we ate goat that our men roasted over an open fire. Ethiopians love meat, and everyone was in high spirits after the river crossing. We sat around the fire together, chewing on the bones, and then Zelalem asked if any of the men could sing for us. A gray-haired porter immediately broke into a strong, rhythmic tune, while the others chanted and hummed in low voices, like the backup singers in a rock band. The singing became stronger, faster, and Kasawol and Adunya jumped up and danced, shaking their shoulders and dodging their heads at one another with quick, snakelike moves. Their eyes glazed over as the singing intensified, and then the song turned to a quick chant, "*Ehskisetah, Ehskisetah, ehsk, ehsk, ehsk.*" It ended abruptly, then began again, and the brothers extended their hands to Nevada and me. We must dance, too.

There was more singing, more dancing, and at last we said good night, leaving the men to enjoy the rest of their meat, and some of the local brew.

I had pitched my tent just below a little hill, and for some reason, as I walked down to it, I thought, "What a great place for someone to hide and watch our comings and goings." I even half-thought I saw some-one duck down as I approached. But it was unlikely. Everyone we had met had been friendly, and they had left our camp as soon as the sun set. In a few places where I'd camped in Ethiopia, the people never left your side for a minute, and you had to get used to having someone spy on you as you brushed your teeth or took a pee. They could be persist-ent, like flies on a piece of rotting meat. You could get angry, or you could laugh or cry; they still wouldn't leave. In such instances, I thought of myself as a biological specimen—just as some European biologists had in fact regarded some of the remoter peoples of Africa. At least, I hadn't been "collected" for display as a few of those poor people had.

The night was cold, and I pulled my sleeping bag up tightly over my head, and soon fell asleep.

Some sounds wake you in an instant. You know even before you are fully awake that something is wrong. First, in some foggy part of my mind I heard the donkeys stampeding past my tent. Had a hyena attacked them? I sat up, then heard the sound of men running. They were shouting. There was the flash and loud crack of a Kalashnikov being fired. One shot. Then another, and a third. I dropped to the floor of my tent, my heart pounding wildly, while two more shots echoed in the night. I flattened myself on the floor, thinking of a close mountaineer-ing friend and his wife who had been shot while sleeping like this in their tent in Afghanistan.

My mind raced. Had someone been hiding behind that hill? Were we under attack by the shifta? There were more shouts, but the gunfire stopped, and we called out questions from our tents. Was everyone all right? What, in God's name, had happened?

Only a donkey thief, Zelalem explained. He'd escaped, but without his prize.

I unzipped my tent and stared out at the night. Kasawol and Adunya walked by, shouting and gesturing. Mike Speaks was out of his tent, too, and walking up and down with a flashlight. Some men were leading the donkeys back to the camp. No one was hurt, everything was okay. I lay down again, but my heart didn't stop racing for several minutes. I had never heard a Kalashnikov or any automatic weapon fired before, except in the movies. And here I'd been close enough to not only hear but see the hot light of the bullets' flash.

A donkey thief, I told myself again. Not a shifta. Our men had done the firing. No harm done, I repeated, it's okay to sleep. But I tossed and turned, and was glad to see the morning light.

The villagers were up at dawn, too. They wanted to know what had happened.

We all did. Sometime after the party ended, a man had sneaked into camp and made off with a mare. He had tethered it down the hill, then brazenly come back to steal her baby, too. That's when the donkeys stampeded, and our men woke up and grabbed their guns.

"They only wanted to shoot him, not kill him," Zelalem said, as Kasawol went through the motions of aiming his Kalashnikov at an unseen enemy. He had fired two of the shots; his brother, one.

"But they should have shot him," complained one of the men from the village. Others insisted that he was "surely not a man from here; we have no thieves among us."

"More likely," said another man in a blue turban and with a pirate's copper ring glinting in his ear, "it was a spirit. A devil from the Gihon that took the form of a thief. That's why you couldn't shoot him."

"The Gihon?" I asked Zelalem.

"That is their name for the Abay, the Blue Nile," he explained.

I had read that some Ethiopians used this very Biblical term for the river, but had not yet heard anyone do so. The name refers to one of the four rivers that flowed out of Eden at the beginning of the world. Gihon was the river in Genesis that "compasseth the whole land of Ethiopia," and in its waters, I now learned, lived a king also named Gihon.

The women we had met the previous evening were worried for us now that a spirit had tried to attack us. "Some nights Gihon comes to the surface with his lights," said the mother, who wore a white shawl pulled over her finely plaited hair. "If he sees you," she cautioned, "he may attack you, so you must look away." There were small devils in the water's depths, too, shape-shifters, like our donkey thief. A gift of bread might keep these jinns away.

Zelalem nodded as she spoke. "We can do that," he said. Later, though, he told me that he didn't believe the thief was a shape-shifter. "That's just something for these people to say."

Zelalem's dismissal of the villagers' explanation, however, didn't mean that Zelalem didn't share their beliefs and worries about the spirits and spirit world. The day before he had told me about seeing men and women transformed into budas in his home town. "They act just like a hyena," he had said. "They run on their hands and knees, and howl, and bite at you. It is terrible."

Some could be saved from their torments with great shows of affection, good food and delicacies, and blessings from the priests. But others died after falling into a fever, and shaking and foaming at the mouth.

Perhaps they had actually been suffering from rabies or another illness, I suggested. Zelalem shook his head.

"No. It was the buda."

Did he worry about meeting such people here, or any of the jinns?

"No," Zelalem replied, touching the small wooden cross he wore on a mateb string around his neck. "I have my God. He will protect me."

"You don't worry, either, Ginny," he added. "You will be okay." Then he laughed. "You know, your name. It is like our word, jinn. Maybe you have a little devil?"

"Maybe," I teased back. "Or maybe my name will give us some protection."

"I think so," Zelalem said.

That was one of the simplest of magic formulas: fighting like with like. We had my "Ginny" to put up against the Blue Nile's "jinns."

eleven

MY STOMACH WAS BAD. IT HAD STARTED ACTING UP THE DAY before, and now was doing handsprings and backflips as we hiked up the trail and away from the village. I passed on lunch, and only nibbled at a granola bar to give me some strength. Mick wasn't faring too well either. He no longer ran ahead of us to shoot film, but trudged along silently, looking pasty in the brutal, midday heat. Every once in a while, the trail would level out, and then the walking was fine, but mostly it was steep and rocky and led through too many old corn-fields. It was like walking over a washboard road that had turned to dust, and my heart sank when I saw that Teno, far ahead, was still walking across empty cornrows. In my travels, I had faced other times that required simple, plodding endurance, and adopted a mantra to go with them: "This too shall pass." I took a sip of water, bent my head, said my mantra, and climbed up the hill through the stubble. Later, Bruce took pity on me and carried my day pack as well as his own up the last, long part of the day's trail. Another seven miles behind us, I thought, lowering myself to the ground. And only five to go. Then we would board our rafts and let the Blue Nile do the work.

Minutes after our caravan arrived, several of the villagers showed up, led by a wiry man wrapped in a white robe and wearing a turban of dark green and blue stripes. Like our guides, he was barefoot and carried a Kalashnikov. His name, he said, as he shook our hands and Zelalem translated, was Atele Asseras, and he was the headman of this village, Abo Gedam, in the area of Genete Maryam. Atele had a direct, cheerful manner, and wanted to know all about us and why we had come. He listened attentively and welcomed us as if he were the head of the local chamber of commerce and not a headman-warrior with a Kalashnikov slung over his shoulder. Then he cleared his throat. He was glad we were here, and yes, we could put up our tents, but first he must see our permits. Mike Speaks produced a thick stack of papers from a plastic case he kept inside his day pack.

For a journey like this in wartime Ethiopia, we'd needed permits for every region we passed through, as well as from assorted government ministries: Customs, Culture and Information, Foreign Affairs, Police, Telecommunications, and Defense. Maurizio, our logistics man in Addis, had spent weeks getting these, writing on our behalf to the Ethiopian Tourist Commission, then pestering their officials to write more letters to obtain the actual permits. Even the American Embassy had written a letter for us to General Tsadkah, the head of the Ethiopian Army, saying in effect, "Please don't shoot our citizens." The letters and permits we carried were written in the distinctive Amharic alphabet, and stamped with the star denoting the Federal Democratic Republic of Ethiopia and signed by an official. We had an all-purpose letter, too, from the Tourist Commission, which listed our names and association with National Geographic, and gave a general outline of the nature of our trip and how it would benefit Ethiopia. It appealed to those who met us along the way to render us "every assistance" and "hospitality."

In the past, when royal caravans traveled through the countryside, the local people were expected to provide their guests with every amenity—food, drink, and lodging. And many travelers tell of the long lines of peasants coming into their camps bearing baskets of flatbread (*injera*), eggs, and honeycomb, crates of chickens, sacks of coffee beans, jars of barley beer (*tella*), and bottles of mead (*tedj*). The peasants weren't paid for their generosity; it was simply the custom to provide such hospitality. Even in Cheesman's day, in the late 1920s, when he began his trek along the gorge, Ras Hailu ordered the Gojami peasants to provide for the British consul in this way. Cheesman would not have it; he did not want to be a burden to the people. Yet it is difficult to turn down any gift in Ethiopia without causing offense, and especially gifts of food and drink. Worried that his offering had been deficient in some way and that the Ras would chastise him, one village headman came to the consul's tent to discover what was wrong: Were the chickens not fat enough, was the bread stale? Would the consul prefer these three fine black calves to the puny red ones the villagers had been so stupid and rude to provide? Aghast and apologetic, Cheesman accepted the first set of gifts.

Atele stood beside Zelalem to read our letter of introduction from the Tourist Commission. He traced his finger beneath each word, and carefully enunciated the syllables. Then he looked up. Of course, we were very welcome to camp here, he said. He was pleased that we had chosen his village. And then, responding to that phrase "every assistance," he asked us what he and his people could offer.

"If we need injera, tella, or tedj, we need only to ask him," Zelalem translated. "He is opening his village to us, and they will bring us everything to eat."

It was spring here, the crops were freshly sprouted, which meant that the villagers were living on the last of the last season's food. What little they had, though, they were willing to share—and with us, a big, wealthy caravan. I felt another twinge of shame about the first night on the trail when Teno and his wranglers had watched us eat, and we had offered them nothing. We weren't, of course, going to take Atele up on his kind offer, but we did tell him through Zelalem that our men would want to buy some injera and meat.

If he couldn't feed us, Atele responded, would we do him the honor of drinking coffee in his home the next day?

We would.

Our camp that night was the prettiest of the trip. Zelalem had sited it on a rounded bluff overlooking the gorge, and the views in all directions were so spectacular that it was easy to understand why the region had been christened Genete Maryam—Mary's Heaven. A soft band of clouds, tinged a cherubic pink and blue, hung just above the canyon, following the course of the river, and the mountains and terraces on both sides looked as if someone had draped them in green velvet. It was grand, Biblical scenery, like in a medieval painting, and easy to imagine Mary and her angels descending from the heavens on the carpet of clouds, while saints stood on the mountaintops blowing their horns and little scrolls announcing her arrival fluttered underfoot. This was a place for dreams and prayers, and once in the past, Atele told us, a group of monks had lived in the forest above the village. The village was named for their haunts: Abo Gedam, the saints' monastery.

People had lived, worshiped, and farmed here for more than a thousand years, yet the land hadn't been tamed; it was pastoral and heavenly and wild all at once.

There was a rocky outcropping on the far side of the gorge, and Yergale shouted, "Look, gorillas! Big ones!"

"Nope," said Mike Speaks, squinting through his binoculars. "Baboons."

"Well, they are big like gorillas," Yergale insisted.

We all grabbed our binoculars. They were indeed baboons, *Papio anubis,* the common baboon of East Africa. Some of the males had large manes, and those were probably the ones Yergale had mistaken in his enthusiasm for gorillas—which don't live in Ethiopia. The primates were walking along the edge of the outcrop, their hips sashaying from side to side with the insouciant air that comes from outwitting humans. They'd probably just finished raiding some poor farmer's crops, and were now heading home to burp and sleep.

I didn't stay up late. My stomach was still unsettled, so I drank a cup of beef soup, ate a couple of crackers, and hit the sack.

MIKE SPEAKS HAD DECLARED THE NEXT DAY A DAY OF REST, SINCE WE didn't need to reach the river's edge until the following afternoon. I was glad for the time off. My legs ached and I felt a little queasy from whatever bug I'd picked up.

Our tents were plopped like big yellow daisies on the green meadow. We also had a large blue tent where we ate when it rained, and where all the porters and guides slept rolled up next to each other in their white robes. They had each other for warmth and company, while we each slept alone. In their culture, Ethiopian men are physically friendly with one another, often holding hands or hanging on each other like lovers. But they are not. It's a brotherly affection, they say, and would be shocked if you thought there was more to it. Adane and Yergale sometimes sat leaning against each other like bookends. Zelalem did not. Throughout the trip he had kept his distance from these Gojami men, and especially from Yergale.

Yergale was always stealing center stage. He would emerge from the tent in the morning, a Somali sarong pulled around his chest like a Roman toga and a porcupine's quill or spotted guinea hen feathers stuck artfully in his hair. Bored with that costume, he'd dress in khaki pants and T-shirt, then wrap the sarong into a turban and hoist one of the wranglers' Kalashnikovs over his head, terrorist-style. He always had a big smile and a little dance to accompany his shows, and Mick and Nevada would crowd around, taking his picture. He had stopped trying to impress me, probably because I often hiked with Zelalem. At times, we ferenjocch were like a bunch of dog bones, I thought—we had to be fought and quarreled over, and divvied up.

Yergale had the sarong arranged like a pair of harem pants this morning—tied around his waist and looped up between his legs—and he stood by the fire, looking very chic while he poured hot water for our coffee. Zelalem was making scrambled eggs, serving them with thick slabs of toasted bread and pots of jam and honey. It all smelled good, but I took only a small helping, then joined the other ferenjocch who sat in a line facing Mary's Heaven.

I'd managed to eat about half of my breakfast when I noticed a little boy standing off to one side, watching us. He was about 11 years old, unwashed, and had a filthy robe wrapped around him. There were bloody wounds on the backs of his legs. He clenched a long stick in one hand and studied us intently, but from a safe distance. We had seen children in all the villages. They liked to gather around us, their mouths agape while they watched our every move. They were poor in the sense that their clothing was patched and torn, and that they already worked for a living, helping with the family farms. Their outdoor lives—tending the livestock, weeding the fields, fetching water—left their faces chapped and raw. Often they were also smudged with dirt and had flies watering at their eyes, but overall they looked healthy, well-fed, and loved. They were full of smiles and would giggle and pull their robes over their faces if you spoke to them.

This lad was different. He had the look of a mendicant, and I wondered at first if he was a *kolo-temari,* a boy learning to become a priest. At one stage in their training, such students are expected to wander the countryside, begging for their food and offering prayers to those who help them. Our visitor, however, lacked the student's begging bowl and he wasn't singing for his supper. But his eyes were.

I set my plate of half-finished eggs on the ground and pushed it toward him.

"*Na,*" I said. "*Belah*—Come. Eat."

He didn't move. I gave the plate another push, and urged him forward. Then slowly, as if he was afraid I might trick him and pull the plate back, or deal him a blow, he stepped toward it. His eyes traveled over me, the other ferenjocch, and our crew like a cur dog waiting to be hit.

Zelalem called to him, encouraging him to take the food. Carefully, gingerly, the boy sat down, picked up the plate, and in seconds had wolfed down every bite. I fixed him some more pieces of bread with honey and a bowl of oatmeal. He wiped up every last drop and drank two cups of tea sweetened with sugar.

Only then did he smile. He moved to the campfire, and found a seat among our men. Zelalem peppered him with questions.

"His name is Abush," Zelalem translated, "and he says he is an orphan—no mother, no father—and that he is from Wollo region. He has been traveling for five days. He was far up there," Zelalem said, turning his head to point at the mountains behind us, "when he saw our tents. He thought maybe this is a wedding party, and he could find something to eat."

Abush had left his Wollo village on foot. Once he'd managed to get a lift from someone, but mostly he had walked. He had reached Bahir Dar, and liked the town. He thought he might stay, but the people there were mean to him. They threw sticks at him to chase him away, so he started walking again. Sometimes the peasants fed him, sometimes they also chased him away. Yesterday, a big dog attacked him. That's why he had the wounds in his legs; they were dog bites.

Kate took him aside to clean and dress his injuries. Then Zelalem said, "You know, he's not telling us everything. He says he is from one village near Lalibela. But that is my home, and there's no village there by that name. He has some secret."

There was a clear stream below Abo Gedam, and after breakfast we walked down to it to wash, our first bath in a few days. Abush followed behind me for a few steps like a page, then more bravely stepped alongside and took my hand. How long had it been, I wondered, since someone had been kind to him? He was a little Christian boy in a Christian country, yet someone had set their dogs against him—right here in Mary's Heaven.

Later that morning, we went to Atele Asseras's home for coffee. Abush again trailed along with me, apparently afraid to let me out of his sight. He sat down on a stone outside of Atele's compound and waited.

Like most homes in the Ethiopian countryside, Atele's was round, built of eucalyptus poles and mud, and had a thatched roof. Inside, a small fire was lit on a central hearth and arrayed around it were several small wooden stools. The only light came from that fire and the doorway, making the interior as dark as a Rembrandt painting. Slowly my eyes grew accustomed to the dim light, and I made out benches of sculpted mud along the walls. These were covered with tanned cowhides and cotton blankets. There were several large storage baskets and huge clay vessels behind the fire, along with other smaller crockery. On one wall, someone had drawn a series of crosses, and several other crosses woven of straw were pinned nearby. Atele grasped us each by hand as we entered and invited us to sit. His wife, Zenev, was seated beside the fire on a small stool, and smiled shyly when he introduced us. She wore her good dress: a deep blue one of homespun cotton, tied at the waist with a brightly striped belt. She had just finished washing the coffee beans in a metal pan, and now set the pan on the fire to roast them.

Coffee is believed to have originated in Ethiopia. Wild coffee plants are found in the mountains in the southwestern Kaffa region, which is said to have given its name to the beverage we drink. The warriors of old made small cakes from the beans, and ate these to give them energy and endurance on forced marches. They may also have brewed them. In time, the coffee drinking ceremony became imbued with great social importance, with many rituals and traditions attached, so that today, the ceremony in its highest form is nearly as elaborate as a Japanese tea ceremony.

When the beans were roasted, Zenev stood and wafted their smoky fragrance over us. It was like ringing a bell for Pavlov's dog. If we hadn't been thinking about coffee before, that warm, rich scent now made us long for a cup.

Zenev scooped the beans into a wooden bowl, ground them with a pestle, then tapped the powder into a black, clay coffeepot and poured in a stream of boiling water. She set the pot aside to brew, and tossed a few chunks of resin onto the pan, filling her home with the fragrance of frankincense and myrrh. She then produced a set of tiny, china demitasse cups, placed these on a wooden tray, and poured us each a cup.

"Do you want sugar or salt?" asked Yergale, who had come to translate for us. "The peasants like it with salt, and they drink, you know, nine cups a day. That's why they have a lot of gastritis."

I glanced his way. At times, I really liked Yergale, and this was one. He was a young man from a city in a far corner of Ethiopia, and yet despite that isolation he had studied his English long and hard enough so that he could correctly pronounce and use a word like "gastritis." Then, again, Ethiopians are fond of eating raw beef, and often suffer with tapeworms and parasites. Maybe the foreign words for an upset stomach were smart ones to learn if you were going to make your living with travelers.

We all declined adding salt to our coffee, preferring it either with sugar or black—which shocked our Ethiopian hosts. "Too bitter," said Yergale, making a horrified, sour expression. To Western tastes, salt seems an unlikely thing to flavor one's coffee, but in the Ethiopian highlands, where salt and sugar are equally rare and goiters not uncommon, salty coffee is a delicacy. Bars of salt, mined in the northeastern Danakil Desert and called *anole*, were in fact used as currency throughout Ethiopia until the 1930s, when Emperor Haile Selassie established the Bank of Ethiopia and the paper Ethiopian equivalent of the dollar, the birr.

Throughout the coffee ceremony, Atele kept up a steady stream of questions, while cradling a toddler of a girl in his arms. She was his daughter by his former wife, he explained. That wife had sadly died, and he had remarried. They called the little girl, Nafkote, for "the one I miss and long for," after she ran weeping to her dead mother's bedside.

How many hours, Atele wondered, did we work each day in our country? Had we traveled by car or airplane to reach Ethiopia?

"He is surprised to hear that there is a big ocean between America and Ethiopia," said Yergale. "You know, out here, most of these people don't know about Addis Ababa or even Bahir Dar, let alone the United

States. He had heard this word 'America' before, but he didn't know it was a country. It's a word the government uses sometimes when they give things; they say, 'This is from America.' But since he didn't have the concept of America, it didn't mean anything to him. Now, he knows this is a country with people. He says if he was a younger man he would like to travel there to see it."

Atele wasn't as out of touch as some of his villagers. He had seen the city lights of Addis a few times, and close to the city he had seen tractors. As a man who tilled his farm with a hand plow and oxen, he could see the advantage of a tractor. "He would like to have a tractor one day," Yergale translated.

Atele was also curious about the food we ate in our country. Yergale used words that had infiltrated the Amharic language since the Italian occupation: "Macaroni, pasta."

Atele looked a little sad at this poor diet, until Mike Speaks interjected, "Meat." "*Sega*," translated Yergale, and our host smiled broadly. *Sega* and *injera*, their bread made from the milletlike teff, are the essence of life for Ethiopians, and people lacking these staples are to be pitied.

Once, when I traveled by bus to the walled city of Harer, an Ethiopian businessman struck up a conversation with me. He had many of the same questions as Atele, and especially wanted to know if we ate injera in America. "No," I said, shaking my head. "No one eats injera." His eyes nearly popped from his head. "Then how can you live?" he shouted. He took pity on me and at our lunch stop ordered a huge plateful of the bread for me, trying, I guessed, to make up for all those sad, injera-less years.

Two other men now came in the doorway, one Atele's neighbor, the other, his oldest son, a boy in his teens. They shook all our hands, then sat on one of the far benches, trying to look as if it was perfectly normal to have six ferenjocch over for coffee.

"Before you came, we hadn't seen a single ferenjocch here," Atele then said. "We only saw pictures of them—photos of them with their intestines, stomachs, and hearts coming out," he added, referring to pictures of dead Italian soldiers taken during the occupation. "We never saw one up close until now."

Atele wasn't the first Ethiopian to mention the Italians to us. No one, it was apparent, had forgotten that bitter period of history, and more than once we'd had to reassure small groups of armed men who eyed us suspiciously that we were not part of an invading army.

"I did see one of you once before," Atele continued. He pointed at Mike. "You were down there on the river in your boat, and I thought, 'What's this? Are these Italians coming to invade?' I had you in the sights of my gun," he said, nodding at his Kalashnikov, which hung against a wall. "I was going to shoot, but then you waved."

"Ohhhh," Mike said, "my mama doesn't need to hear this."

We laughed and sipped our coffee—and decided that we would continue our practice of waving to everyone we saw.

ABUSH WASN'T THE ONLY ONE WHO HAD LOOKED DOWN ON OUR TENTS that morning from the plateaus and mountains far above. A small posse of vigilant militiamen had, too, and early that afternoon they tramped into camp. They looked like trouble. There were six in all, three in their middle to older years, three in their twenties. Four of them cradled Kalashnikovs; one of the younger men held a transistor radio. The older men wore turbans and old suit coats with robes slung over their shoulders; the younger men were dressed more Western-style in slacks and printed shirts and wristwatches. They were Christians, the mateb strings around their necks attested to that, but most of them had Arab features:

thin faces, hooked noses, narrow black eyes. The forgotten progeny, I thought, of Ahmad Gragn's 16th-century jihad, or of a passing slave and salt caravan.

None of them smiled. They stood in a row and stared icily at us. Their leader stepped forward. He was one of the older, turbaned set, and he had a wide face, full lips, and a prominent gap between his front teeth. Mike Speaks, Zelalem, and Yergale shook his hand; the rest of us formed a small semicircle around them and kept quiet. He was the head militiaman in the main town of the Genete Maryam district, he said, jerking his head toward the distant hills, and he wanted to see our travel permits. Zelalem explained that we already had shown them to the headman here, Atele, and he had approved them. But Atele, our visitor countered, was only a local headman.

"I am from the district, and I must see your permits," he said.

Mike produced the plastic case again, and handed several of the letters to Zelalem. He and Yergale took them and sat down next to the militia leader, who had squatted on the ground. Maybe it was the Kalashnikov that lent him his imperious air, but he had a haughty way of looking at us as if we were nothing more than some annoying ants that had worked their way into his picnic basket. He could squash us with his little finger, his look said. One of the dark-eyed young men stood off to his side. He glanced my way, and I felt a sudden chill. His eyes were black with anger and colder than death, and I whispered to Nevada, "They could kill us if they wanted to." She nodded.

The militia leader wasn't happy with our permits. He waved aside the ones from the Commissioner of Police, the Tourist Authority, the Defense Department. Zelalem's voice rose a notch. He pushed one of the permits toward the leader, and again the man waved it away. Yergale spoke up. The militia leader shook his head, then held forth for a while.

Yergale stepped away and came to us. "He wants you—or at least Mike Speaks—to go with him to their police station. He wants to send a telegram to Addis to make sure about your permits."

I glanced up at the mountains where our visitors had come from. It would be a six-to-eight hour hike to reach their distant town and police station.

Zelalem continued to argue, talking softly at times, then raising his voice angrily. He did not seem to be afraid of these men. Mike Speaks sat beside him, I guessed for support, since there was nothing much he or any of us ferenjocch could do. If they insisted that we go to the police station, then we would.

A long half-hour of negotiations ensued. I kept waiting for one of these militia men to smile, to at least register that we were human. They didn't. Another 20 minutes passed, and then to my surprise, the black-eyed fellow who had cast such hateful looks our way, walked to me and asked softly in excellent English, "Have you finished your work here? Then you can go."

I stuttered something about this being a day of rest, and that we were leaving the first thing tomorrow morning.

"It's better that you go now," he said. And he smiled.

We were humans after all. I smiled back and said that it would be hard for us to leave now when the sun was high and so hot. He nodded sympathetically.

"Can you walk down there in the desert?" he asked, pointing to the gorge.

"Well, we will tomorrow."

"I cannot," he said. "It is too hot there for me."

The other men, even the militia leader, had also started smiling; Zelalem's voice was now soft, placating. They asked for water and tea, and soon were drinking their fill.

What had been the problem? I asked Yergale.

"Well, you don't have the right permit. You have a permit to walk over there in Gojam, on the other side of the gorge. But you don't have one to walk here in Begemder. So they don't want you to stay here two nights. They want you to go. But now they say you can go tomorrow."

It was that old Ethiopian xenophobia. Foreigners were never to be trusted. You could welcome them, offer them food and drink, but really, you were much happier when they left.

A few moments later, Yergale joined me again and whispered, "Zelalem has made a big mistake. A big mistake! He gave them 100 birr."

One hundred birr, or a little more than eight dollars. Maybe it was wrong to bribe the local officials, but somehow these turbaned vigilantes had seemed more like brigands than law enforcers anyway. I thought Zelalem had done exactly the right thing in paying them off. They didn't linger after he slipped them the cash. They tossed their robes over their shoulders, hefted their weapons, and disappeared into the hills like the shifta of old.

ABUSH CAMPED WITH US THAT NIGHT. HE JOINED THE MEN AT THE FIRE and ate from their communal pot of injera and meat. We'd given him lunch, too, and he looked far different from the morose, worried child standing by our tents in the morning.

Abush had a round face, darker skin and eyes than our guides', and lashes so straight and thick they looked like little brushes. His teeth were white, uneven, and slightly bucked, and angled out at you when he smiled and talked. He held the center stage at the campfire, and chattered away about his life and his plans, as Zelalem and the other guides tried to pry his secrets from him.

"I told him I know he's not telling us the truth," Zelalem said. "There's no village like that one he says he is from. I told him, 'If you don't tell us, we'll make you pay for your supper.' " Zelalem chuckled. "I think he ran away, maybe."

Abush sidestepped the questions. His stomach was full, he had new friends and protectors, and he wasn't interested in his past. He wanted to tell us about his future.

"He says he is a traveler, like us," Zelalem announced with a giggle. "And he wants to see all of Ethiopia."

"Oh, yes," Yergale added. "He is a traveler: the original Budget Traveler."

"He wants to earn money," said Zelalem. "He'd like to be a shoeshine boy in Addis, and he says, 'I'd make money then and I'd have me a house and a bed and one little wife.' "

"Oh, he has big dreams," Yergale said, spreading his hands wide. "*Big* dreams."

Abush carried on, both ignoring and enjoying the men's laughter. He was outfitting his dream kitchen, describing the burner he would buy, and the big stewpot, knives, and serving dishes, and baskets. "I'd have a bowl for grinding coffee, and a nice black coffeepot, and eight coffee cups," he added. There'd be a little bowl for sugar and one for salt, and he and his one little wife would serve coffee to everyone who called.

"And after that," teased Yergale, "he can become the president. He has plans!"

And why not, I thought. Poor Abush—"no mother, no father, he is a poor," as one of the porters described him—his big dreams cost him nothing.

In the afternoon, one of our younger porters, a boy about 16 named Maru, had asked me if I liked Abush.

"Yes," I said, wondering what his question really meant.

"I don't like him," he said, turning up his nose. "He is black and he is ugly."

Maru pronounced the word "ugly" with an extra syllable, "ou-ugly." I ignored that remark and asked why couldn't this orphan seek help from one of the churches.

"Oh, he is too young to kiss the church," Maru replied. I didn't understand. Perhaps Maru thought I was suggesting that Abush become a *kolo-temari*, a student-priest, something he was still too young for. The Orthodox Church does take in orphans, although it is difficult for those in the countryside to do so, since they have neither the facilities nor funds.

And maybe Abush didn't want to go to an orphanage. Maybe he'd run away to escape that fate, and had chosen a wanderer's life instead.

I knew we couldn't take Abush with us on our journey, although the idea appealed to me. It would be like the journey of an Ethiopian Huckleberry Finn. But I'd seen the rigid muscles forming in Mike Speaks's neck as I handed Abush some lunch. He wouldn't let Abush come with us; I knew that without asking.

I would do the little that I could, though, for him. I would give Abush the money to buy his shoeshine box. He had become a tiny part of my *eddileh*, my destiny, that the priest had told me about so long ago.

twelve

~~~
~~~

N THE MORNING, ABUSH WAS WAITING OUTSIDE MY TENT.
I greeted him in Amharic, then led him over to the campfire for
breakfast, where Kasawol and several other guides were already gathered. Unlike Maru, Kasawol seemed to like our orphan, or at least he
approved of our charity. He moved aside to let Abush sit next to him.

After breakfast, we quickly struck our tents and loaded our gear on
the donkeys for the last time. Atele Asseras and several of the villagers
came to say goodbye.

"Come visit us again," Atele said. "We will always welcome you."

I liked the idea of returning to Genete Maryam, in spite of the ruffi-
ans who'd called on us. But I'd have that letter of permission for
Begemder, too—although I had a hunch our uninvited guests would have
figured out another way to weasel a "tax" from us, even if we'd had one.

Today's walk was to be a short one, just five miles, which suited me.
I couldn't shake my bad stomach, and again had eaten only a handful
of food. I'd been living on soup, crackers, and toast for the last couple

of days, and had already pulled in my belt a notch. I didn't want to complain, but I also thought I needed some help, and asked Adane if he could carry my day pack.

"Yes, yes," he said, hoisting it on his back. He looked around for our priest, and spoke to him quickly in Amharic. "The kes will look out for you."

One of the porters handed a small bag of gear to Abush to carry. He reached for it politely with both hands and smiled with elation. He was part of our caravan. Then Mike Speaks pulled the handle of his imaginary train whistle—"Whoo!! Hoo!"—and we were off.

The trail stayed to a beaten path, now; there were no more cornrows to tread through. We hiked along the slopes of the hillsides, and angled our way down toward the gorge. Springtime here was in full flower, and we walked past fields of yellow *meskal* daisies and cornflower blue flax. Tall spears of peppermint, pink morning glories, and frothy Queen Anne's lace waved in the sun, while swallowtail butterflies with turquoise-and-black markings, and dozens of smaller marine blue butterflies hovered about. Food and sex seemed to be on every insect's mind, and the air buzzed, hummed and clattered with the sounds of bees, locusts, and beetles.

I trailed along at the back of the line, and stumbled a few times, much to my annoyance. Our warrior-priest always reached out to steady me.

"*Ayezoch, ayezoch,*" he would say. "You'll be okay."

I knew I would, but in the meantime I hated feeling weak like this, and decided that I'd ask Kate for something stronger than the Pepto Bismol pills I'd been popping. I needed to get my appetite back.

Abush was doing fine. He traipsed along with Kasawol or Zelalem, his dirty robe flapping in the wind, his belly full. For the moment, he had "no worries," as Mick liked to say.

The trail finally swung down sharply toward the river. We were on the edge of the gorge again, and there was the Blue Nile, all nasty, red, and angry. Its loud, throaty roar carried up to us, drowning out the insects and birds. We'd heard the river every night of our trip, but usually as a distant, steady purl. Here, however, the Blue Nile sounded exactly as it looked: a big, rushing river at flood stage. It crashed, thundered, and boomed, and if there'd been any wooden rafters overhead, the river would have made them ring.

A series of sharp switchbacks cut down the hill, and around one bend we spotted what we most hoped to see: the three rafts. Mike Speaks was a little ahead of me and he paused to take in the scene.

"There's my home over there," he said. "My raft. I can't wait to get to it."

Two of the rafts were gray, one was orange, and they were tied up to the black rocks on the far shore, a little ways below the Second Portuguese Bridge or Broken Bridge. Like the bridge we crossed below Tis Isat Falls, this one was built in the 17th century by Portuguese and Indians working in the court of King Fasiladas. At one time, its five brick-and-mortar arches spanned the Blue Nile, but in the 1930s Ethiopian patriots tore away the center one with picks, shovels, and their bare hands in a desperate effort to keep the invading Italians out of Gojam. During the demolition, 40 of the bridge-busters lost their lives when the center arch collapsed and they were swept downstream and drowned. In retaliation for wrecking the bridge, the Italians shot a half dozen more men in a nearby town. The advancing forces made many bombing raids against Gojam, and they gassed thousands of people in Addis and the other major cities. And while all of that had happened 70 years ago, these cruelties had not been forgotten. They were spoken of as if they had happened yesterday. Little wonder that Atele Asseras and some of the other militiamen we had met seemed a bit trigger-happy when they spotted a ferenji—they were determined not to be at the mercy of foreigners again.

The closer we got to the Blue Nile, the more it sounded like we were approaching the beach at Malibu when a winter's surf is breaking onshore. The river was crammed tight in its canyon, and it pounded against the bridge's footings as if determined to finish the patriots' job. We walked down to the bridge, where several other groups of travelers were gathered. Although broken, people still use the bridge, relying now on the stoutness of a rope and strong men on either side to pull them and their goods across. Everything from sacks of grain to crates of chickens and Kalashnikovs crossed the river this way, as did everyone wanting to travel to Gojam, including a mother with a tiny, sleeping baby strapped to her back.

"I can't watch," said Yergale, hiding his eyes as the woman stepped off into space. Everyone seemed to hold their collective breaths while she and her baby dangled over the white, foamy rapids where Gihon and the jinn dwelled below. But neither she nor the men faltered, and soon she was walking safely down the bridge on the other side, her baby still asleep on her back. "Thank you, Mary and Jesus," Yergale said, crossing himself.

Behind us, at the end of the trail, Teno and his men had herded their donkeys beneath some shady acacia trees. They started unloading our gear, while Teno, Kasawol, and Adunya argued with Mike Speaks over their payment. Kasawol's eyes were glistening with that "I know your cheatin' heart" look again. There was some dispute, Zelalem explained, because they had been hired for only three days, but our trip had lasted five. They needed more money. That made sense to me and the other ferenjocch, and the dispute was quickly settled. The three Ethiopians raised their hands, palms out, as if surrendering, and smiled. Speaks counted out the cash.

A policeman stationed at the bridge crossed to our side. He had learned that our men had shot at someone—the donkey thief—and he needed to take a report. How many shots had been fired? Who had done the shooting? Kasawol and Adunya went off to one side to talk to him.

Then suddenly all of our men wanted their pictures taken—although certainly not as donkey wranglers. They were militiamen, and they posed like the gritty, fierce warriors they were, training their Kalashnikovs on unseen enemies, while Nevada clicked away. Even our warrior-priest got in the act and scowled menacingly into her lens.

And then, the next minute, we were bidding them good-bye. Teno made a short farewell speech, telling us through Yergale, that he was glad we had reached our destination peacefully and without any problems. "You have become our good friends," he said, "and we have taken good care of you. Now our responsibilities are over, and we are sad to say farewell. But you are in our hearts." Teno then crossed his hands and placed them on his left breast. Yergale did the same. He was leaving, too. His efforts to supplant Zelalem (if indeed that was what he had been up to) had not succeeded. He was going home, as was Adane. One-by-one they started across the rope bridge, giving us a final wave good-bye. They would hike up the other side of the gorge to a town called Mota, where they would catch a bus to Tis Abay. Maru and one of the other guides would lead the donkeys back the way we had come.

I was sorry to see them go. They'd drawn me back into Ethiopia and I wanted to linger. I wasn't sure what this next stretch of the trip would bring—but it was certain to be different. We were no longer a group of some ferenjocch and many Ethiopians; we were now going to be a group of some ferenjocch and a few—two—Ethiopians, Zelalem and another assistant, Ephrem Abdi Wayis, who was on the far shore, waiting to join us.

The social dynamics of our group were already beginning to change. Any remaining questions about who was in charge or who was going to give the orders were quickly put to rest. Mike Speaks raised his voice and summoned us all together.

"Okay. It's hot down here, and we're going to have to wait awhile. So keep your hats on, drink plenty of water, and wet your heads, hats, and shirts. Keep yourselves hydrated. Keep in the shade. Keep an eye on your personal effects. There are a lot of people here. Bruce and I are going to go over and get the boats. Zelalem, watch us—you'll need to catch the ropes on this side. It'll be a hard, tough row."

He delivered each sentence as if it were a singular pronouncement, then left with Bruce to cross the bridge.

On the far side of the river, we'd spotted Maurizio. "I have good news," he called across the roar of the river. "I have the last permit."

That wasn't just good news; it was excellent news. We needed that permit to pass beneath the next bridge, the big, modern Abay Bridge that was now heavily guarded because of the Ethiopian-Eritrean War. Without that permit, we would not have been able to complete our journey to Sudan. We joined Mau in a cross-river cheer.

We also spotted our two remaining team members: Mike Borcik, a boatman, and Kelly Shannon, Nevada's friend from Santa Fe.

There were various tasks our teammates needed to see to on the far side of the Blue Nile, and after watching people cross the river for awhile, I sat down under a big euphorbia tree to work on my notes. Abush had been up on the bridge, his eyes widening every time someone grasped the rope to cross. He'd turned to me with a smile and said something, but Zelalem wasn't at hand to translate. I guessed Abush wanted to try this crossing, too. I figured we would part here—but not until the next morning. There was no reason he couldn't spend one more night with us, and eat his fill again. That way I could quietly slip him a few birr. It was impossible to give him anything now with so many Ethiopians about. Someone would see and if they didn't start begging from me, they might try to rob him.

I patted his shoulder. "*Ishi*. Okay. But wait now; you can go tomorrow." I hoped he understood my poor Amharic. He seemed to; he nodded his head, then turned back to watch the daring bridge-crossers.

It didn't take long for Speaks to come back with his boat; he neatly ferried it through the big waves while everyone on both sides of the river stopped whatever they were doing to watch. Mike Borcik then rowed his boat over, tied it up with Zelalem's help, and climbed up the big black rocks to meet us. He had a fireplug's build and a hatchet-shaped nose, and was as clean-cut as a freshly shaved soldier. He was smartly dressed, too, in a white shirt and dark shorts, and wore a white Panama hat over his dark crewcut. He had a silver stud in his right ear, and the earring and hat combined gave him a slightly raffish air. Borcik's skin was tanned a deep, nut brown as if he'd just stepped off another rafting trip somewhere—and he had, one on the Colorado. He shook our hands and told us about the trouble he, Mau, and Ephrem had getting the rafts and gear down to the river's edge. A big thunderstorm had suddenly come up, drenching everyone and raising the Nile's volume considerably.

"It made the river even more gnarly than it was," Mike Borcik said with a laugh.

Borcik also had news about Conrad for us. He'd stopped in Nairobi on his way to Ethiopia and spent a day with Conrad. Zelalem was standing nearby and I called him over.

Borcik was shaking his head, "I hate to say it, but Conrad looks bad. He's aged about 20 or 30 years. He looks like an old man. And he has trouble with his left leg and arm. He has to use a cane now."

I could hardly grasp the image he was painting. Conrad as an aged, crippled man? It didn't seem possible.

Zelalem didn't seem to fully understand. He was simply happy that Mike Borcik had seen "his father." That meant that Conrad was fine. He was in Nairobi and recovering.

"He's very broken up about not being here," Borcik continued. "He really wanted to do this trip." Borcik's voice trailed off.

"He sends his greetings to you," Borcik added. "And to you, Zelalem."

"You've seen Conrad; that is good," Zelalem replied. "I'm happy for that."

Borcik nodded. "Well, let's see what needs to be done here."

A few moments later, Bruce rowed his orange raft across the waves, bringing Kelly with him. Again, there was a round of introductions. Tall, thin, and fair with blue eyes, Kelly was Borcik's mirror opposite. He was an older gent, too, about 65, I guessed. And he was dressed like an experienced river-hand, in a T-shirt, quick-drying shorts, and Teva sandals. He had a friendly smile and asked immediately about Nevada.

"She's up on the bridge, taking photos," I said.

He laughed. "I figured she'd be off with her camera somewhere."

Mike Speaks suddenly appeared. He climbed on top of a rock so he could project his voice over us: "Okay. I want to get our little band back together. I'll be happy when our little band is all in one place." He had apparently already passed these instructions to Nevada and Mick because they soon joined our gathering.

We stood silently, waiting.

"Okay," he said. "We're all together, and everything looks good." He paused a minute, uncharacteristically uncertain. "Okay. I guess we just need to do everything we've been doing: keeping cool, keeping our eyes on our stuff. So, well, I guess you can go back to whatever you need to do."

Nevada looked steamed. "I *was* doing what I needed to be doing," she said curtly, and turned on her heel.

WE HAD TO CAMP ON THE DONKEY TRAIL THAT NIGHT. EVERYTHING HAD happened a bit slower and later than Mike Speaks had planned, so he, Zelalem, and Ephrem walked along the trail and found more-or-less flat places to pitch each tent. That didn't trouble me, but Speaks seemed increasingly agitated. He got this way, I'd noticed, whenever we were close to gatherings of Ethiopians. But it was getting late in the afternoon. Fewer travelers were coming down to cross the river. We'd soon be alone.

After crossing the river, many of the travelers had stepped onto the rocks above the bridge, undressed, and sat in an eddy, while others poured the waters of the Blue Nile over their heads.

"They are being baptized," Zelalem explained. "They'll take some holy water home for their families, too."

Our party interrupted some of these religious activities as people stopped to marvel at what few had ever seen: not only white people but also boats on the Blue Nile.

"They look like airplanes," a short, wiry militiaman named Kassa Mongenet told Zelalem about our oar-powered rafts. "Surely, this is *tarik*—a major historical event!"

I thought Kassa was just a passing militiaman like many others we had met, but Zelalem said, "No, no, he is coming with us." Mau had hired him—and his Kalashnikov—after hearing about our trouble with the donkey thief. Kassa lived and farmed in a village outside of Mota, where he had a wife and three young children, but he'd left all on the spur of the moment to join us. "He's a little worried," said Zelalem.

Kassa sat on a rock and looked down at the boats, his weapon resting on his knees. He could swim, he said, but he also knew there were devils in that water, and he eyed its brown boiling surface warily.

Our river bags with our individual gear were piled at a bend in the trail, and while we were waited for whatever was to happen next, a couple of kids asked me if they could move them down to the tents for us. They each wanted one birr (eight cents) for this big job, so I said okay.

No sooner had they carted a couple of the bags off to the tents than Mike Speaks appeared.

"Who told them to do this?," he shouted.

"I did," I said. "They wanted to help and…"

"I *am* the one giving orders here, and I don't want these bags moved yet." He picked up both bags and hefted them back to their original position. The two kids flew off like baby quail.

"Sorry," I said. "I thought it might be helpful."

He wasn't listening; he'd turned his back and was already walking away.

I called the two kids back and gave them the money I'd promised.

Twenty minutes later, Speaks told us to carry the bags down to the tents.

STUFF WAS STREWN ALL ALONG THE DONKEY TRAIL: BAGS, COOKING gear, a table for cooking. You had to pick your way among the things and people, but everyone was being polite about it. I'd just finished stashing my gear in my tent and was walking toward the dining area when Nevada walked up. Kate was standing nearby. It was one of the first times the three of us women had been alone together, and we all looked ready for a chat.

"I just have to get this off my chest," Nevada said to me in a half-whisper. "I can't stand Mike Speaks."

"He makes my skin crawl, too," I said sympathetically.

"No one tells me what to do," she continued. "It's the one thing I can't stand."

"Me either," I said.

We started laughing, relieved to know that we felt the same way. I hadn't noticed that she and Mike Speaks were getting along badly—maybe because I'd generally hiked with Zelalem or Teno—but apparently Speaks's order to her to join the group wasn't the first. "He's been telling me how to take pictures, how to pack my bag, how to look after my gear. I've got to stay away from him."

Nevada had worked as a river guide herself for many years, she went on to say, as well as a guide for photographic expeditions. She knew the business, knew how to travel, how to work with clients, and how to take care of herself.

"Maybe he's threatened by that," I suggested.

"The last thing I wanted on this trip was some macho, ego-hungry river guide. It's why I left the river business in the first place," she said. "His pose is wearing thin fast."

She thought that Mike Borcik seemed a more kindred spirit, and proposed that we join him on his boat in the morning. "I need someone who's going to row me where I need to go to get the pictures I want," she said. "We'll take Zelalem, too, so he can talk to you about Ethiopia."

That sounded like a smart plan. We'd just keep out of Speaks's way and tend to our work.

Kate hadn't said a word. She looked puzzled, then surprised, then slightly aghast. She wasn't part of our rebellion.

I'D LOST SIGHT OF ABUSH WITH EVERYTHING THAT HAD BEEN happening. It was late afternoon, twilight would be on us soon, and I wondered aloud, as I fixed a cup of tea, where he was. Nevada and Mick spoke at once.

"Oh, he left us."

"He crossed the bridge at least an hour ago," Nevada continued. "He really wanted to try that rope, but he was terrified. He was crying and shouting, and hanging on to my neck. I didn't know if he'd let go."

My heart sank. I hadn't found the opportunity to give him the little gift I'd planned. Bruce had also wanted to give him some money for the shoeshine box, and he too looked disappointed.

I walked down the donkey trail and found Zelalem.

"Do you see Abush anywhere over there?" I asked him.

We searched the shore, studying the people, looking for a castoff kid in a dirty robe. Zelalem whistled and then waved.

"There he is!" He shouted and whistled again, and caught Abush's attention.

Abush at once ran down to the rocks and shouted to us. He started crying.

"He thinks our rafts are cars," Zelalem said, "and he wants us to come back with one and pick him up. He thought he would get a ride in one of the boats, but they wouldn't let him."

Poor Abush. The men who hauled people across the broken bridge had gone home; he was stranded and on his own again. It was impossible to row a raft upstream through this maelstrom, and impossible for us to explain this to him over the roar of the Nile.

"Tell him to find someone to stay with there, and we'll send him some food and presents in the morning," I said, still hoping to find a way to help our orphan.

One of the police officers noticed the commotion and walked down to Abush. Zelalem shouted to the officer to help our young friend. He nodded, and put an arm around him. Abush walked off with the officer, his robe slipping off his shoulder, his bandages flapping at his legs.

I never saw Abush again.

thirteen

∿∿

WE WOKE TO THE MORNING CALLS OF ROCK DOVES, FINCHES, and chats—and the steady crash of the Blue Nile. Mike Speaks was itching to get on the river, and we soon had the camp dismantled, our gear, including Kassa's Kalashnikov, stowed in waterproof river bags, and cameras, notebooks, and binoculars locked in watertight cases or old ammunition boxes. Then he called us together. We sat on the big boulders on shore while he gave his river safety talk.

"The gorge here is very confined as you can see," Speaks began, "and so we've got a lot of upwellings, pillows, and big strong waves over the rocks. That's the nature of the Blue Nile. So I'm going to go over some of the scenarios we need to be aware of on this river."

We were going to encounter crocodiles. Some of these could be aggressive, and he didn't want any biting the boats—which would cause a leak, and possibly the raft to collapse—so we'd have paddles on board to smack the crocs with. "You can also use them to hit hippos, if they attack, or to help in a jam with the waves."

Most river rafting accidents happened when people were getting in or out of the boats, or while hiking on shore, so we should walk carefully and assist each other. On the boats the passengers—us—were "moveable ballast. You can shift your weight to adjust the movement of the boat. And you'll be doing that whenever I—or Mike [Borcik] or Bruce—calls out, 'high side.' "

Speaks didn't expect any of us to fall overboard, but if we did we were to wave and shout, "'Hello, I'm here.' This is a tough current to swim in, so we'll toss you a throw bag with a rope in it. Take hold of the rope, let the bag trail, turn your back to the boat and put the rope over your shoulder so we can pull you in."

We were to stay with our raft if it happened to capsize, and we were to keep our life jackets on at all times. If someone was unlucky and ended up beneath the boat, well, that was "a bad place to be. Try to do a belly crawl up the raft, rather than to swim out." Speaks did, however, think that we could make it down the river without flipping any boats or having any swimmers. But if someone took a plunge, that person should keep his feet out in front to take the brunt of any collisions with rocks. "If you're in the waves, you'll have to concentrate on getting your breath, then swim, swim, swim. Go for it like it's the Olympics."

Even when we were safely on the rafts and entering the big waves, we were to face them like we were "moving toward the enemy. You'll be leaning in toward them, and kissing the waves, kissing the front tubes, and you'll want to keep your head down. The boat will be going forward, facing the wave and then you'll hit it, boom!" He dashed one hand against the other. "You'll be up and over."

"If I yell, 'High side,' I want you to get on the downstream end of the boat, where the enemy is, just as fast as you can. This water can wrap a boat around a rock like tin foil on a baked potato, and I don't want that to happen. I think it's mostly going to be, like the Ethiopians say, *'chig-ger yellum'*—no problem. We're a good, strong group and all systems are go."

Speaks brought his fists up to his shoulders, like a double-barreled Black Power salute. "Okay. Let's go."

He jumped off his rock and walked down to Nevada, who had started to carry her camera boxes to Mike Borcik's boat. "I think it'd be great if you, Ginny, and Zelalem came with me this morning," said Speaks.

Nevada was momentarily speechless. "Uhhh. Okay."

Maybe he's trying to patch things up, I thought. I gave Mike a smile as I walked down to his raft and said, "That'd be great, *Captain* Speaks."

I meant it half facetiously, and as a way to distinguish between the two Mikes (Speaks and Borcik). Speaks didn't seem to mind, so "Captain Speaks" became my sobriquet for him for the remainder of the journey.

Speaks showed Nevada and me where we could stow our camera boxes and things, like sunscreen, that we wanted to get to in a hurry. Then Zelalem untied the raft's line and jumped on board. Untethered, the boat shuddered for a second as if feeling for the first time the power of the Nile. Speaks wrapped his hands around the oars, leaned backward, and pulled. One stroke, two, a third, and a small pivot, and like every other bit of flotsam tossed into the Blue Nile's muddy waters, we were on our way to Sudan.

It was a fast ride. The river coursed along dark and lathery, forming two- and three-foot white-capped waves that we slapped across. Muddy spray and water sloshed into the boat and crashed against us, which felt good. The morning was hot, the water was cold, and dirty though it was, I didn't mind.

The canyon walls shot straight up on either side, the black basalt arrayed like vertically stacked timbers that some giant had used to shore up the cliff. Spiny and snaky euphorbias twisted over the edge of the gorge, and thirsty fig trees shot brown roots down to the river's water like long, fat straws.

I looked at Nevada and laughed. "We're here. We made it."

She laughed, too, then turned to put her cameras away. She'd been busy taking photos of the two other boats as they pushed onto the river. It was about eleven o'clock in the morning, and the light had changed from blue and misty to simply harsh. Not the kind of light that photographers favor.

I wanted to give Nevada a toast—or something—for having pulled this all off. As far as I knew she had never said anything to the group about all the work she'd done to make our adventure happen, perhaps because, as I'd discovered, she had a Buddhist's sensibilities. She didn't like calling attention to herself, or acting in what she would consider an egotistical manner. She had wanted to travel along the Blue Nile and meet and photograph the people, and she was doing that.

Just then Speaks spoke up. We were about five minutes from the shore, and he'd turned the boat so that we were facing downstream, which gave him a view of the rapids up ahead. He pushed his oars into the water with a nice tight, cycling motion. "Well, we're out of the highlands and finally away from the villages and the people. We won't have to be with them anymore."

What did he mean, not be with them anymore? I looked at Nevada. We all had on sunglasses, making it difficult to tell what anyone was thinking. I knew she didn't want another confrontation with Speaks, and certainly not right now, having just put on the river. We'd talk about it later.

WE RODE DOWN RIVER FOR A FEW MILES, UNTIL SPEAKS SIGNALED TO the other boats, curving his left arm over his head to point to a pretty gravel beach with a freshwater stream pouring into the Nile. Clean water. Zelalem jumped onshore to tie our raft up to some rocks, and Nevada and I grabbed our soap and headed for the stream.

We hadn't had a bath since Abo Gedam, two days earlier, and my skin was oily and grimy from the accumulation of dirt, sweat, and smoke. Washing in the Blue Nile's gritty waters, as I had that morning, did little more than smear the dirt around. Kelly had it right when he'd commented that we'd soon "become the mud people" if we had only the Blue Nile to bathe in.

A short walk up the stream led to a thundering, silver waterfall. We splashed in fully clothed and sat at its base, letting the cool water beat down on us. The fall boomed and crashed and pounded its hard wet fingers on our backs. Back onshore, I rubbed at my clothes and body with the soap, then splashed back in for a rinse. I wasn't squeaky clean, but I knew I never would be on this trip—the next wave I caught from the Blue Nile would see to that.

Zelalem and Ephrem had stayed down by the boats, taking the big water containers off the rafts to fill them with fresh water. They scooped the water up with a bucket, then pumped it into the jerry cans through a filter to rid it of possible parasites and bacteria. Speaks also added a couple drops of iodine solution to kill anything that survived the filter.

It was hot in the gorge. The sun beat down on the black rocks until they shimmered like the high polish on a black Cadillac. My wet clothes and hair were bone dry by the time we got back to the rafts. I opened my water bottle, drank every drop, and refilled it with some from a freshly pumped container.

Zelalem and Ephrem knew each other from Addis. Ephrem was younger, about 25, and taller, with a basketball player's long limbs. His head was long, too, and angular, like the paintings of the long-faced priests in some Ethiopian churches. He wasn't an Amhara like Zelalem, but an Oromo. The Oromo people—whose name means "the strong men"—had moved into the highlands of Ethiopia in the late 13th century. They were great warriors, as their name for themselves suggests, and they chipped away at the Amhara's mountain stronghold, every year moving a little farther north. They were culturally adaptable, too, and wherever they moved picked up some of the local customs. Oromos could be pagans, Christians, or Muslims; they could be fishermen, nomadic herders, traders, or farmers. The Amharas in contrast were almost uniformly Christians and farmers. "To say that I am an Amhara is to also say that I am Orthodox," a friend once told me.

Ephrem was shy. He spoke his language, Orominya, as well as Amharic and English, but he hesitated about speaking English with us. He understood us, and smiled when we spoke to him. But generally he said little in return.

Kassa, our new guard, looked even more uncertain. He sat on the side of one of the rafts, his Kalashnikov resting over his knees, and studied our group. I smiled and asked him in Addis street-lingo, "*Tadias?*—So, what's happening?"

He started and gave a short laugh. "*Amharinya tichelalish?*—Do you know Amharic?"

"*Tinish bicha*—Only a little."

But it was enough to make him smile. The other members of our crew did what they could, too, to make Kassa feel welcome.

We pushed the boats back on the river, but traveled only another couple of miles before stopping for a light lunch on another gravel beach with another thrumming waterfall. The opposite shore was also graced with a waterfall, which shot down a slick chute of limestone that was folded as neatly as a curtain. Above it in an old snag, a pair of fish eagles (which resemble bald eagles) sat on a nest. We thought they were keeping a close watch on us, until one lifted into the air and dived into the river to bring up a fat fish.

Back on the water, we coursed along on a southeast heading, much as we had on the hike. Speaks used his handheld global positioning (GPS) device to calculate our river speed: ten miles an hour. "I hadn't expected that," he said. "We're moving along at a good clip."

All that afternoon, the Blue Nile continued to fight its way through the narrow basalt canyon. The river's water felt bunched up and reined in, and it kicked up short, choppy waves that we splashed across light-heartedly. These small trains of rapids always ended in a series of deep-sucking whirlpools that sent our boats spinning helplessly downstream. It could catch us any time it wanted, the river seemed to say, and toss us about like so many rubber ducks. Kassa mistrusted the swirling dark waters and studied them intently as if searching for the passage to the devil's world. But it was daytime, the sky a clear blue above the sheer canyon walls, and if the Nile harbored any demons, they were content to let us pass.

It seemed far more likely that any dangers were going to come from the canyon above. From there people could see us long before we could spot them. If we were rubber ducks to the Nile, we were sitting ducks for anyone with bad intentions perched along the gorge's rim. We knew the stories: the two gun battles the British Blashford-Snell team had fought with the shifta, the disappearance of the American hikers, the rocks hurled at some river travelers, the shooting deaths of others. And we knew that many of the village men had Kalashnikovs, and were not hesitant about using them. Our friend, Atele Asseras, had very nearly shot Mike Speaks after all. How would the local people react when they saw three boats bearing eight white foreigners downstream?

Our first hint came shortly after lunch as we rounded a bend and saw a group of people running along the canyon's rim. They were clapping and dancing, cheering us on.

"*Konjo!* —You are beautiful! *Gobez!*—You are brave! *Melkam gouzo!* —Good travels!"

Their shouts and trilling calls followed us downstream—an outpouring of goodwill and innocence that we hadn't expected. Where were the bullets, rocks, and thieves?

"You are *tarik*—history—for them," Zelalem said, using Kassa's expression to explain how wonderful and novel our journey was for these countryfolk who celebrated our passage with such joy. "They will never forget you."

We traveled 16 miles that day, riding along with the Nile as it wound through the canyon in tight bends, twisting first left, then right, cutting under the cliff in places and hollowing out caves and arches in others. Hundreds of clear streams and waterfalls spilled down the canyon's walls into the river. Along some of these grew tangled thickets of ferns and tall reeds, lending the silver waterways a tropical air. In contrast, the bare rock of the canyon felt harsh and unfriendly; not without reason had the angry, young, dark-eyed fellow with the ruffian crew at Genete Maryam referred to the bottom of the gorge as the desert. Occasionally we passed wide, sandy banks, and on one we spotted our first crocodile. But it was only a small crocodile, and it slithered at once into the safety of the river.

A few moments later, Nevada opened one of her waterproof cases. She had told me she'd arranged to bring along an iridium satellite phone, but since I'd not seen her use it on the hike, I thought perhaps her plan hadn't worked out. But there, in her box, was a black telephone like an oversize cell phone. She held it nonchalantly in her hand. Our boats were in a tight formation, like bumper cars, and she asked, "Who should we call?"

The idea of phoning someone while riding a raft down the Blue Nile made us laugh. Zelalem shook his head. "Can it be?"

"Ginny," said Nevada, "it must be about 7 a.m. on the West Coast. Do you want to call Michael?"

"Can I?"

"Sure, let's call him." She dialed our number. "It's ringing," she said, and handed me the phone.

Three rings, and Michael answered. "Hi honey!" I shouted.

"*Ginny!*" His voice shouted back, astonished.

"I'm calling from the Blue Nile, and we're okay and we've just seen our first croc," I said.

"You're on the Blue Nile? Right now?"

"Yes. We're floating down the Blue Nile."

The connection was fuzzy, like talking to someone as far away as Mars, and our voices faded in and out, but we managed a short conversation. Everything was fine at home, Michael said. The roses were still blooming and our dog and cat missed me. I then tried to tell him about the donkey thief and the shooting, and just as I got to the point about the five shots, the line went dead. Our satellite link had moved on to another portion of the globe. I handed the phone back to Nevada.

"Well, that wasn't the best place to end my call," I said. "But I don't think he'll be too worried; I think he could tell everything was okay," I added, knowing in my heart that Michael was probably worried sick.

I could call him back as long as I was willing to ante up the five bucks a minute fee, which seemed a small price to pay.

"We'll have to wait until the satellite comes back into our zone to call again," Nevada said. "We can try someone else tonight."

The phone could also receive short text messages, which was handy for getting news from Maurizio in Addis.

It felt strange to have reached out and touched someone from this isolated spot on the planet. I might as well have been on the moon, and I thought about the astronauts who relied on communications not unlike this to keep themselves connected to this world, to their loved ones. It was like having an umbilical cord, but one as fine and flimsy as silk. With luck our phone would be fun and useful, and never necessary.

Camp that night was on a small wedge of sand tucked up along a wet drizzle of a stream that ended in a small swamp. It wasn't one of the prettier spots we had passed, but it was late afternoon and Speaks wanted to get the tents up. Earlier he had explained the routine we should follow once we hit a camping beach: form lines to unload the boats, pitch the tents, set up the kitchen, have a cup of something warm. There wasn't much room to spread out on this beach, and we squeezed the dome-shaped tents into a rickrack pattern close to each other.

As Captain Speaks had promised, we weren't close to any villages or people. For the first time on our trip, we had no guests in camp. It wasn't just the threat of shifta that Speaks seemed worried about. Over lunch, he had talked about camping along this section of the gorge on his 1996 trip. Two highland Ethiopian men, much like those we had met in the other villages, came into their camp.

"They were talking to us, all friendly-like," said Speaks. "And another guy and I were chopping up some veggies for dinner. We had two knives we were using for the job. We set them down for a minute, turned around to check something on the fire, and when we turned back the knives were gone." So were their two visitors.

Could this be why Speaks was always nervous when any Ethiopians appeared in our camp; why he had been so agitated along the donkey trail when many Ethiopians were passing by on their way to the bridge, and why he had no plans to camp near any villages now? He didn't come right out and say that he thought all Ethiopians were thieves, but the curtain on his views had been raised, if only for a second.

I didn't want to challenge Speaks any more than Nevada did. And I knew that saying I'd never had any problems with thievery on my camping trips in Ethiopia would mean little to him. He didn't easily turn to other people for either their opinions or advice. He'd had a bad experience and he had made up his mind. It would be tough for Nevada and me to budge him (even though—and this is the part that scrambles my brain even now as I write it—we were the ones who, through National Geographic, had hired him). In his mind, we were clients and he was our leader.

There wasn't much privacy in camp and whispered voices at the edge of the campfire would have been rude. Nevada and I didn't discuss Speaks's edict that night. Instead, I sat with Zelalem and Kassa and asked Kassa about the proverbs the men of Gojam told. Kassa was proud of being a Gojami, a man born in the region that held itself to be the truest repository of Ethiopian culture, and the proverb he sang made us laugh: "*Abayna Tana tetaletew bemeret/ Abay achenefer yeGojam gorabet*...Lake Tana and the Abay River had a contest, but the Abay was faster because he is a Gojami!"

Kassa had a good singing voice and chanted his proverb in a soft, lilting melody—until he hit that keyword. Then his voice dropped and he barked it out—*yeGojam!*—like a cheerleader at a pep rally.

I asked him if he could tell us about the buda people, those carriers of the evil eye. Weren't there an abundance of them in Gojam?

"He says, 'No,' " Zelalem translated. "That's just something people say because they are jealous of Gojam. He says he has a proverb about that, too."

Kassa sang again. *"Gojami buda no/ Bleshiyawrashew/ Sewun sew sibelow/ Yet honish ayeshew*... People say that the buda is a Gojami. But the Gojami people say, 'Why do you say that? Has anyone seen a man's eye eat another man?' "

"That's what they say if something bad happens," Zelalem explained. "They say, *'Alyegn yebelowal*—The eyes ate you.' Sometimes, if you want to look at a child, the parents will say, 'No, because *alyegn yebelowal.'* They don't want him eaten by your eyes."

What about metal and hide workers? I asked. Weren't they thought to possess the evil eye because of their work, transforming iron ore and animal skins into something else?

"This was the old belief," Zelalem said. "But the new government is trying to change that. If an ironworker is called a buda now, he can complain to the government."

"So they've got an anti-Buda Defamation League," joked Mike Borcik, who was sitting nearby and obviously interested in the stories.

The Oromo people, like Ephrem, used to be called "Gallas," too, an Amhara word that means immigrant, or more bluntly, barbarian. Again, "Galla" has not only fallen from fashion, it is understandably considered derogatory and no one in polite company uses it. (At the beginning of this trip, I had once or twice used the term, since it was the common word for the Oromo in Haile Selassie's day. Zelalem shuddered and shook his head, "Ahhh, don't use that word. It's not good for them.")

Somehow, political correctness had managed to make it all the way to the Blue Nile—or at least a greater sensitivity to the words and actions that can cut so deeply they cause lasting rifts in a society. The Emperors

Menelik and Haile Selassie had forged a nation through force. They'd brought all the disparate peoples, cultures, and religions together by conquering and subjugating them. Without a king in the center to hold these peoples in check, some had questioned whether the country could survive. It had lost Eritrea, and nearly lost much of its southeastern region to Somalia. Even now, Zelalem told me, there was a group of Oromo who had banded together with Somali Ethiopians to create a separate country. They made sporadic raids throughout the south. The government fought them sometimes. But what the government really wanted was to create a country where everyone, regardless of ethnic background or religion, felt himself or herself to be an Ethiopian.

"That's what we're trying to do in America, too," I said.

On a far smaller scale, that's what we were trying to do on this trip, as well: get along, despite the differences in our backgrounds and experiences, our worries and needs and fear.

Speaks was off checking on the three rafts, making sure they were tied securely, that there wasn't any danger of them being swept away. He checked, too, on the rising waters of the Nile. It had come up a little bit since we'd camped and lapped at the shoreline only five feet from our tents. "I'll let you know if we have to break camp in a hurry," he'd said. "I don't think we will, but I'll keep an eye on it."

Speaks seemed most comfortable in moments like these, when there was the possibility of some natural threat. He moved with an athlete's grace whether on shore or on his raft, and his body and jutting chin projected a confidence that said, "I'll get you through this." That was his mandate: to get his "little band," as he liked to call us, down this river and through this country safely and intact—and for him, that meant avoiding the unpredictable people. And that's what put us at odds. Nevada and I had a separate mandate: to get our story. We needed to be among the people, and welcomed every chance encounter or village visit that might come our way. Our two different mandates, unfortunately, put us at cross-purposes and it wasn't clear how the matter would be resolved.

But for the moment, seated on this sandy beach next to the Nile, we'd put all that aside. We were friendly, polite, and interested in each other. We were doing the job Speaks expected us to do: We were building a team.

I CLIMBED INTO MY TENT A LITTLE BEFORE 9 P.M. IT WAS STIFLING INSIDE, and I unzipped the outer door and flaps over the mosquito-net windows. Kate had started me on a short course of antibiotics to cure my bad gut, and I'd finally managed to eat some lunch and dinner. I wasn't 100 percent yet, but I was on the mend.

I pulled out my notebook and counted the days. We'd only been gone one week. It felt like a year. Time could do that—expand like a rubber band—when it was packed with events, new sights, people, and sensations. That was one reason I loved to travel in exotic lands: it gave you the chance to rekindle your sense of wonder and awe.

For Michael, at home, on the other hand, the last week had surely felt just like that—a week at home. We'd been married long enough and traveled apart enough times to know that we were momentarily off-balance. I was sorry we'd lost the phone connection at that critical moment, when I had just mentioned the shooting. He was at home and now he was worried. And I was lying on top of my sleeping bag, feeling sweaty and gritty, while I listened to the last high, piping notes of an owl, the boinks of distant frogs, and trill of insects here along the edge of the Blue Nile. I was far from home—as was Nevada, Kate, Kelly, and the rest of our crew. We were all far from home.

fourteen

~~~

THE NEXT MORNING WE GOT UNDER WAY A LITTLE AFTER NINE o'clock. Nevada and I switched to Mike Borcik's boat, saying we wanted to get to know all our boatmen. Zelalem came with us, while Kate, Kelly and Kassa, transferred to Mike Speaks's raft. Mick and Ephrem rode on Bruce's boat as they had the day before.

Nevada, Mick, and I had held a small, swift meeting beforehand. Since Mick was also here on National Geographic's behalf, she wanted him to join with us in persuading Speaks to alter his "no people" dictate. "I've got to have people —Ethiopians—in my photos," she'd said. "And Ginny needs them for her story." Mick nodded. He was making a film about the trip and Nevada's role as leader-photographer, and would, of course, support her. He also wanted people scenes. "I'll talk to Mike Borcik, too," Nevada promised. "I think I can get him to intercede for us."

Borcik, we learned that morning as we drifted down river, had grown up in central California, and he had a West Coaster's laid-back manner. He was unassuming and not easily ruffled, and, as Nevada predicted, the two of them got along fine. He was also sympathetic to our work needs and said he would discuss the issue with Speaks.

It was a pretty morning with the light illuminating all the shades of red, brown, and gray in the water. The canyon walls rose starkly above the river, adding texture and depth to the scene, and Nevada was having fun. She stood just behind Borcik on a wooden platform that covered one of the big food-storage bins, asking him to row the boat this way or that, and using a telephoto lens to frame the two boats ahead of us as they traveled down the Nile. She had her camera on a motorized setting and shot with such abandon that Zelalem began laughing.

"Oh, this is all so good," Nevada said, lowering her camera for a moment. "If everyday is as good as this, I'll soon be out of film." She tossed her head back and laughed at herself.

Later, with the sun fully up and the light grown harsh, she sat down next to me to say that Mick was having a little trouble adjusting to the rafting portion of the trip.

"He's still got his adrenaline up from being in the war zone in Bosnia," she said. "And he found yesterday really hard. He said it was too passive for him, just sitting on the boat. He's crawling out of his skin."

"Well, we should be getting off sometimes for hikes and to meet people, I hope," I said. "But I know what he means; sitting here is very passive."

I used the raft time to catch up on my notes, and to study the river and country. We were headed down a long incline, steadily if slowly losing altitude, and the river and land changed from one moment to the next. Speaks had promised us this morning that we would travel along the stretch he called "the Gorgeous Gorge," one of the prettiest sections of the part of the river he had rowed in 1996.

Before reaching it, we stopped at a freshwater stream to fill our jerry cans and bathe. This stream was bottle green, and it ran down through a canyon and along a wide gravel bar. We waded up through its cool waters for some distance, choosing separate pools to splash and swim in. Once I looked down, and a school of tiny fish shot fearlessly between my feet.

Like most of the lands we had traveled through, these above the canyon and on both sides of the Blue Nile's gorge were heavily farmed. Corn seemed to be the main crop people grew at these lower elevations (around 3,000 to 4,000 feet), and most of the people waving and calling to us along the river were farmers or their children out tending the crops and livestock.

We had started to head back to our boats, when we spotted a wizened, gray-haired fellow running toward us. He was barefoot and carried a small wooden ax in his left hand. As he ran, he patted his chest with his right hand and called to us.

"He's telling us to wait," said Zelalem. "He wants to meet us."

We stopped and he soon caught up. He stared at us amazed, and covered his mouth with both hands in wonderment.

"He is too surprised to see you," Zelalem laughed. "He says he is a *Wunz Sew*, a River Man, and he wonders if you are all men, too. I told him, 'No, that three are women.'"

That response elicited another cry of surprise. How could women wear pants?, the River Man demanded, studying the trousers and shorts we wore. We should spread our legs and show him the truth. Nevada instead good-naturedly gave him a peek down her blouse, but even then, he told Zelalem, he could not understand how a woman could wear a pair of pants.

Our visitor was a small, burnt twig of a man, weathered and misshapen from his years of farming, and his shorts and shirt were nothing but pieced-together patches of cloth, like a tattered crazy quilt. He pointed to them now and shook his head forlornly.

"He says he lives up there, a three-hour walk," Zelalem said, pointing to a distant hill. "But he ran to meet us because some years ago some friends of his saw ferenjocch on the river like this, and the tourists gave them T-shirts. He is so happy to meet you, he says, because this is his lucky day. He would like to present you with one goat and you may give him one shirt."

We all stood in a circle around this small man, and I thought that one of the guys would hand over his T-shirt. I was wearing a thin camisole and long-sleeved shirt to protect myself from the sun, and didn't see how I could take off what I was wearing. Besides, he might not want a shirt from a woman—even a woman wearing pants. None of our male teammates, however, made a move to give up his shirt. Perhaps it was the direct way the old fellow had asked for it, but Mike Speaks seemed to recoil.

"Well, he doesn't need to give us a goat, and we can't take off what we're wearing," he said. "And all the other clothes are packed and tied down on the raft." He wasn't going to unload anything.

Speaks offered the River Man some yarn and needles and fishhooks instead.

The old gent took the gifts, but shook his head. "He says he can't catch anything with these," Zelalem said about the fishhooks. "They are too small, and he has no wife for sewing."

We were close to the region where the British expedition had their two big shifta shootouts and trying to change the subject, I asked if he'd heard any reports of bandits hereabouts. "No, he says there are no shifta here in Begemder," Zelalem said. "He says maybe there are some in Gojam, on the other side of the river."

Kassa was standing with us and he objected at once, as if he'd been insulted. "No," Kassa told Zelalem. "There are no shifta in Gojam, either."

Kassa and the River Man were both so adamant; I wondered how they could be this certain. Was it just their pride? The Brits had been attacked simultaneously from both sides of the river and by large groups of armed men, a couple of whom had even sounded war trumpets. True, that had happened 30-odd years ago, and Ethiopia had made many changes since then, but I didn't think losing the shifta tradition was one. It had existed for centuries.

What about wild animals?, I persisted. Did he lose many animals to leopards or lions?

"There are no lions, he says. But sometimes he sees leopards and there are hyenas and jackals. He has some medicine to kill the hyenas and jackals." The River Man reached in his shirt pocket and produced a piece of blue cloth containing the "medicine": plastic vials, which we guessed, held strychnine. "The government gives it to him, and he has killed many jackals."

The old fellow brought the conversation back to his own interests. He patted his chest and asked again for a shirt. "He says, 'Look at my clothes. Please give me one shirt,'" Zelalem translated.

By now, Mick had started to circle around our visitor and us with his video camera. He filmed for a while, then stopped and replayed part of the film for the River Man, who again reacted with astonishment. This time, he placed both hands on top of his head, and let out a series of sharp cries, which made us all laugh.

Mick apparently hoped to get more of a rise or some other reaction out of him because he now began jabbing his microphone (which was wrapped in a furry covering) in the old man's face as if it were a rat.

"*Nee, nee, nee*," said Mick, imitating a rodent's call.

The old man wasn't impressed. "He says you cannot frighten him with that thing," Zelalem translated.

Mike Speaks had turned away and was walking back to the rafts. Soon the others followed, leaving our visitor spluttering. I was unsure what to do, but then I saw him make a move I'd seen before. He was raising his arm and getting ready to spit—a sign that he would curse us.

"Tell him to wait," I said to Zelalem. "What can we give him?"

"Maybe two or three birr," Zelalem said. "Something small. It will be okay."

I was going to break the group rule about not giving out money. And there was no way to do it without being seen. I didn't look at anyone, but walked straight to the raft and opened the small waterproof case where I kept my notebook and wallet, and pulled out a few birr. I walked back to Zelalem, feeling every pair of ferenjocch eyes on my back, and handed the bills to him.

Zelalem took the River Man's hands, and pressed the money into them, saying as he did so, "Thanks for your visit; we appreciate you. Take this small gift for a good day."

The old man looked puzzled. "Birr?" he said. He had not asked for money; he was not a beggar. He had only had the good fortune of seeing our boats and thought it was his lucky day. Instead, he'd run into a bunch of cheapskates, one of whom had tried to make him look like a fool.

Zelalem smiled again. "It is a small gift. We thank you and we say goodbye."

The fellow shook his head, muttered a puzzled thanks, and walked away.

We got back on our raft and no one said or asked anything.

"He ran all the way from his home to meet us," I tried to explain to Nevada. "We couldn't let him go away empty-handed." But she looked at me skeptically. For a while, I felt like the traitorous and self-ostracized Marlon Brando in the film *Mutiny on the Bounty*, and only wished there'd been a stateroom down below where I could go and hide.

There's an art to getting along in groups, and I didn't have it—at least not with some of the people on this trip. I didn't want to apologize for breaking the rule, and I didn't understand why Speaks did not consult more with Zelalem about the customs of his country.

A LITTLE DOWNSTREAM, THE GORGE CHANGED: THIS WAS SPEAKS'S gorgeous section, he called out. On the left-hand, Begemder side, the canyon was somewhat scruffy and open, with a low, rocky rise, while on the right-hand, Gojam side, it continued as a grand, curved wall of basalt. It formed a swooping cliff of rock, decorated here and there with fig trees, mosses, and epiphytic plants, and rose ever higher, from 60 to more than 100 feet, as we swept down the river. Rock doves cooed from their perches on the cliffs, fish eagles soared overhead, and every shrub and branch that hung out over the river held dozens of nests of buffalo weaverbirds. The weavers were busy mating and nest building, and carried on a constant chatter while darting in and out of their homes like big golden bees.

The high cliff continued for several miles. In one section, we spotted two caves, one triangular, the other semicircular, once perhaps the dwellings of reclusive monks. The only way, it seemed, to reach the caves was by climbing up from a boat on the water, or dangling a rope over the cliff. In 1968, a few members of the British team had explored the caves, taking with them pieces of black pottery and bits of old baskets; but they'd lost their treasures during the bandit attack. Richard Bangs and Jim Slade had also climbed inside the caves in 1974, and found an entire black clay pot inside. Bangs took this to the Institute of Ethiopian Studies in Addis for analysis, but was told only that pottery of this sort had been made for a very long time.

We stopped for lunch close to the caves. The skies had clouded over, and there was a short, sudden downpour like we'd had on the trek.

"What's with this rainy season?" groused Bruce as he pulled on a rain jacket.

"Kassa says it can last some more days," said Zelalem.

Actually, we didn't mind the rain. It cooled off the gorge and washed away the layer of dirty film that coated our skins and that seemed to be part of living on the Blue Nile.

We were getting into the rhythm of the river journey now, and after lunch continued our ride through the grand gorge, enjoying a few big waves and surprise splashes. At one point, two basaltic towers rose some 120 feet from the river like crumbling chimneys, and around the next bend, we entered a world not unlike the Grand Canyon. The land above the gorge rose in a staircase of terraces, and as before, every flat piece was farmed.

"This is what the Grand Canyon must have looked like in the days of the Anasazi," I commented to Nevada. "What a lot of work for the farmers."

All the farming was done with hand plows and teams of oxen; the irrigating with rainfall. We sometimes saw men in wide-brimmed straw hats working the land. They waved and called to us, and then shouted down the river canyon with long, looping cries that rose and fell, and must have carried great distances, alerting everyone who heard them to our visit.

"Konjo! Konjo! Konjo! (Beauty! Beauty! Beauty!)" two little boys with goat skins tied on their shoulders cried out as we swept past. Close to them, some men stood on shore and made a kind of hitchhiking sign, patting the air as if signaling us to slow down and stop. They want a ride, Zelalem explained.

We were in midstream, a hard row from shore, when we saw the would-be travelers, and couldn't of course stop to pick them up. Mike Borcik devised an answer, "Tell them there's no reverse on this airplane."

We waved and shrugged our shoulders to the importuning farmers, while Zelalem shouted an Amharic version of Borcik's reply.

On the slopes and hills between the farmlands grew a tangle of bushes and trees.

Many of the trees were the oaklike *hagenia* (known to the Ethiopians as *kosso*) whose seeds, Zelalem told us, are burned as incense in the coffee ceremony. Their leaves were turning red and gold, imparting an autumnlike look to the hillsides, despite the fresh green, springtime shoots of the crops around them. Along the cliffs near these forests, we spotted small bands of gray-and-white vervet monkeys. They would watch us for a few seconds as we glided down stream, then leap into the trees for safety, crying out in alarm, *"Nee! Nee! Nee!"*

With every mile, the river grew wider. At the put-in, it was about 200 feet across, but had now grown to at least 300. The Blue Nile was leaving the hard, black rock of the gorge behind. It had cut its way down to the old Mesozoic seabed, exposing layers of red sandstone and pink limestone. These were softer rocks, and the river moved through them easily, carving a wider channel for itself and shaping the land into cliffs and plateaus that looked like the high, stepped pyramids of the Maya. Broad bands of sandstone ran along the tops of the cliffs, and in some places, these had been eroded into long arches and caves. There were wide, sandy beaches along the river now, too. Crocodiles lined many of the banks like old, yellowed logs. Most of them were small, about four feet in length, and slender; we had yet to see the ten-to-twenty foot behemoths some of the other Blue Nile travelers had reported. The crocs invariably headed for the water as soon as they sensed our approach, hurtling their overgrown Gila monster-style bodies into the river with a surprising burst of speed. They might have looked small and sleepy, but there was no mistaking the predator's intent of their moves, or the cold, snaky glint in their eyes. Like evil jinns, the crocs vanished at once into the Nile's black depths.

Around two in the afternoon, we stopped for the day on one of the wide (crocodile-free) beaches, just above the confluence of the Blue Nile and Bashilo Rivers.

The Bashilo River and its canyon were nearly as big and wide as the Blue Nile and its gorge, and the whole scene, with massive sandstone arches and cliffs fronting the Nile, and big plateaus stacked up in all directions, was as grandly masculine as parts of the Wild West. This was John Wayne country.

A large, spreading fig tree shaded the sandy beach where we'd tied up our rafts, and we pitched our tents above and behind it. The land beyond the beach rose up to a plateau, where the browning leaves of a stunted corn crop waved in the sun. Beyond the plateau lay one of the large arches we had drifted past, and Speaks announced he was going to explore it. It sounded like a fun adventure, and almost everyone decided to join him. I reluctantly stayed behind. My starvation days had taken their toll, and I did not yet feel strong enough to tackle a hard, fast climb.

Kassa and Ephrem didn't go either, and Kate only hiked as far as the top of the plateau, which, she said, gave a smashing view across both canyons. I decided to try it at dawn, when it was cool.

Kate and I chatted awhile when she returned. She was the gung-ho member of our group, ready to pitch in whenever Speaks announced a job to be done. She was always first in line to help unload the boats and pitch the tents, and very willing, too, to lend her medical skills to the people we met. In the mountains, she told me, she'd quickly devised a system at her impromptu morning clinics. She would help the ones she could do something for. Those who had minor complaints, like a headache, she sent on their way; those who were in a truly bad way, she suggested seek medical help in Bahir Dar.

"Boy, I would have packed differently if I'd known what I was getting into," Kate said. "I'm so much smarter now than I was three weeks ago."

"What do you mean?"

"Well, I would have brought a lot more medicines for stomach ailments; more antibiotics. Things that could really do some good. And more of everything, actually. I thought I was only going to be treating our little group, not the whole Blue Nile Valley."

We laughed.

"I'm used to treating someone and then getting to see how they recover," Kate continued. "But here, I have no idea of what's going to happen to them. Like Abush. His legs looked pretty good the last day we saw him. I hope they heal."

Neither of us said it, but we also hoped that Abush had not contracted rabies from his bites.

There were lots of birds, warblers, finches, and the brilliantly colored red-and-black bishop birds in our fig tree. I left Kate to watch them through my binoculars for a while, and then turned them on the gorge across the way. People had shouted to us when we first landed, and I wondered if I could find them. First, I spotted their livestock: cattle and goats. They were moving up a sharp series of switchbacks that apparently led from the water's edge to the plateau at the top of the gorge, a good 300 feet. Then I saw the dark stick figure of a man right at the canyon's edge. He was looking my way, so I lifted my arm overhead and waved. He waved back. We were watching each other. There were cliffs and arches on that side of the canyon, and I shifted my view to these, not wanting him to think that I was spying on him. After a few minutes, I turned back to the man. He was now herding his animals through the thick scrub along the plateau. I wondered how far he had to travel with them each day. There appeared to be no village nearby. Indeed, we had yet to see any village. We saw people occasionally, either individuals or small groups. There were always farms and sometimes livestock about, but no homes or larger settlements. No one seemed to live along the Blue Nile.

It was ironic. All our fretting about Mike Speaks's edict may not have even been necessary. Maybe there weren't any villages or people to camp with. I leaned back against the folding beach chairs that we set up each night and closed my eyes. I was at the junction of the Blue Nile and Bashilo Rivers, I thought, laughing to myself, and I was content.

The hiking party returned a couple of hours later. They had made it to the arch, although the trail had been nasty in places, leading through masses of plants with sharp stickers and thorns. There were so many of these sharp stickers in Nevada's pants that they looked like they were made of bad fake fur. The arch was really more like a shallow cave, but there wasn't anything in it except for lots of goat droppings. The views, though, had been spectacular. Even more impressive was the row of enormous crocs lined up along the Bashilo's shingle beach.

"The biggest ones we've seen," said Mick. "Monsters."

A few moments later, two naked men came walking up the beach, from the Bashilo River side. They had swum across that river to meet us, somehow managing to avoid the toothy crocodile gantlet, and now came up shyly, covering their genitals with one hand, to greet us. They were young men in their late teens or early twenties, and thin and angular. They each wore several wooden and brass earring studs and had a mateb string around their necks, denoting their Christianity, and their faces were square with the fine planes and lines of a Greek sculpture. Nevada took one glance and welcomed them with outstretched hands. They were shy, but willing subjects, and seemed to enjoy having her take their pictures.

Then another man came into camp, but he appeared from the opposite direction. He had just swum across the Blue Nile, which left us shaking our heads. The river was broad and swift here, with small rapids and crocodiles about. His crossing seemed even more daring than that of our other visitors. Like them, he was also wet and naked, but he held his clothes bundled in front of him. (Later, we learned, he'd carried them across the river in a small goatskin bag.) Although older than the two teens, he was equally spare, and had flaring cheekbones and dark curly hair. Hesitantly, he walked up to Nevada and me, held out his hand and smiled. As we shook hands, Zelalem came over to translate, and I learned that this was the man I had been watching through my binoculars.

"He says he saw us when we stopped our boats, and he wanted to visit, but he was afraid," Zelalem explained. "But then he saw you looking at him through your binoculars. You waved at him. So he thought it would be okay to visit."

His name, we learned, was Melese Menesha, and he was the medical officer in Mertule Maryam, a village so far up one of the distant plateaus we could not see it. He was an Amhara, and of course, a farmer, too, and he had just watered his animals and was leading them to their night corral when we saw each other.

It was nearly dusk by now, and our other visitors left to recross the Bashilo, apparently having chores of their own to tend to, but Melese seemed inclined to stay. We were curious, too, about him and his medical career, and invited him to warm himself by our fire and to join us for dinner. Later, Nevada, Zelalem and I sat up, peppering him with questions.

Melese explained that he had taken a two-month medical course the government had offered in Debre Markos, the capital of Gojam. He looked after pregnant women, dispensed pills for stomach ailments and headaches, and gave quinine injections to people suffering from malaria. He was also a big believer in birth control, and gave out birth control pills and condoms. His own wife was taking the pill.

"We have two children, a boy and a girl," he said through Zelalem. "And that is enough. A person can start out wealthy," he added, "but if he has ten children, he will soon become poor."

"He has never met a white person before," Zelalem continued. "Because of that, he was at first afraid to come here." But he had heard that ferenjocch have "excellent medicine, and so he decided to come anyway." Melese wondered if we had some new knowledge to teach him or some of the latest miracle drugs to give him.

Nevada and I shook our heads. Kate had retired early, unfortunately, so we could not turn to her for possible samples, plus she might have been reluctant to give him anything anyway, given her worries about not having sufficient supplies. We explained that we were not doctors; that he had far more medical training (and probably a better medical chest) than we. Our government, we added, also regulated the sale of the kinds of drugs he was asking about, and the average person had to get permission from doctors to buy them.

Melese gestured at the big fig tree by our camp. "This is the place where the men in this region have a big meeting every May," he told Zelalem. The borders of three provinces—Gojam, Begemder, and Wollo—meet at the confluence of the Blue Nile and Bashilo Rivers. "Men come from all three regions to feast and renew their vows of peace as their grandfathers have done," Zelalem explained. The Begemder men, who live the closest to the tree and do not need to cross a river, bring a white ox and a white goat. The men from Gojam and Wollo pay some money for the animals, and bring baskets of *injera* and *kolo* (a toasted mix of seeds and grains), and bottles of *tella* (barley beer). They sacrifice the animals and pour their blood into the Nile, while the elders from each region stand and vow that they will not quarrel with each other for the coming year.

"Then they have a feast for two days," said Zelalem, continuing his translation. "They eat the best parts of the ox as *kitfo* [a raw meat dish something like steak tartare], and the rest is boiled and eaten in strips. And they crack the bones and suck the marrow."

That was the biggest feast of the year. There were also feasts in late October and November when the harvests begin, and people seek marriage partners. "He [Melese] says a father who has a son may know someone who has a daughter. The father goes to that man's house with many gifts, and he asks if their children can marry. But the father of the daughter must refuse the first time. He says, 'Oh, I can't let her go. I love her too much.'" The visiting father protests, and after a few weeks returns to press the issue. "A second visit is always required," Zelalem said, nodding at Melese. And it is in that meeting that the marriage is arranged. People in the three regions do intermarry, Melese said in answer to our query, and that also helps to prevent quarrels.

Melese and Zelalem talked together for a while, and then Zelalem turned to us. "You know, he has a radio," Zelalem said, clearly impressed. "He listens to the news. He says the soldiers are still fighting Eritrea. He says it is getting worse. I don't like to hear this," Zelalem added, shaking his head.

Melese mentioned something else, and Zelalem again reacted with surprise, his eyes growing wide as he translated. "He is telling me now about the Kurdish leader who was arrested last year in Kenya! He wonders if he is being treated fairly in Turkey."

We all agreed that the rebel leader was likely to be executed, but we were marveling, like Zelalem. We'd not expected to discuss world affairs with a man who had just swum the Blue Nile. His own questions for us about America were more prosaic. Did we have cattle, sheep, and goats? Did we travel here by airplane? He again expressed his disappointment that we had no special medicines to give him. We were disappointed, too.

Melese stayed the night, sleeping in the same tent with Zelalem, Kassa, and Ephrem. In the morning, he was anxious to get home. His cattle and goats were waiting for him. We walked with him along the bank of the Nile to his ferry point. On the way, he picked up a short log and carried this with him to the river. He stripped off his clothes, stuffed them in his goatskin bag, and waded into the water. As the water came up over his waist, he pushed the log in front of him and used it like a boogie board to kick his way across the rough current of the Blue Nile. The river caught him and swept him downstream, but in a few minutes, he had reached the far shore. He stood and waved farewell.

"He is a progressive thinker," Zelalem said, watching Melese in admiration, "and look at where he lives."

I was thinking the same thing, and winced again at how ill-prepared we were for meeting men of progress along the Blue Nile. We had expected bandits and spear-throwers, not paramedics who listened to the Ethiopian equivalent of the BBC.

fifteen

~~~

OVER THE NEXT FEW DAYS THAT WAS OFTEN HOW WE MET people: They came swimming across the Blue Nile to greet us at our lunch stops and camps. And we never ceased to be impressed with this most basic mode of river travel—or that people (always men) would make these crossings in order to meet us.

We also met people (again, always men) working along the river. Some had brought their cattle to water, others were tending beehives, or working in their fields. Many called to us, imploring us to stop. When we could, we did. As Nevada had hoped, Mike Borcik had discussed our need to visit with people, and Mike Speaks had relented— a little. It had become increasingly clear that there weren't villages along this stretch of the river, and Speaks didn't mind our daytime visits with the small groups we occasionally spotted, as long as we didn't spend too much time. He was on a tight schedule, we learned, and had another trip to lead in Bhutan about four days after this one ended.

"As long as we get in the right number of klicks [kilometers] each day, I'm okay with some stops," he said. "We've been doing about 50 kilometers [about 17 miles] a day, and I'd like to keep up that pace."

That would put us at the border town of Bumbadi in three weeks, right on schedule.

Speaks was less happy about visitors who came to our camps in the evening, fearing another stolen-knife episode. After that incident, and for the rest of that trip, he did not allow Ethiopians into his camp, and he clearly intended to keep them out of this one, too. Indeed, the night before, he had stepped forward, his jaw clenched, ready to throw out the young men and even Melese, but stopped when Nevada and I protested.

Speaks didn't trust us on this score, and we thought he behaved like a bully. In a way, it was like a Keystone Kops routine: We were all trying to do our jobs, but we kept bumping into each other. Nevertheless, with luck, we might stumble into an arrangement that made us all happy.

Just beyond the Bashilo River, the Blue Nile made a deep curve to the right. We were now heading due south into an arid land of big castellated plateaus.

"If I wasn't looking at acacia trees and baboons, I'd think I was in the [American] Southwest," Nevada said as we drifted along.

It was true: The plateaus with their layers of pink sandstone and beige limestone looked remarkably like parts of Arizona and New Mexico.

"Almost makes me homesick for Santa Fe," teased Kelly.

We also hit our first big rapid, which may have been the one the British team was forced to run in the dark, after their second bandit attack. We stopped some distance above this stretch of water, and hiked to a spot where the boatmen could study it and pick the best route through the waves. A lone log happened to come downstream as we stood above the rapid. The log's course kept to the left of a big churning hole of swirling water that spun just below the largest wave.

"Would you look at that?" Speaks said. "It's taking a good course, a wise, conservative one. We'll do something like that. We do want to keep to the left of that hole, and the right side of that rooster tail," he added, pointing to a series of tall waves that broke in a ragged fashion. "Other than that, it's 'hey diddle, diddle; right down the middle.'"

Kassa was riding on Speaks's boat, and this was the largest rapid he had yet seen. A glum look settled over his face. Zelalem gave him a few pointers, and Kassa nodded. Then they were off. We stood onshore, taking pictures, and filming Speaks's run.

The river's force and energy seemed to increase foot by foot as the water rushed downstream, heading toward this cascade. A slick, brown watery tongue formed where the force was strongest, and Speaks guided the boat onto it, letting the river do his work. He kept the boat sideways for a moment, then with a strong stroke, pivoted the raft into the center. *Crash!* They hit the big drop, plunged from view for a second, then rose up the other, lathery side of the wave, and were soon bucking and tossing through the rest of the rapid.

I'd switched boats again that morning, in order to ride with Bruce and Kelly, and we followed Speaks. Bruce was the low man on the boatmen's totem pole, and he knew he was being watched. But this was a straightforward, "fun run," in rafting lingo, and he said as we headed onto the brown tongue, "Do you want to get wet?"

There wasn't time for an answer. We fell like a big beach ball into the drop, hit the bottom and climbed back through the foam. A wave crashed over my back from the right; another hit Kelly from the left. And then we were plunging up and over a series of high, peaked waves that dropped into deep troughs, where there was nothing to see but red-brown, angry water. It was fun and exhilarating, and we were laughing by the time we reached the eddy on the Gojam side of the river where Speaks was waiting. We pulled up alongside, and I asked Kassa if he'd enjoyed his first real white-water ride.

In response, Kassa opened his eyes wide, put his hand over his heart, and then thrust his fist out at arm's length—a fair indication of the distance his heart had leaped in the midst of that maelstrom. We all laughed, then turned to see the last part of Borcik's run as they crashed through the waves.

As Borcik rowed into the eddy, several farmers came running along the shore, shouting.

"They are surprised that we are still alive," Zelalem translated.

An older fellow came closest and shook his head. He looked pale.

"He is saying, 'I thought you must flip. We were afraid for you.' They are thanking Mary and Jesus that we are safe."

Zelalem told him that the boats were designed to travel on rivers like this. He could come sit on one of the rafts, if he liked. Slowly, the man stepped forward and put out his hand to touch the boat's round, inflated rubber tube, then very cautiously lowered himself to a sitting position. His friends stayed farther away, under an acacia tree, and watched, while he called out to them what it felt like.

"It is strong, like a hard cowhide," Zelalem translated. "He thinks this is an airplane, and he tells them there is a floor in it."

These inland, mountain people, we guessed, had never seen a boat before, maybe not even the tankwas on Lake Tana, which was a long journey by foot for them. Like everyone else we had met, they pointed to the highest peaks when we asked them about their homes. Some of the mountains behind the plateaus soared to heights of 9,000 and 10,000 feet. That's where the villages were.

We camped on a sandy beach near the confluence of the Bashilo and Blue Nile Rivers on day eight of our journey. Melese Menesha, a paramedic in a village in the western Gojam highlands, swam across the Blue Nile to meet us here.

About 120 miles from the Second Portuguese Bridge, we take a joyride through the canyon on some of the Blue Nile's choppy white water.

Descending from Ethiopia's highlands, the Blue Nile winds through lonely country for some 540 miles to reach the border with Sudan. The region is so remote and rugged that the river remained unmapped until the late 1920s. Our 1999 expedition was the first to travel the river's length in an unbroken journey.

Ethiopian *Borana* farmers gaze westward over the Blue Nile Gorge toward Gojam. We met many Borana livestock traders along the river. They swam with their animals across the Blue Nile, then trekked back up the other side of the gorge to markets in the Gojam highlands.

Some of the Borana
people Nevada
and I met worship
in a mosque in Debat
village, high above
the Blue Nile.

Halfway down
the Blue Nile, we left
the highland people
behind and entered
the land of the
Gumuz. In the village
of Botuma, a woman
in labor shelters
behind a reed mat,
assisted by a midwife.
Her grandmother
sits outside.

At Meten village, two groups of Gumuz men blast their *duwa* horns for us in a friendly contest. "My girl is the shapeliest and most beautiful of all," they trumpeted.

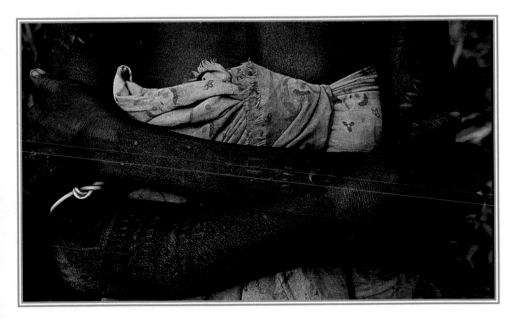

In the past, the Gumuz people wore little clothing, adorning themselves instead with scar patterns like these. But clothing is now in vogue, following a government order, and such scarification is rare among the young.

A Gumuz boy holds all the weapons— rifles, a bow and arrows, a spear—of his companions who had dashed off to their homes to fetch *duwa* horns to play for us.

While at Gishe Abay, the priests of Saint Michael's Church invited us to attend a memorial service for a beloved nun and priest who had recently died. After the river journey, Nevada and I spent several days at the source of the Blue Nile located at Gishe Abay.

Many Ethiopians make sacrifices to Gihon, the spirit of the Blue Nile. At the village of Gilgel Abay, a woman prepares coffee for Nevada and me to present as an offering. The springs at Gishe Abay give rise to the Little Blue Nile (or *Gilgel Abay*, as the Ethiopians call it). It flows into Lake Tana, joining the waters of other rivers and streams to form the Blue Nile proper.

Just a few miles from the Sudan border, we stop to ask villagers of Libet how close we are to Bumbadi, our takeout point. "You are nearly there," they told us. About half an hour later, we were.

The Little Blue Nile meets the waters of Lake Tana. By the time Nevada and I reached the confluence, we had made a wide circle around Ethiopia, just as the Blue Nile does.

"They say it is not good to live down here," Zelalem explained. "There is too much malaria. They come only to the river if they have some work to do."

A few miles farther downstream, we met other men who were livestock merchants. They had bought goats, donkeys, and horses at a good price in a market in the Wollega highlands, and they were taking them—swimming them—across the Blue Nile to a market in the mountains of Gojam. The men made small floats from bundles of sticks, stuck their clothing inside, then tied two or three goats to their twiggy rafts (called *jandies*). Like Melese with his log, they then laid their upper bodies across the float and kicked the whole lot across the Blue Nile. Donkeys and horses had their ears wrapped shut to keep the water out before crossing, and were held on a tether. They were expected to swim alongside their dolphin-kicking owners.

Watching one man crossing the river like this while simultaneously holding the heads of his three goats above the waves, I was struck by the limited use the highland Ethiopians make of all this water. They seek it out as a holy source, and those who live close enough lead their herds to it to drink. But although a team of Ethiopian and American engineers drew up plans for dams and irrigation projects some 40 years ago, none have been built on the Blue Nile. The American engineers came on behalf of the United States Bureau of Reclamation. Between 1958 and 1963, they worked with their Ethiopian counterparts to survey the land and water resources of the Blue Nile River Basin, and to prepare an overall development plan. The final proposal recommended 33 projects, including the construction of four large dams on the Blue Nile itself and several others on some of the larger tributaries. None of these were built, partly because of political and financial concerns. There is a dam on the Akaki River, a small tributary of the Blue Nile which flows past Addis Ababa; it provides power for the city. There is also a small conduit below Tis Isat Falls, which channels some of the Blue Nile's water through a hydroelectric station, generating power for Bahir Dar.

At least in the immediate future, the Blue Nile will likely remain free-flowing, although the Ethiopian government does intend to build dams on several of its tributaries.

Local farmers along the river itself depend solely on the rains for irrigation. The rains had been meager in the past few weeks (despite the sudden downpours we'd witnessed), and we could only imagine the farmers' frustration as their corn and barley turned brown while the Nile's waters rushed by below. The previous night, we had camped close to some of these withered crops, and on this day had seen many more.

"They have a proverb about this," Zelalem said, when I raised the subject with him and Kassa. Kassa sang it.

"Abay taresealew/ Betikur beri/ Machila bezerraw/ Bekele berbere."

The proverb's literal (wax) meaning translates to something like, "In the summer, the Abay plows with black oxen. He sows corn, but only pepper sprouts." But the true, gold meaning of the saying was simple, Zelalem said. "The Abay carries all this water, but gives us nothing."

Why, the farmers wonder, can't the Blue Nile slow down and linger for a while?

BABOONS, VERVET MONKEYS, AND CROCS. THESE, AND THE BIRDS, WERE our constant river companions. Baboons leaped from rock to rock, barking their disapproval at us, the vervets fled into the acacia and hagenia trees, and the crocs slipped sullenly beneath the water like stealthy criminals on the prowl. Near rocky cliffs, wire-tailed swallows appeared, skimming over the river, and in the mornings, half-collared kingfishers livened the air with their long, chattering cries. Sometimes we spotted pairs of goliath herons walking along the sandy beaches. They were stately birds, like princes of the realm, and would slowly turn their necks to peer at us. Then, as if the rabble had come too close, they would spread their wings, give a small, discrete jump (with knees held tightly together), and soar majestically downstream. We saw the dark-plumaged hammerkop birds, too, which look like herons that got stuck in a clothes dryer for too long: shrunken, squashed and misshapen. The hammerkops, whose heads resemble hammers, liked to gather in small groups of three or four along the sandy deltas where other rivers fed into the Nile, and poke their long beaks in the water, searching for tadpoles and frogs. We also saw a couple of their nests: massive, haystack-like affairs of sticks, twigs, and grasses piled high in the crotches of the shoreline trees. A single opening led to the nest's interior, where the young were raised. Presumably, the hammerkops build such huge nests as a way of protecting their young, since both parents are often away for long periods of time, foraging.

Mike Speaks was a great birder, and kept his well-thumbed Collins' *Field Guide to the Birds of East Africa* close at hand. Whenever he saw a new species, or one he hadn't expected to see along the Blue Nile, he'd stick one oar beneath his leg to steady the raft, and write a note in the book's margin with his stubby pencil.

The river widened and contracted and widened again. It bent left and right and left, and ran right along at a steady seven miles an hour.

"For a river this forceful, it sure does have a lot of twists and bends," Kelly commented at one point. "You'd expect it to be more straight."

Kelly was an old riverhand, I learned. He'd been down the Colorado River three times, as well as Chile's Bio Bio, and several smaller rivers. But mostly he was an adventurer. At camp at the end of each day, we would spread out a blue tarp on the sands and arrange our beach chairs on it. We'd get a cup of soup or tea, then sit back to rest or write up our notes or talk. Kelly was a great notetaker and we often sat next to each other, helping each other remember all we had seen and done. Kelly wrote his notes on lined, yellow legal-size pads. When he got home, he would give them to his secretary to type, and then have them printed and bound into books for his friends and family. He had self-published a whole series of these "Kelly Adventures."

Kelly was in the real estate business, and had always made money. He used some of it to finance his trips. "I started off as a hunter," he explained in a slight Texan drawl. "I did that for 30 years. I hunted every-where: Asia, South America, Africa. I wasn't really after the trophies. I went for the journey and adventure."

He had even been in Ethiopia once before, in 1988. "I came here to hunt the mountain nyala [an antelope with beautiful, spiral horns]," he said. "We went down in the southeastern Bale Mountains for it. That was my last trophy." He decided he didn't need to hunt any more to have his adven-tures. A few years later, he met Nevada and began joining her on treks in India's Ladakh Range, the Pamirs of Tajikistan, and the steppes of Mon-golia. "Then we came up with this idea of seeing the Blue Nile," he said.

Yet Kelly wasn't going to see all of it. He had missed our trek because of business obligations, and he planned to leave at the second modern Abay bridge (about ten days down the river) because he wanted to sur-prise his wife. "Anne's going to St. Petersburg with our friends," Kelly told me, a sly smile crossing his face. "She thinks that I'll be here on the river, and that I'll meet her later in Paris. But I'm going to show up early, surprise her." They'd been married 26 years, and he knew how to keep the sparks going. He had a good suit and tuxedo packed in his suitcase that was waiting for him at the Addis Ababa Sheraton Hotel. He'd grab that and be on his way.

From his previous river trips, Kelly knew the river camp routine and was always the first to have his tent pitched and first to have it down. He was fastidious, too. Every morning, I heard his battery-operated razor humming in his tent for a few moments. His clothes were worn, but clean and tidy. Even his fingernails were clean. I never did figure out how he did it. I felt like a dirt bucket in comparison.

We stopped at a clean stream or river each day to wash and collect fresh water. I had started off by trying to wash one set of clothes at the same time that I bathed and shampooed. But it usually rained in the afternoons, and the clean clothes would still be damp by the time we reached our next camp. Sometimes they were even damp the next morning—and beginning to smell like an old shower curtain. I had another good set that I kept at the bottom of my river bag, but I didn't touch them; I wanted to keep them clean for the end of the trip, when we reentered society.

By our fourth day on the river, I gave up on the two-set idea. I would wear the same clothes all day, every day for the rest of the trip: my khaki-colored nylon pants, and khaki-colored, long-sleeved shirt. My clothes were as drab and shapeless as a prisoner's uniform, but at least they were color-coordinated. I still made an effort to keep them clean, washing them out every day, even rubbing at the black dirt streaks on the cuffs and collar. It was hopeless. They were usually damp when I put them on again, and every wave or splash from the river turned them a slightly dingier hue.

I also had a colorful Kenyan sarong, and I wrapped this like a turban around my white sun-hat to cheer myself up about my sorry-looking wardrobe.

Nevada and Kate looked far more stylish in their blue sleeveless shirts, and cute river shorts. They didn't seem to mind the hot, equatorial sun.

Speaks had taken the big step of changing his shirt at the beginning of our river trip. His trekking shirt had been badly torn at the neck, when Adane grabbed hold of him during their scary river-crossing. Speaks ripped it off and switched to another faded, long-sleeved T-shirt with holes along the shoulders. His exposed skin soon became so sunburned that he developed a row of festering blisters. They were large and red and watery, and poked through the holes in his shirt, but he ignored them. Every few days, he bathed. I saw him walk down to the river on hot afternoons with a bucket. He'd scoop up the river's water and pour it over his head. Then, he'd shake all over like a big dog.

Heat, sweat, and dirt aside, we actually weren't that uncomfortable. There weren't many insects to speak of, although we sometimes heard mosquitoes in the early evening, and there were sand fleas on some beaches. We weren't even very hot. The mornings were often cloudy and cool enough for jackets. And in the late morning and afternoons, when it was hot, we were generally on the river, where the water and a breeze or two kept the heat down. If we stopped to explore a canyon or to take a break onshore, though, the temperature instantly soared, as if someone had just switched off the air conditioner. Many afternoons, it rained, sometimes for a good hour, and then we were cold. We zipped up our rain jackets and life jackets to keep warm, and huddled beneath our umbrellas—and said repeatedly to each other that this was the last thing we expected, to be wet and shivering from a cold rain on the Blue Nile.

KASSA WAS HUNGRY. IT WASN'T THAT WE DIDN'T GIVE HIM FOOD OR invite him to eat with us. He couldn't bear our bad diet. Pasta and rice, vegetables and salads, stale bread, some brown goo called peanut butter, rubbery orange stuff we called cheese. He looked on sadly at first, then wanly as he grew ever hungrier. He always ate a little of our food, but not enough to fill his belly. He started putting fishing lines out every night, hoping to catch a nice, fat catfish. But he had no luck.

Then, on the morning of our fourth day, Kassa's luck changed. We met a group of Borana men with goats and cattle they'd brought to water at the Blue Nile. The pastoral Borana are part of the Oromo people. Those who live here along the northern stretch of the river are descended from clans who migrated north from southeastern Ethiopia in the 16th century. At that time, the Amharas were still recovering from the terrible jihad of Ahmad Gragn who had laid waste to the land, and the Borana found an easy path into the cool mountains along the Nile. They were skilled cattle herders and soon established a strong enclave, almost a small kingdom, giving their name "Borana" to the highlands above this stretch of the river.

The Borana are a beautiful people, somewhat taller than the Amharas and with softer features and hair, which they oil with their butter. Those we met appeared to be the healthiest people we had seen, and we all commented on their good, strong looks.

Like every other group of people we'd seen along the river, they shouted and called to us to stop, and were delighted when we did. They were dressed simply in shorts and shirts, or white robes, and most had a few bright beads and amulets on leather cords around their necks. They gazed at us with great curiosity and asked us the usual questions about our airplanes, and then told us that most of them came from a village a three-hour walk away. "Those who live in that village come here every day in this season to water their animals," Zelalem told us. "But some live in another village that is a six-hour walk. They stay somewhere near here for one month at a time."

Then they asked a question which made Kassa's heart—and stomach—soar. Did we want some milk?

"They want to give us milk as a gift," Zelalem said.

"We'll take it," said Speaks.

A young boy was dispatched to one of the nearby camps. He ran off at a trot, and did not return for a good half-hour. Once, someone in our group suggested that it was taking too long, perhaps we should leave, but Kassa looked so forlorn at that idea that it was quickly dropped.

"We can wait," Speaks said.

While we waited, we asked about their life along the river. They crossed the Blue Nile regularly to take animals to the markets in Gojam, and yes, they lost livestock regularly to the crocodiles. The crocs had taken 20 of their cattle in the last year. One boy told Zelalem that he was a student. "What grade are you in?" Zelalem asked in Amharic. "Five," the boy replied in English. We English speakers took over. "What is your name?" "How old are you?" He ducked his head shyly, then asked us, "How are you?"

At last, the milk boy reappeared carrying a large gourd sealed with a leather cap. The gourd easily held two gallons, and the milk inside looked like yogurt and had a rich, smoky scent. The boy presented the gourd with both hands, and we told Kassa to take it.

Kassa put the gourd to his lips and drank…and drank. We started laughing, but Kassa didn't stop until he'd finished about a quarter of the milk. He filled his canteen, and another container, and looked about for a third. I handed him one of my two water bottles, and he poured more milk into it. Then he drank what was left in the gourd.

What could we give the people in return? we asked Zelalem.

"They say they want nothing. You are tarik for them. They are so excited to see you, and this is their gift. If you have some malaria medicine, they would like that."

That was the one thing we didn't have. We each had our own stash of preventive pills, but not enough to hand out, and besides only taking one or two pills would likely make them more susceptible to the disease. It was better, we suggested through Zelalem, that they go to a government health clinic for help. One of the herders had a bad eye infection, which Kate treated, and then gave some directions about keeping clean.

Several of the boys ran along the riverbanks as we shoved off. They raced like marathoners, shouting and waving goodbye, until we disappeared around a bend.

We rowed on. The river had widened to 350 feet, and cut through more layers of sandstone, limestone, and mudstone. It looked slower and fatter with all the water that its tributaries poured into it. Yet every time Speaks checked his GPS, he found the river moving at a steady five-to-seven miles an hour. Speaks's GPS reading also gave us an elevation of 3,200 feet.

"We started at about 6,100 feet, so we've lost a fair bit," he said.

The mountains and plateaus were no longer jammed up close to the Nile, but set back a mile or more behind a row of rocky hills. In the foreground, the riverbank rose only three or four feet and was capped with an undulating, gravel-covered plain dense with shrubs, acacias, and tamarisk trees. Many of the acacias were in bloom, covered with fluffy, white rosettes, whose sweet, honeysuckle fragrance followed us downstream.

In the early afternoon, on the Gojam side, a small group of men stacking up long wooden poles called to us, and we pulled ashore.

The eldest, a man of about 65 with dark eyes shaped like crescent moons, came forward to greet us. He was wearing a patched blue suit jacket and knee-length shorts, and sandals made from rubber tires. One by one, we stepped off our rafts and shook his hand.

"His name is Abate Abuye," said Zelalem, "and he and his nephews are cutting these poles to make new houses." The poles would serve as the center support for their round homes. One of the nephews came closer and listened, while leaning on his walking stick.

We wondered if this was the first time they had seen ferenjocch.

"No," Zelalem translated. "They have been to Addis because they have relatives there, so they have seen tourists before, but only from a distance, never to talk to like this. He says, 'In my conception, the ferenji didn't speak with black people. So I'm very happy about meeting you. For us, it is just like seeing the sun up close.'" He had never imagined, Zelalem continued, that a ferenji would shake his hand, "because my hands are very rough."

Nevada caught her breath at these words, and pressed both his weathered hands once again in hers.

"It is not because he is an Ethiopian and black," Zelalem explained to me later. "It's because you are rich. In our country, poor farmers are not accustomed to shaking hands with the rich. The rich don't do this."

Abate had a couple of questions. He wondered why Bruce and Mick weren't wearing shirts; in his culture, men only went shirtless when they were sick.

"It is because they come from a cold land and are hot," Zelalem said.

"Well," Abate replied through Zelalem, "I've heard that ferenjocch make all kinds of clever medicines, so they should make one to warm up their countries, too."

His other question was why was Nevada, a woman, wearing shorts? In his culture, it was impolite for women to show their upper thighs. Nevada quickly removed the sarong she had draped over her sun hat, and wrapped it around her legs.

Abate nodded approvingly. "He is more comfortable now," Zelalem said.

Mike Speaks had fished out a gift of yarn, buttons, needles, and threads, and presented these to Abate. Unlike our River Man, who regarded these presents as useless, Abate became choked up.

"He will give these to his wife, who will be so happy to have them," Zelalem said. "He says, 'God be with you, wherever you go. I wish you good travels.'"

We shook his hand good-bye, and stepped back onto our rafts.

The nephew, a boy of about 15, followed. He hadn't spoken a word while his uncle talked, but now he asked, could we please take him to America with us?

We shook our heads, no. We were on our way to Sudan now. Zelalem untied the line on Speaks's boat. Speaks dipped the oars in the water, and we shoved off.

The boy stayed at the water's edge, watching us—and his dream of going to America—slip away.

sixteen

W E CAMPED THAT NIGHT, OUR FOURTH ON THE RIVER, ON A wide, sandy bank with acacias overhead and wildflowers underfoot. This was cattle country, and we heard a few lone cows mooing in the distance. Closer to camp, a cow stood licking her stillborn calf. A half-dozen vultures hunched nearby, waiting. In the morning, the mother was still standing protectively over her calf, and the vultures were still patiently waiting.

I walked up to join the others for breakfast, when Kassa appeared. He was visibly annoyed.

"Something has been biting me," he said. He extended his hand to Zelalem to show the "something," pinching it between his thumb and forefinger.

"A mosquito," Zelalem said. He began laughing.

"This is a mosquito?" Kassa replied.

"Yes," said Zelalem, who could by now hardly control his laughter.

Bruce and I began laughing, too.

"He's never seen a mosquito before?" Bruce asked, incredulous.

"No," said Zelalem. "I think many bit him last night."

Kassa rubbed the bites on his face and neck, and spoke again to Zelalem. "He says, 'That because of mosquitoes many people die,'" Zelalem translated. "And he says, 'If I am killed by a mosquito, I'll be sorry about that.'"

"We would all be sorry about that," Bruce and I agreed.

"He should be careful," added Kate. "Tell him he should go to the clinic if he gets a fever."

Kassa was clearly a man of the cool highland country, where mosquitoes—and malaria—are not found. He was also not protected against the disease, and we hoped he took Kate's advice seriously.

We all liked Kassa. He was very musical, and was constantly composing couplets and songs about our journey as we floated down the Nile. In many of these, the "boat-plane's pilots" were all lions, the ferenjocch women "beautiful," and the men of Gojam, strong and brave. "We wrestle with the crocodiles/ We break their necks/ We are strong men of Gojam!" He taught us to sing a nonsense chorus—"*Janjero! Janjero!... Baboon! Baboon!*"—between his couplets. At night, he played a bamboo flute Bruce had purchased from a child at Lake Tana, stopping to break into song or to drum on the bottom of an aluminum pot like a one-man band. Once at the campfire, he sat between Nevada and me, and sang about how he had protected us from the *azzoch* (crocodiles) and bandits on the Nile, all the while aiming his Kalashnikov at make-believe enemies.

Kassa took his guard duties seriously. At our first camp, Speaks told us that when he got up to check on the boats in the middle of the night, Kassa was right at his side, his Kalashnikov at the ready, asking if there was a problem.

"He sleeps only one hour or two," Zelalem concurred. "He's always waking Ephrem and me, saying 'Get up, let's talk, isn't it time for coffee?'"

Like most Ethiopians, Kassa had never spent any time with feren-jocch, and he found some of our customs puzzling. He was very surprised that Bruce and Mick had long hair "like a woman's," but he wasn't worried that the boatmen sometimes consulted with Nevada and me. "Even in our country," he told us through Zelalem, "women participate in the government and can be leaders. Besides you are educated, so of course you should lead." He wondered why we all slept one by one in our tents; it seemed so lonely. And he was most astonished—actually horrified—that the boatmen would fart during meal times. "Making that sound is very bad," Zelalem said, "and especially when eating. He cannot believe you do this." I imagined Kassa returning to his village to tell of our scandalous social behavior, and thought of a story I'd once read about a man on the island of Lamu in Kenya (where breaking wind is also regarded as the worst of social sins) who was known as "The man whose grandfather farted." (After Kassa's etiquette lesson, the mealtime farting subsided.)

Saddest of all, though, to Kassa was our pathetic food. "I'm really sorry that you have to eat this bad food, and that you have no injera, or kitfo," he said through Zelalem, one night. "He is surprised," Zelalem added, "you are all really strong in spite of your bad food."

And in spite of having to subsist on our bad food, Kassa was enjoying the trip, although Zelalem said, "he misses his wife and three young children too much. He dreams at night that he is holding them like he does at home. They all sleep together, and he is lonely for them."

We were luckier in one regard perhaps: We had the iridium phone. If we became lonely, we could call home, and did so every few days. I had telephoned Michael again, and let him know that the donkey-thief incident had turned out fine. He sometimes sent short text messages to the phone (until that feature stopped working), as did Kate's daughter and Nevada's boyfriend. I loved receiving such messages, but they seemed strange, too, somehow utterly disconnected from my new life on the Blue Nile. It was like receiving a letter 20 years after it had first been sent, and all the circumstances of my life had changed.

THE RIVER SLICED FARTHER SOUTH. ONCE IT MADE A BIG *S* MEANDER, turning back on itself to head northwest for a while, then lazily curving southeast again. A little past this meander, we left the Wollo region on the left-hand bank behind and entered a region Zelalem called "Semi-Shoa," or northern Shoa. There were many cattle herders about, and we stopped to visit one group who had a small cluster of huts—the first semblance of a village we'd seen since our trek.

The people—a small group of men and young boys—had waved from the shore, but they did not come down to greet us. Zelalem called to them, asking if we could visit, and they said yes, but they didn't seem particularly excited. We were not tarik for them.

We hiked up a small incline, and a man of about 40 wearing a white robe finally broke away from the others and walked up to greet us. He was reserved and quiet, and did not smile as we all shook hands.

"Yes, it is okay if we go to see his home," Zelalem translated. "It is just a temporary home for two or three days when they water their cattle."

The man had built a large corral of peeled poles lashed together with leather strips, and along one side had built small A-frame huts on stilts. One served as a place to sleep, and his two little boys scrambled up a ladder to show us this; the other was a storage room. They had several gourds of milk inside, and we bought more milk for Kassa, along with some injera and barley bread. Like many other people we'd met, they asked for medicine to treat malaria, and as before we had to say, no, we didn't have any.

We shook hands again, and said goodbye.

"These are typical Semi-Shoans," Zelalem said, after we pushed off. "They are Amhara, but special. They are tough, you know, very independent, and they cause every government trouble because they don't like any government. They even killed some soldiers from the new government." We weren't to feel bad because of the cool reception they'd given us; they were simply suspicious of everyone and anarchists at heart.

The anarchists were more carefree once we'd left their shores. The boys ran along the bank, hooting and calling, and racing our rafts. Their cries—and our boats—were soon spotted from the other bank, and men and boys ran and shouted at us from both sides of the Nile.

"They are saying, 'Come here! Don't go to them! Please come to us! Slow down and stop with us!,' " Zelalem translated, laughing.

Around the next bend, we did. There were large herds of cattle and donkeys here, and a big camp of herders, perhaps as many as 30 men. They, too, were Semi-Shoans, but maybe less political ones. They welcomed us with smiles and warm handshakes.

"They say you can come see everything," Zelalem translated.

The herders had dug water troughs in the gravel shore about five feet from the river. The troughs were close enough to the river to easily fill with water, and far enough away to reduce the threat of crocodile attacks. Nevertheless, they regularly lost animals to the big reptiles. Certainly, the crocs in this region appeared to have plenty to eat. We had seen far more than usual and several big ones. A couple had been brave enough to swim like submarines toward our rafts, and Speaks had slammed one on the head with an oar. It sank at once, then obstinately surfaced close to Borcik's boat. Kelly threw a rock, and the croc vanished, slapping the water with its tail. The men had built some small wickiups on shore to shelter themselves from the sun, and their axes, milk gourds, and baskets were lined up near these. In one, a boy was tending a day-old calf, and in another, a young and very ill boy lay suffering. A bull had gored him in his leg three days before. Kate took one look, and went back to the rafts for her medical kit. The wound was swollen and an infection had set in. She gently washed it, then made a poultice with a disinfectant and antibiotics, all the while telling the boy through Zelalem how to care for his injury after she left.

Speaks had stayed on his raft, and to pass the time, he started humming one of Kassa's tunes, pitching his voice high then low like Kassa did. Some of the herders shook their heads. They had a better song, and they launched into it. "*Oooohh, Whoa-oohh*," their song began. Other men came running, and the entire group formed into a block formation and trotted down the beach, singing and chanting. Zelalem, Ephrem, and Kassa joined in, too, locking arms with the others. The men then formed a circle, and two of the teenage boys danced in the center, shaking their shoulders and darting their heads at one another as Kasawol and Adunya had at our mountain camp. It was a frenzied dance, sexual and athletic and surely designed to put the dancers in a trance. And indeed, the boys' eyelids drooped and quivered as if they were on the verge of passing out. The dance ended abruptly. The men chanted their opening bars again, and trotted farther down the beach, singing as before.

"It is a song of joy," said Zelalem, who had left the group. "They sing it when herding and when going to work in the fields. Now they are singing a patriots' song. It means something like, 'The hero says our country has nothing to give the outsiders/ Let them stay away.'"

"That sounds like the kind of song a Semi-Shoan would sing," I said.

Zelalem laughed. "Yes, but we all sing it," he said.

Kelly had asked Zelalem once what most Ethiopians thought about having tourists visit their country.

Zelalem looked hesitant. "Well, we like tourists to come to see things, but…it's better if they don't stay," he said, searching for a kind way to phrase his countrymen's notorious xenophobia.

"So it would be hard to live here as a foreigner?," Kelly asked.

"Yes, I think so," Zelalem replied. "It's better for you to stay in your own country."

The songs and dancing had given Nevada and Mick many wonderful scenes to photograph. One of the young dancers was particularly handsome, with a jaw line and tousle of brown curly hair a male model would envy. He had five tiny brass crosses strung on black cords around his neck, and Nevada shot his portrait from many angles. He and all the others followed us back to our boats and stood looking at them longingly as we climbed on board. "He wants to come with us," Zelalem said.

"Is he sure he wants to go to Sudan?" I asked.

"He says, 'Yes, he would go wherever you are going.' "

We couldn't take him there, but I thought we could give him a short boat ride. Speaks acquiesced to this, and the dancer-herder and several others quickly scrambled on board. The river was wide and slow here, and we rowed them downstream for about a mile.

"What do they think about the river?," I asked Zelalem, thinking about the farmers farther upstream who saw it taking their soil away and leaving them nothing.

"For them, it is good," Zelalem said, after talking with the men on board our raft. "They say there is nothing bad in the river. Also, they are Christians and don't believe there are bad jinn in the water. But they say that over there in Gojam," Zelalem said, pointing to the opposite bank, "the people do spirit-worship. They see them sometimes killing a goat or sheep, and putting its blood in the water."

They had questions for us, mostly about the boats, what they were made of and how excellent it was that they had floors. Speaks guided his raft into a little eddy, and our Semi-Shoan friends jumped off. Then they raced along the banks, calling their thanks and cheering us on— "*Melkam gouzo! Melkam gouzo!* Good journeys! Good journeys!"— until our royal flotilla vanished from view.

NOT ONE OF THE MEN IN THAT CAMP HAD A GUN, I SUDDENLY realized, after they left. In fact, no one along the river seemed to have a gun. None of the farmers and none of the herders we'd met had one— or at least they didn't have them in view. Yet when I had lived in Ethiopia, you seldom met a man in the countryside without a firearm on display; it might be a battered World War I antique, but an Ethiopian man always had a weapon.

Something had changed, and one night after dinner, I asked Zelalem about it.

"We haven't seen any armed men along the river, and everyone says there are no more shifta. What happened?"

"It's because of the EPRDF [the Ethiopian Peoples Revolutionary Democratic Front]," Zelalem said.

The EPRDF had defeated the old, Derg government in 1991, and its leaders now ruled the country. The Front had grown out of the combined forces of Tigreans and Eritreans who'd fought together to win Eritrea's independence. With Meles Zenawi (now Ethiopia's president) at its head, the EPRDF expanded to include all peoples of Ethiopia.

Peasants joined en masse and swept south, taking Wollo and Gojam. Along the Blue Nile, Zelalem said, the peasant soldiers encountered many shifta gangs. They brought them into their army, and used their hideouts to avoid the Derg soldiers.

After overthrowing Mengistu, President Meles gave the shifta gangs a chance at amnesty. If they turned themselves and their weapons in, he would forgive them. Those who did not would be shot or imprisoned. The government was serious about the order, and the EPRDF tracked down their former allies to enforce it.

That had taken care of the shifta. And strong gun-control laws assured that the tradition wouldn't soon be revived. "You can only have a gun now, if you belong to the militia," Zelalem said. Men who did not belong to a militia, and who were seen with firearms could be imprisoned for life. "They maybe have them at home, but they don't bring them out." All our guides and donkey wranglers on the trek who had Kalashnikovs had very likely fought with the EPRDF against the Derg; that entitled them to membership in a militia and a Kalashnikov.

Kassa, too, was an EPRDF member, and a commander in his militia group. He'd been a young soldier in the Front when it defeated the Derg.

"And what about you?," I asked Zelalem. "Were you with the EPRDF?" I'd seen him cleaning Kassa's Kalashnikov the evening before, and thought that for a tour guide, he knew an awful lot about automatic weapons.

Zelalem shook his head, a slight smile on his face. We'd been traveling together now for almost two weeks, and had become friends. I'd told him about many of my earlier experiences in his country, the time of the revolution, and how I feared many of my students had died. And I'd told him about the old priest's dream for me.

"Sometime, I'd like to do something about that dream," I told Zelalem. "I've thought about finding some child in the countryside, maybe an orphan, and helping him go to school. Maybe after the trip, you could help me do that?"

Zelalem didn't hesitate. "I have one," he said.

"You have a child?" I was surprised, since Ethiopians seldom keep such relationships secret.

"He is my sister's son, Hailu. But she died, and his father is gone." Hailu was now Zelalem's charge, and he worried about him. Zelalem looked at me intently, trying to determine if I was serious about wanting to help a child. "Hailu is a little boy, 11, very nice. You would like him."

I'd said, "Okay. I'll think about it." And the more I thought it over, the more it seemed like a good thing to do. I liked Zelalem. He was honest and forthright. He'd been helping support Hailu, who had lived with Zelalem's parents in Lalibela since Hailu was a toddler. "It is a big worry for me," he told me when I brought up the subject again. "My parents are old. If something happens to them or to me, what will happen to Hailu? It is on my mind." I didn't make any fast promises, but I knew in my heart that I would help Hailu.

Maybe finding one's eddileh—destiny—didn't have to involve grand gestures or plans. Sometimes it could appear right in front of you and all you had to do was say yes.

Zelalem had not been at home when his sister died, leaving Hailu an orphan. He had been serving—unwillingly—in the Derg's army.

"I was 19," Zelalem told me. "I was a 12th-grade student at a school in Dessie," the capital of Wollo province. "The EPRDF had already captured most of north Wollo, even Lalibela. Then the Derg soldiers came to our school. They made us stand in a line, and they took all the boys away. We could not say good-bye to our mothers, our fathers."

The Derg soldiers loaded Zelalem and his classmates, all teenagers, onto heavily guarded buses and drove them south into the desert beyond the Blue Nile. They traveled for three days to an army training camp close to the Didesa river, one of the Nile's big tributaries, which we would be floating past in about a week's time. "They shaved my hair, took away my student clothes, and gave me a soldier's clothes. They trained us to use the Kalash," Zelalem said, using the Ethiopian abbreviation for the weapon.

Many of the student-soldiers died, either from disease or from trying to escape. "The desert there was just a wilderness, like this," he said "The Shangalla [Gumuz] people lived there, and they would spear you if they found you." Malaria, though, was the biggest killer. "Too many students died from that," Zelalem continued. "But the soldiers didn't care; they'd just throw the bodies somewhere. Even if your own brother died in the camp, you must not cry or say something sad…because why? Because you are a soldier." After their training, many of the students were sent to the north to fight the EPRDF. Zelalem was lucky. The camp's commander had taken a liking to him, and kept him there as his attendant. Only at the end of the war, as the Derg was collapsing, was Zelalem's unit dispatched to the front, near Addis.

"We saw the EPRDF soldiers," Zelalem said. "But we did not fight them. The war was over. Why fight?" Instead, he and his fellow students surrendered, laying down their Kalashnikovs. For a few days, the EPRDF held them in a large camp, and then asked them what they wanted to do.

"We said, 'We want to go to our homes.' So they said, 'Then go.'"

Zelalem headed for Addis where he had relatives. "They were very frightened when they see me dressed in the Derg uniform. But they hid me, gave me clothes, food. That was when I wanted so much to see Thaitu, my sister. We were very close." But Thaitu had died in childbirth while he was gone; the baby had died, too. "That was very hard for me," Zelalem said. It was then that he had assumed the responsibility for Hailu, telling his parents that he would help to support and raise his nephew, although he had no idea how he would do so.

After the war, his cousin Yohannes, who had started a small tourist business, introduced him to Conrad. "Conrad taught me this work: how to be a guide, how to cook for the tourists, how to make a camp. He gave me work, money, so I can help my family. That is why he is like my father."

We were sitting on some large boulders next to the Blue Nile, and after he finished his story, we sat there awhile longer, listening to it flow by, steady and soothing. But I thought, even all the waters of the Nile could not wash away some of the sorrows in Zelalem's heart.

IN THE MORNING, I TOLD NEVADA AND MIKE SPEAKS ABOUT Zelalem's comments about the shifta, and why Kassa and the River Man were both probably right: There were no shifta in the gorge.

"Maybe that's why Conrad was certain this trip could be done without any bandit problems," I said.

"Let's hope it's true," Speaks said.

Zelalem's story made sense, but we also knew that we could still be mistaken for an invading force of foreigners and killed by patriots, even if there were no shifta about. That's why traveling with Ethiopians like Zelalem, Kassa, and Ephrem was sensible; they could explain our journey to any suspicious militiamen or soldiers.

We were now one day's journey from the big Abay Bridge, which would mark the first real test of our permits and how seriously armed Ethiopians perceived us. Kassa would leave us at the bridge, since the next stretch of the river took us through an uninhabited gorge where we presumably would not need the protection of a militiaman and his Kalashnikov.

The wide, river canyon we were floating through on this day, however, was very much inhabited. Densely planted cornfields stretched along both banks, and the farmers were busy plowing more land. They stopped to shout and wave, making Zelalem laugh.

"You know what they are saying? 'Look what's coming down the river! Boats on the Abay! *Konjo! Konjo! Konjo!*'"

We were once again tarik.

Past the cornfields, the land rose up again in big, rocky hills. A smoky haze hung over them, and a large group of people were busy close to the shore.

"Is it a fire?" I asked.

"No, they are making charcoal," Zelalem said.

It was against the law, he added, for people to chop down the forest, like this, to make charcoal, since everyone knew that doing this would cause bigger problems, like losing more topsoil to the Nile. But the government had not been able to enforce its ban. "Everyone in Addis likes to use charcoal for heating and making coffee," he said, shrugging. "The police sometimes check the trucks and buses to look for charcoal, but they can't stop it." There was too much demand.

We tied up our boats below the charcoal makers' camp and climbed the hill. There some small homes nearby, and women and children—the first women we had seen on the river. They were dressed in Western-style dresses and wore plastic shoes, a sign that we were close to a highway and a big town. That's what made this small industry possible, too. They didn't have to travel far to get their product sent on its way to the city markets.

All the people were Amhara. The women and children tended their corn and sorghum crops, while the men made the charcoal. They chopped down the trees, dug the pits, tended the fires, and packed the finished product in gunny sacks. It was hard work, and although several of the men were in their early twenties, they were all as gaunt as the tree limbs they cut, and as crooked, too. Their faces, hair and skin were coated with black soot from the smoke, and they looked tired and unhappy.

The nearby hills had been nearly denuded from this charcoal enterprise, and Mick asked the men if they knew the harm they were causing.

"We tried to replant, but the seedlings failed," said Belay Alebachew, through Zelalem. "And we worry, because we know this can make the hills like those in Wollo [where there were bad droughts and famines in the mid-1970s and '80s]. But what can we do? We have to make a living."

Another man stepped forward. He was angry. "We were born here, so we are working here. We can't change our country. And the new government doesn't give us other work. This is work we can do."

He turned away, a bitter look on his face.

For all their hard work, they made very little money, about 10 birr, or $.80, for each bag. And they had to cut down almost five trees to fill a single bag. They had depleted most of this forest, and knew it. "We're going to have to move," Belay said. "We have to find some other place."

The people here didn't think about the river at all, Zelalem said, when I asked. It flowed past their homes, and their dry, sooty hill, and it gave them water. But it was the trees that gave them a livelihood, and now they were gone.

Farther downstream, the forest reappeared.

"I think maybe the charcoal people will be here next year," Zelalem said.

We all thought so, too.

AROUND TEN O'CLOCK THE NEXT MORNING, WE ROUNDED A BEND AND saw our first goal: the big Abay Bridge. Speaks slowed down and studied the bridge with his binoculars.

"There are some soldiers…and there's Mau and Yohannes!"

Our men from Addis were right on schedule with fresh supplies and news. Their presence also meant that the soldiers knew we were coming. No one was going to fire a protective shot on their country's behalf.

We rowed ashore to shouts and cheers from the soldiers and our friends. Mau and Yohannes had brought a big cooler of beers and cold drinks, and a basket of injera drenched in a meat sauce. We climbed up beneath the bridge to the shade of a cool fig tree and ate and drank, while answering a hundred questions about our journey.

Yes, everything had gone smoothly. No, we'd had no trouble from any of the people, and the crocs weren't bad. It was a good, a wonderful trip, and we were ready for more.

Mau had printed out a stack of e-mail messages that our friends and family had sent us, and we each sat quietly reading news of home. Nothing much had changed in the world, although there had been a terrible earthquake in Taiwan, Mau said. Two thousand people had died. And, yes, the war with Eritrea was still being fought. Some American diplomats had tried to get both sides to negotiate, but their efforts had failed, and they'd left the country. Zelalem, who hated the war, looked disgusted.

Mau and Yohannes had also brought us fresh vegetables, tomatoes, eggs, and frozen chickens. "We're going to have a feast tonight," Speaks said, after packing the food into his raft's cooler. "We could have finally impressed Kassa."

But Kassa was getting ready to head to his Gojami home. Mau counted out his wages, and we gave him a handsome tip. It was enough, he told us, to buy a new ox, and clothes for his wife and kids. He was going to name his ox *Daragote ferenjocch*, "Gift from the Tourists."

Kassa gave us each many kisses on both cheeks, as is the Ethiopian custom, and his eyes filled with tears.

"He says he never expected to be part of our group," Zelalem translated. "He thought he would be doing things alone. So he thanks you for including him, and he wishes he could go with you all the way to Sudan, but he does not have permission to take his gun there. He thanks you and wishes you good travels."

Many of the soldiers on the bridge gave us letters they had written to take with us to the next modern bridge, about 150 miles farther down the Nile, where their friends were stationed. They imagined their friends laughing when they received their mail via our boats. Nevada packed the letters in one of her waterproof cases. Then we bid the soldiers, Mau, Yohannes, and Kassa a final farewell.

By 12:30 in the afternoon, we were once again traveling along the Blue Nile.

~~~

seventeen

"LOOK AT WHERE WE'RE GOING. WAY OUT THERE...JUST WAY out there," Mike Speaks said as we left the Abay Bridge behind and followed the river into a vast, open valley framed by long plateaus and distant peaks. The Blue Nile was turning again, completing its circle around Gojam, and setting us on a westerly course. The sun shone brightly on the water, drawing us on like a guiding star.

No foreigners had traveled on this part of the Blue Nile for almost 30 years. We were likely to be a great surprise to those who lived along the river, particularly as we got closer to Sudan. The countryside here was again heavily farmed with big fields of corn and sorghum close to the water's edge. The gullies and hills between the crops were thickly forested in acacia and hagenia trees. Euphorbias, too, grew in dense clusters, raising their spiny arms to the sky as if in prayer.

Down on the river, in the narrower sections of the gorge, it had been easy to lose sight of the immense canyonlands the Abay and its tributaries had carved. But now with the vistas opened up, we could see the basaltic capstone at the tops of the plateaus, some 6,000 feet above us. The black basalt had been our geological marker on the first several days of our trip; now it towered over our heads. In most places, the basalt was just a crown at the top of a mountain that descended like a wedding cake in ever widening tiers of cream-colored limestone and red sandstone. Although it was difficult if not impossible to see from our perspective, we knew that the distant plateaus on either side of the gorge were more than 12 miles apart. No warriors here could ever hope to leap across the full width of this canyon.

Without Kassa to sing our way downstream, our group fell quiet. A few hornbills flew over the water in an up-and-down pattern, as if riding an invisible roller coaster, and huge colonies of buffalo weaverbirds chattered and flitted among the shoreline elephant grass.

"Hippo!" Mike Speaks shouted, nodding to his left. The animal was nearly submerged, only its nose, eyes, and ears poked above the waterline. It snorted, sank from view, and resurfaced, twiddling its ears as if trying to fine-tune its scanner—what were these strange things coming down the Nile?

Aside from the baboons, monkeys, and crocodiles, we'd not seen many animals along the Nile. Kate and Kelly had been lucky and spotted a lone lioness coming down to the river one afternoon. We could expect to see more wildlife after we entered the Black Gorge as the British team had dubbed the stretch of canyon we expected to reach the next day. It was said to be uninhabited, the shoreline too steep for crops, and thus wild and densely forested.

At our camp that night, there were already signs of more wildlife. Hyena, civet cat, antelope, and baboon tracks covered the beach. There were crocodile tracks, too, but close to the water's edge. We pitched our tents higher up the beach, far away from their claw prints.

The moon was full that night, and cast a soft, silver light that flickered across the Nile. A bright planet—Jupiter—hove into view a little later, and the two rode the black waters of the night, a diamond in pursuit of a pearl. *Konjo!* I thought to myself. Absolutely *konjo.*

In the morning, a thick fog hung over the Nile, muffling the river and the calls of the morning birds. It didn't keep the baboons away. They crept down a cliff and sat in a tree above our camp to bark at us. They were probably used to stealing from people, and watched us to see if we might leave a pot open or a loaf of bread untended.

Downstream, we traveled into birders' territory. Black-capped chattas, red bishop birds, and weavers sang from the riverside grasses, and a flock of dark green hoopoes swept by, flashing the white undersides of their wings. White-rumped swallows skimmed along like daredevil speedsters, making sudden turns to catch a fly, and emerald green beeeaters darted into the air after their prized food—bees. A lilac-breasted roller flew along the shoreline, its plumage a rainbow melange of turquoises, lavenders, and blues. There were Egyptian and common plovers on the beaches, prying the sands with their beaks, and fish eagles, fantailed ravens, and black eagles soaring overhead. Speaks was having a grand time, and nearly brought his raft to a complete stop when he spotted a verreaux's eagle. It was a large bird with black feathers, except for its rump and the middle of its back, which were snowy white.

"That makes the trip for me," Speaks said, smiling broadly. "Don't see those too often."

I'd taken to riding on Speaks's raft. He almost always rowed the lead boat, and we were more likely to see wildlife and people first. I usually took notes and kept a record of the passing scenery, people, and animals.

Mick and Bruce, in another boat, were sort of a team, since Bruce was also working as Mick's assistant cameraman. He was the big talker in our group. He'd settled down a little bit, but still had difficulty simply sitting on a raft after the work he'd done filming in Bosnia. I sympathized. I'd preferred trekking in the mountains, and sometimes felt, as we drifted down the river, as if we were watching a movie. I was always happier when we pulled ashore and went for a hike or met the local people. Then I felt part of the river and its ways, not just a passive spectator.

Mick could barely abide the silence of the river. You had to be a listener if you traveled on his boat. He told of his peripatetic childhood, when his parents uprooted the family year after year. They'd lost their home in Rhodesia, after it became Zimbabwe, and then traveled the globe. His father was a doctor, and they lived everywhere from Indonesia and New Guinea to New Zealand before settling in Australia. Over the years, they'd moved in and out of something like 30 different homes, and he described them all in great detail. He told about his sexual escapades in equally great detail, and wanted to nose his way into mine. And he told about Bosnia, the excitement of working alongside hardcore war correspondents, the adrenaline rush of getting caught in an angry crowd, and the horror of watching that crowd turn against a young man identified as a Communist. "They beat him to a pulp, and they told me and my brother to just stay away, to leave him lying there, and threatened us if we tried to help him." Mick was torn over his Bosnian experiences. He'd loved the heart-pounding thrill of filming the riots and war scenes, but hated what he'd seen.

When Mick ran out of things to say, he opened Walt Whitman's *Leaves of Grass*, and read aloud. He had a good reading voice, and Whitman's rich words were just right for traveling down the Nile: "Out of the cradle, endlessly rocking…"

At mid-morning, we passed the broad delta of the big Muger River, which spilled into the Blue Nile from the left-hand, Shoa side. You could almost feel the Abay burp as this fresh volume of water poured into its stomach. It let out its belt, and widened again, increasing to some 400 feet across. Despite the added volume, the river still chugged along at a steady clip, and gave us some good, fun runs up and down several short haystack rapids.

Just below one of these, we spotted a lone man on shore, and pulled over to greet him. Zelalem had told us that today (September 27) was an Ethiopian holiday, a Church celebration called Meskal, which celebrates the discovery of the True Cross as well as the arrival of a piece of that cross in Ethiopia. Many Ethiopians believe that Jesus's cross was discovered by an Ethiopian princess, although other Christian traditions say that Britain's Empress Helena found it. Either way, some of the cross was enshrined in the basilica of the Church of the Resurrection in Jerusalem, and the rest carried to Rome, where a Church of the Holy Cross was built to house it. Then in the late 14th century, during the reign of Ethiopia's King Dawit I, a priest brought part of the cross from Jerusalem to Ethiopia.

"It is a very special holy day," Zelalem said. "Everyone makes big fires to celebrate, and they kill a cow or sheep to feast on." Earlier in the day, he'd told us that we shouldn't expect to see many people on the river, since most would be at home for the festivities.

We were, thus, surprised to see this man working in his corn patch. He was tall and terribly thin, his skin stretched drumtight over his high cheekbones. He stopped his hoeing when he saw us, and introduced himself.

"His name is Maru Zambate," Zelalem translated, "and he is an Oromo. He has been living here for two weeks to grow this corn. His village is three hours away by foot."

We wondered if there were any villages closer to the river where we might see some of the Meskal celebrations.

"No, he says the people don't come to the river for that. But they do come next month for a big baptism celebration." If we could wait four days, we could see this.

That wasn't possible, we said, we had to keep moving downstream. Maru nodded, then said something quietly to Zelalem, while pointing to his patched and torn clothing.

Zelalem smiled. "You know he is a little embarrassed to meet you, because he is dressed poorly. He says he is so poor because he has eight children."

We protested that we were pleased to meet him, that it was always interesting for us as travelers to meet the people who lived on the Nile. But why wasn't he at home with his children on this feast day?

Maru looked down. "He says, 'Because I am poor. I have nothing to give my children.' Six of his eight children have malaria, even his wife is sick with it. He says she is thin as a stick." Zelalem shook his head. "This is a hard life."

Maru spoke again. "Poor people come here to grow corn," Zelalem translated, "because there is nowhere else. But if you come here to farm, you will also get sick with malaria. It wasn't always like this, he says. But now the malaria is worse. We don't know why, he says, because we are not educated." Later Zelalem told me that the incidence of malaria had increased dramatically in Ethiopia after the Derg stopped the mosquito-control program that had operated during Haile Selassie's reign. The new government, he said, was trying to reintroduce the program. Their job is all the more difficult because, for a variety of reasons, the strains of malaria have grown increasingly lethal as well as resistant to drugs used to treat or prevent the disease.

Speaks had gone back to the raft and put together a gift of yarn and needles and buttons. Then he added a stack of one birr bills, 20 of them (the equivalent of $1.60). To Maru's utter astonishment, Speaks placed everything in his hands.

"Tell him that because he is a proud man and a working man, we want to help him," Speaks said to Zelalem. "He can take this money and buy a feast for his children."

Overcome, Maru dropped to Speaks's feet and hugged them, and wept.

"*Baca, baca*—It is enough," Zelalem said softly to Maru, lifting him gently by the elbow.

Maru still could not speak, and simply dropped to his knees again, once more hugging Speaks's feet. Zelalem leaned forward to talk to him. Maru slowly rose, pressing his gifts in his arms.

"He says he is going home now to tell his family of his good fortune, and your kindness," Zelalem said. "He thanks you and he says that Mary and Joseph will bless you."

Maru stood next to the river as we boarded our rafts, and waved farewell.

"He can maybe buy one or two chickens now for his family," Zelalem said, "and have a small feast."

WE SAW ONE MORE GROUP OF PEOPLE ON SHORE THAT MESKAL DAY. The river was narrowing again, squeezing its bulk down to fit between the hard, metamorphic rocks of the approaching Black Gorge. The land was shifting, too. It tilted up in sharply pitched but rounded hills. Park-like glades of tall grass grew amid the broad-leaved trees, and Zelalem said that was the best grass for making thatched roofs. We rounded a bend, and there standing among a stack of big boulders on the Gojam shore was a group of about ten men and teenage boys. They were dressed in shirts and shorts, with turbans wrapped on their heads, and the moment they spied us, they fled. Turbans, walking sticks, and baskets flew in all directions as they raced up the slope and into the bushes. Some even climbed the trees. It was as if a cat had pounced on a flock of birds.

"*Ayezoh! Ayezoh! Ayezoh!*—Don't worry!" Zelalem shouted, standing up on the raft so that they could see there was an Ethiopian on this airplane.

We began slowly rowing to shore, while Zelalem continued to call to them, telling them that we were friends and tourists, and we meant them no harm. It was okay, we wanted only to greet them.

Hesitantly, some of the older men came back down the hill. But they stood far back from the rocks, ready to make their escape again if need be. Some of the younger boys still hid in the trees and watched the proceedings from their safe perches.

The boatmen butted the boats against the rocks, using their oars to hold us in place, while Zelalem talked.

"They live on a mountain up there," he said, pointing his chin toward a distant spot beyond the hills. "It is a three-hour walk, and they say they only came to the river today to get a drink from the Abay. It is holy water for them. They will take some back to their village, and then they will have their Meskal feast."

"I don't think they have seen a ferenji before," Zelalem added. "They were worried when they saw us. They thought maybe we are coming to invade."

One of the men spoke to Zelalem, then shook his head and took a few brave steps forward to get a better look at our rafts.

"He wanted to know what we are doing and I told him we are going to Sudan. Really, he cannot believe this."

They talked a little longer. Then Zelalem wished them a good feast, and Speaks pulled on his oars, pivoting his raft back into the river's mainstream. A couple of the men spoke with each other as we left, and Zelalem caught their words and began laughing.

"You know what he is saying? He says, 'I feel so lucky. If I hadn't come to the Abay today, I would never have seen this, or met these people. Now, I have something special to tell when I go home.'"

They were the last people we saw on shore for the next three days.

A few miles downstream, we spotted the remains—or more accurately, the beginnings—of Castanio's Bridge. Two well-designed and constructed abutments of mortar-and-granite blocks faced each other on the opposite shores. A tangle of vines and bushes grew across them, but otherwise, the abutments looked like the building blocks of any sturdy, modern bridge. What was missing, of course, was the bridge.

The British consul Cheesman had actually met Signor Castanio in Addis in the 1930s. The signor worked for the Ethiopian government as an engineer, and he was, by the time Cheesman met him, well advanced in years. Thirty years before, at the turn of the century, the Emperor Menelik had given him a choice commission: to build the first modern bridge spanning the Blue Nile. Castanio took a team of hard workers to the gorge, a ten-day mule journey from Addis, and chose this spot, where a bridge about 200 feet long could be built. They found a granite outcrop in the hillside, and quarried and carved the blocks by hand there, then mixed the mortar from limestone they brought from Addis. All was finished on schedule. Castanio had ordered the massive iron girders to complete the bridge from a firm in Milan. With the abutments in place, he rode back to Addis to check on the girders' delivery. There, he learned that the ironwork had been lost somewhere between the coastal port of Djibouti and Addis. As Cheesman notes in his book, "One would scarcely think the ironwork of a bridge an easy thing to lose, but the story goes that there was no trace of it."

Castanio placed and paid for a second order with the Milanese firm. It, too, arrived safely in Djibouti. And it, too, vanished, as if by magic, somewhere between that port and the Ethiopian capital. Castanio did not try again, and the bridge project was abandoned and then forgotten. The bridge would have "connected Addis Ababa by road with the rich and powerful province of Gojam," Cheesman wrote. "[I]t is conceivable that the people of Gojam were not…enthusiastic over a bridge that would weaken their power," and may have had a hand in the ironwork's disappearance. Not for nothing did the people of Gojam have a reputation for being skilled magicians, although probably the only wand the Ras of Gojam needed to wave was money.

The abutments were still in good condition in Cheesman's day, and not long after he inspected them, the government installed a ferry. Using a system of cables, ropes, and pulleys that ran through the abutments, a 16-by-12 foot, flat-bottomed iron boat was pulled from one shore to the other. But even this slim connection was severed when the Italians invaded.

The day we floated past Castanio's folly, the abutments still appeared perfectly sound, and one of the old pulley cables was still in place, 30 feet above our heads.

The canyon continued to narrow, and the river followed a pronounced zigzag course, although each bend was short, about a half-mile long. Then we entered the Black Gorge. The British named it for the dark, sculptured rocks along the shores. These are some of the oldest rocks in the gorge, dating to Precambrian times, some 700 million to one billion years ago, when multicellular life was just beginning to explode on Earth. Marbles and gneisses, quartzites and schists, the rock is hard, shot through with intrusions, and beautiful.

In some places, the shores were solely paved with icy white-and-blue marble, like a king's palace. Beyond the marble, dark cliffs of gneiss rose out of the water like the walls of a moat, and on every turret, a baboon perched like a sentinel. Some barked out alarms, others were content to let us pass, although they scrutinized us closely. The cliffs were hung with mosses, ferns, and grasses, like delicate hanging gardens, and fig trees draped their roots left and right like living ropes, binding everything in place. Pretty vines with heart-shaped leaves wove in and out of the forest's trees, lending the woods a fairy-tale quality, too, as if some sorcerer had charmed them into being. Once or twice, we saw tiny klipspringer antelopes balancing like ballerinas on their dainty hoofs at the water's edge, but they spun and leaped into the forest as soon as they spotted us.

More crocodiles appeared, too, and they were bold. They slipped into the river and made straight for our boats. Some were belligerent and rode high on the water, so we could see every jagged, rough scale on their backs; others were secretive, and it was only the bowline of their snouts that gave them away. But they all dived into the depths or turned away when they realized we were too big to tangle with, or smelled that the rubber boats were unpalatable.

There were bugs, too, hard, black sand flies that swarmed in thick flocks, and pelted our faces like sharp bits of pepper. We all stopped talking and bent our heads to the side, trying to avoid them. They liked Nevada the most, but she claimed, all insects always liked her the most. I had only a couple of itchy bites, but she had scores of them, and from insects I had never seen. Indeed, a swarm of the sand flies seemed to settle right over her head as we rowed downstream. "I can't believe it," she said, swatting at them. "They're fornicating on the wing—and right in front of me!"

We camped that night on a broad beach next to the Guder River, another huge tributary that comes into the Nile from the left-hand, Shoa side of the river. The canyon was narrow here, and the mountains rose steeply right from the water's edge, as we'd been told. There wasn't a sign of a soul about. And there wasn't a breeze. It was still and black, hot, and dark, the kind of country a jinn could most appreciate. I shoved my sleeping bag aside and slept only on my mat, feeling the sweat trickle down my sides.

eighteen

THE BLACK GORGE HELD THE BLUE NILE'S BIGGEST AND rough-
est rapids. This was the section of the river we had scouted from
the air, and the next morning, Speaks went over what we could expect.

"We're going to hit a series of big V-waves," he said, raising his arms
in the air to form that letter of the alphabet. "They won't all come at
once; there'll be some smooth water in between where we'll regroup.
But we'll be going up one side of these waves and crashing down the
other, and there's a huge potential for inundation from waves coming
over the side and top of the boat. We want the boats to be facing straight
into the waves, because we don't want any flips. This is big water and
we're going to have some big drops. I want everyone holding on tight."

Speaks thought we would run the first big wave sometime that morning. "This is the one that caught Arne Rubin [the lone kayaker who ran
part of the Blue Nile in 1965] and the Brits by surprise. It was bigger,
rougher than they expected, and that woke 'em up, made them pay attention to the next ones," he said.

None of the other rapids matched this first one, however, and our predecessors had finally settled back and enjoyed the ride, said Speaks. He thought we could do the same.

Speaks wanted us alert and ready, our river bags well-sealed and every piece of gear lashed down tight.

By 9:30 a.m. we were once again on the Nile. The river wound its way through a canyon of big, sculptured boulders. Its pace was steady, determined, and its level was high—although not as high as it had evidently been in the past. Mike Borcik spotted wads of brushy debris jammed in tree crotches about 20 feet above us. "Guess that would be your highwater mark," he said. "Wouldn't want to be here then."

I was riding with Nevada on Borcik's boat, having agreed to play the role of "photo victim" during the rapids. Borcik could position our raft for the wildest, wettest ride—one that would dump plenty of water over my head—and Nevada could shoot away with her underwater camera while I screamed and (I hoped) laughed.

An hour downstream, a crocodile surfaced, a big one. As usual, Mike Speaks's boat was in the lead. The croc raised its head, opened its jaws, and launched itself toward the raft. Speaks saw it, grabbed a rock from his "croc rock bucket," and threw a pitch that smacked its target on the snout. The crocodile sank below the surface, and Speaks pummeled the water with an oar. But then the croc resurfaced inches from the raft. Speaks flailed with his oar, and the croc finally gave up the chase, sinking again before reappearing close to shore.

"Hey, that was pretty wild there, Captain Speaks," Borcik called out.

Speaks looked back at us, his mouth wide open, and thumped his chest with his hand to illustrate just how fast and hard his heart was pumping.

Another hour downstream, and we heard the telltale roar of white water. "That's got to be Arne Rubin's surprise wave," said Speaks.

We tied the boats onshore and scouted the rapid.

The three boatmen stood on a boulder overlooking the crashing waves to find the best route. The river was the color of dark chocolate, and heaved over a five-foot drop, then rolled right back up into a six-foot-high fist of a wave. The Ethiopians had it right, I thought, when they called this river the Tikkur Abay—the Black Nile. It was darker than mud, and that fist was just waiting to hit something. Beyond the big drop and wave, the Nile pitched along in several tall, pointy peaks before settling into a little riffle. Nevada stood watching the river with me.

"It's a pretty straightforward run," she said. "It's just that the first wave is so big. They've got to be prepared for the hit."

The boatmen rejoined our group.

"We'll run two boats together, one right behind the other," Speaks said. "That way at least one should be upright at the end and can pick up any people if the other has trouble. Then we'll wait for the third boat."

Nevada and I were in the last boat, Borcik's. She climbed down close to the water to photograph the other two as they slammed into that wave. Speaks went first, swinging his raft into position on the wet slide into the rapid. He stood up on his boat, balancing his oars with the poise of a tennis player, watching the water for the right moment. Then he sat down, grabbed the oars, pulled hard against the current to steady the boat as it fell over the drop. The wave rose up and the fist slapped down mercilessly on Kelly and Ephrem. They disappeared under buckets of brown-and-cream water, then came up laughing. Speaks pulled hard again, and his raft rode high up and over the wave and down the other side, and bucked its way downstream through the high-peaked train of rapids.

Bruce's run was equally smooth and fun, and Kate gave a thumbs-up as they pulled into a downstream eddy. Since this was her first white-water trip, she'd been a bit anxious about going through the Black Gorge's rapids. Now, the worst one was behind her.

Borcik set our boat up for the wettest run possible, and when we crashed into the hole, it felt like we'd gone over Niagara Falls. A mountain of water fell over my head and back, knocking off my hat and sunglasses. I screamed, I laughed, I gave the photo-victim shots my all. Then we were airborne over the top of the wave and crashing up and down the next set like a tiny boat on a big sea.

"Well, if that was Arne Rubin's worse, I think we'll be okay," said Speaks. "That was just a good, fun run."

We crashed through some smaller rapids that day and we had—or Speaks's boat had—more croc attacks. The reptiles liked his raft so much that Borcik began referring to it as the "SS Croc Bait."

And we saw more wildlife: black-and-white colobus monkeys, sitting high in the acacia trees, dusky-colored kudus, tiny forest dik-diks, the smallest of the antelopes, hippos, and monitor lizards that climbed like robots over the rocks, then leaped into the Nile to swim away.

The woods were full of animals, and at night even over the roar of the river, we heard the high-pitched, unearthly cries of tree hyraxes and the puppy-doglike whimpers of bush babies. They could leave your nerves unsettled, as if someone were being mugged out there, but then, there'd be the softer sound of a scops owl, like a small, tinkling bell, signaling "all is well, all is well" even here in the Black Gorge of the Blue Nile.

FOR THE NEXT TWO DAYS, WE JOURNEYED THROUGH THE BLACK GORGE. It was always hot and stifling, and it rained a little every night. Once, after dinner, we sat onshore entranced as lightening flashed over the river and mountains, and the thunder rolled like boulders crashing down the Nile.

Then slowly, almost imperceptibly, the river began to widen again. The mountains still rose in a steep pitch from the water's edge, but they were rounder, softer, less forbidding. We were coming to the end of the Black Gorge, and would soon be at the Gumare (Amharic for "hippopotamus") Bridge, where we would bid Kelly adieu. That morning, October 1, we raised our coffee mugs and gave him a toast to thank him for dreaming up this wonderful trip. Kelly turned momentarily shy and tried to pass all the credit to Nevada, but she shoved it right back.

"No, it was you, Kelly, who first said, 'What about the Blue Nile?'" she teased. "And we're glad you did."

Like the Abay Bridge, the Gumare is a modern, highway bridge with a concrete-and-steel span crossing the river. The cement was heavily pockmarked with what appeared to be bullet holes, and when I commented on this to Zelalem, he said, "Yes, there was a big soldiers' war here. The EPRDF attacked the Derg and chased them away."

That was probably the most activity the bridge has ever seen. Today, very little traffic crosses its expanse (two vehicles a day on average), and the soldiers guarding it find their duty dull and tedious. Our appearance was, thus, a cause for celebration. Every man on duty came down to the river to shake our hands and ask about our trip. Their smiles grew even bigger when Nevada gave them the letters their friends at the Abay Bridge had sent.

Maurizio was once again on hand to welcome us. As before, he had a lunch basket of injera and meat for us, a cooler stashed with cold drinks, and fresh supplies to replenish our food stores. He had also brought an outboard motor, which the boatmen planned to use farther down the river, close to the border and Roseires Dam, where the current grew sluggish. The river would be wide there, and they intended to lash the three boats together in a triangle, attach the motor to the raft in the rear of the formation, and cruise the last 60-odd miles.

Past the Gumare Bridge, we would be entering the land of the Gumuz people, a Nilotic tribe, utterly different from the highland peoples we'd come to know. These were the people the Amharas had used as slaves in the past. For centuries, the Amharas had raided the Gumuz and other Nilotic peoples, capturing men, women, and children, then marching them up into the mountains. Some they kept as slaves for themselves; others they sold to traders traveling to Egypt or the Arabian Peninusla. The raids had fully stopped only after World War II, but the Gumuz had not forgotten how they had been treated.

Zelalem had been stationed among the Gumuz during his military training, and he knew full well how they disliked the highlanders. "They don't trust people who wear clothes," he said, pulling at his pants. "They may throw spears first when they see us. So it's better if we have someone with us who can talk to them, who knows their language."

Maurizio had the same idea and had already sent his assistant to a nearby village to locate a suitable Gumuz guide. About a half hour later, Mau introduced us to our new protector: Melesse Sima. Tall and fit, with skin of a lustrous black hue, Melesse was in his late twenties. He had a round face and a ready smile, although at first we saw little of it. He had a slightly serious demeanor, and like Kassa before him, was unsure of what he was getting into. Melesse, we were told, spoke three languages: Amharic, Gumuzina, and Orominya. He could thus translate the words of the Gumuz people to Zelalem, who would then translate them into English for us. Melesse was also a member of his village's militia, and of course had his Kalashnikov with him.

Zelalem and Melesse struck up a conversation, and Zelalem turned to me. "He is singing in three languages," he said. "He knows proverbs and songs and will teach us."

We were going to be a musical flotilla once again, it seemed.

The new stores were loaded on the rafts, and the motor secured in a box. It was time to get under way. And in what was becoming something of a trip ritual, we all stood in a line as we had for Kassa's departure to hug and say goodbye to a good friend. We knew Kelly would have fun surprising his wife in St. Petersburg, but we would miss him. He stood on the bridge next to Mau and waved a long farewell as we floated away downstream.

We were about 325 miles from Lake Tana and had some 145 miles to go before we reached Sudan. The river continued to cut through the Precambrian metamorphic rocks, although the shoreline boulders were smaller and the canyon wider with big, broad banks of rich soil planted with sorghum and cotton—a sure sign of people.

We'd only traveled a few miles when we spotted our first group of Gumuz: men, women, and a few young kids, tending their cotton crop. They had long spears, bows, and arrows, and a couple of Kalashnikovs, but no one reached for a weapon. Instead they called to us, and Melesse, riding in Borcik's boat, called back.

"*Nehgay! Nehgay! Nehgay!*—Greetings! Greetings to all! Greetings!"

"Some of them are his [Melesse's] relatives," Zelalem told us.

Like Melesse, their skin was a deep, almost true black, and their faces oval, with wide, broad planes and small, flaring noses. Their eyes were black as obsidian, and almond-shaped, and their hair was short, black, and tightly curled. They were also wearing clothing: shorts and well-worn T-shirts for the men, and knee-length skirts and T-shirts for the women. The women stayed in the background, eyeing us curiously. They'd been gleaning the last tufts of cotton from scrubby little plants, and would later pick out the seeds.

"They come from a village that is a two-hour walk away," Zelalem said through Melesse. "And they come every day to work on their crops, or just to come to the river. They say they love this Abay River because he does good favors for them. He gives them good soil, good crops. They really believe in the Abay, and they give him a goat or a sheep to thank him."

When they sacrificed an animal, they also "read" its liver, looking for signs of the future.

They were, of course, surprised to see us. But we were not the first ferenjocch some of them had seen. Tule Balkachew, a well-wrinkled, gray-haired fellow who was barely more than five feet tall, said he remembered the 1968 British expedition.

"The British came here for one week. They came by boat with motors." And then Tule imitated the sound of the boat's motor: "*Brrrrpppppp...*" He shook his head and laughed.

"Because of that," Zelalem continued, "he says he knows very well what you are—tourists—and what the rafts are—boats."

Speaks produced a sharpening stone, and offered to put a fresh edge on the men's spears. The spears were stuck butt-first in the sand, and the men pulled them up and handed them to Speaks.

"They are using these weapons to kill animals to eat," Zelalem explained in answer to our questions. "And to protect themselves if people attack. This spear is too small for killing hippos, but they can use it to kill crocodiles and people, they say. They also kill antelopes and leopards, but no lions, because they don't see them now."

It was late in the afternoon and tall columns of thunderheads had built up behind the hills along the Nile, casting a blue-and-gold light over the land and our Gumuz hosts. When Nevada began taking photos, they asked her to please wait a minute, and sent a boy running back to a shelter. He returned with their robes of dark green and gold cotton. The men wrapped themselves in these, took their freshly sharpened spears in hand, and then posed for the camera.

We camped only a few miles farther downstream on one of the wide, sandy beaches. It was cool and cloudy and a few raindrops spattered as we ate a stir-fry dinner of fresh chicken and ginger. The weather matched our group's mood: Mike Borcik and Bruce had sore throats and were feeling feverish, several of us (including me) had a nasty, burning foot rot, and we all missed Kelly. We turned in early.

THE GUMUZ AND THEIR COTTON CROPS WERE A SURE SIGN THAT we had entered the lowlands of the Blue Nile. Our elevation was now about 2,500 feet. We were in tropical Africa, we kept telling ourselves, even though the weather said otherwise: the morning was cold, and as rainy and gray as London in March.

We pulled out our rain jackets and shuffled to the campfire for breakfast and to warm our hands. Speaks had red pepper and green onion omelets and bacon on the grill, and Bruce had a stack of toast ready to serve with jam and honey. And there was a newly opened bottle of fire-hot, hot sauce to cheer the Ethiopians on our crew. The guys were trying. But they couldn't outdo the weather. We ate huddled under our umbrellas, and the rain fell even harder.

"Melesse says it can rain all day," Zelalem said. "It is good; it will make the crops fat."

We nodded glumly and headed back to our tents. We were supposedly traveling in the "dry season," but learned that the rainy season had come a little later than expected in the highlands, while down here, it was right on schedule. "It should rain this time of year," Melesse told Zelalem.

Melesse was about as on-target a weatherman as most, and around 11 a.m. the rain stopped. The sun came out and suddenly it was hot. We packed quickly and got back on the river, where a cool breeze was blowing, but we didn't travel far. A man and woman stood on the opposite shore, waving, and we rowed across to greet them.

Melesse shook the man's hand and introduced us. "His name is Demechew Banga, and his wife is Dunguch Tefere," Zelalem translated. "They saw us camping here last night and were at first afraid. Then they saw Melesse was with us, so they decided to stay here and try to meet us."

Demechew was thin, but strongly muscled, and had a handsome, square-jawed face with high, flaring cheekbones. His wife, Dunguch, had broader features and pretty, almost Asian-shaped eyes, and wore a row of copper and brass bracelets on each arm. She had a large gourd filled with colored corn cobs hung on a stick that she balanced over her shoulder. Dunguch barely looked at us, and when she did, kept her expression flat and emotionless, until I caught her eye and smiled. Her eyes sparkled then, and she smiled back, then set her gourd on the ground and offered us an armload of fresh corn.

They had a little yellow cur dog with them, the first dog we'd seen on the Blue Nile. Most of us were a bunch of sappy dog-lovers and we tried to make friends, calling to it by name, *Lemcha! Lemcha!* (Lion), but we must have smelled strange, if not downright bad. Lemcha stood off by the cornfield, ears and tail down, until Dunguch tossed a rock at him and he skipped away.

In answer to our queries, Demechew told us about their crops—corn, cotton, flax, and sorghum—and their six children, who were back at their village, a five-hour walk away, and the wonderful Abay that gave them this good life. Like other people along the river, the couple was curious about our rafts, and we invited them to take a closer look. They ran their hands across the rubber, and shook their heads when Zelalem told them that the boats could be deflated and rolled up. Zelalem translated: "He is saying that when they saw us in our camp and in our boats, they thought, 'Can this be? Is it a dream?' And he says, 'I don't mind if I die now, after seeing this.'"

"He also has one question for me," Zelalem continued, laughing. "He asks what country Ephrem and I are from. He is surprised we are Ethiopians like him, because he says it is not usual for Ethiopians to travel like this."

Before we climbed back on our boats, we gave the couple a few bars of soap and razor blades. Zelalem had told us these would be the best presents on this stretch of the Nile, since most people lived far from markets and such goods were difficult to obtain; Maurizio had brought us a supply of each, along with pens to give to any school kids we might see. Borcik and Speaks had a couple of empty plastic bottles, and we handed these to them as well, along with a few birr for the corn.

Demechew had one last question before we shoved off. He had lived all his life along the Blue Nile, tilling the soil, harvesting his crops, watching the Nile's waters rise and fall with the seasons, and he wondered: Where does this river go?

IT WAS GOOD TO SEE PEOPLE ALONG THE BLUE NILE AGAIN, AND WE waved and called to every Gumuz we saw. Most waved and shouted back, although some stood thunderstruck, as if they could not make out what we were. Melesse called *"Nehgay, neghay,"* and no one threw any spears.

A few big tributaries wound their way down to the Nile through grassy, tree-dotted hills that reminded me of California's gold country. The river was broad and swift here with fast little riffles that made us bounce and always made Melesse laugh. He liked the feel of the raft on the river, he told Zelalem, and he liked watching the other boats pitch across the waves.

Melesse and Zelalem discovered that they had a shared history. Melesse had also been conscripted into the Derg army when in his late teens. The soldiers had grabbed him when he was working with a crew of men on the Gumare Bridge, and packed him off to the same Didesa training camp that Zelalem had been dumped in. "He only stayed two months," Zelalem said. "That camp is in his country. He knows the land, so he could escape." For two weeks, Melesse hid in the dry forest, living on fruits and roots he knew how to find, and finally made his way to the city of Nekempte, where "it was easy to find civilian clothes and hide from the military police."

Last year, he joined the EPRDF and received "good training" from them, and was subsequently elected to his town's militia. Yet, although he was a patriot, a militiaman, and member of the EPRDF, he did not like the war with Eritrea any more than Zelalem did.

"Some of my friends have gone there," he told Zelalem, "but they have not come back."

Zelalem frowned. "That is the problem. Many men go there, but they never come back. We know why. It is not a good war. But joining the army, it is the only job the government gives. They don't do this by force, like the Derg did. But if there are no jobs, it is the same thing. If you want a job and money, you must go to the army—and to this war."

He was quiet for a moment, then said with a sigh and a shrug, "You know, that is the problem with my country: It always has war. It is why we are poor."

Melesse wasn't as critical of the current government as Zelalem was, but Zelalem said that was to be expected: Melesse was a man from the countryside, and it was the peasantry who had built the EPRDF, overthrown the Derg, and made Ethiopia anew. "The government has many projects and work for the villages," Zelalem said. "They have schools now, new clinics, and if they have their own land and crops, then their life is good. They don't want anything more; they are not like people in the city." And because the government had done little to stimulate the urban economy, those in the city had trouble finding jobs. "It is why the city people are not so happy with this government."

Melesse and Zelalem were perfect examples of this Ethiopian dichotomy. Melesse, the countryman, had a contented quality about him, a surety about his future. He had a good piece of land that he farmed, and he had his militiaman's job which paid him a little extra money. Zelalem, the city dweller, was the opposite. At the end of this trip, if Conrad did not recover, he did not know what would become of him. He might try to make a living as a taxi driver, he once told me, but really he did not know what he would do, since Addis was filled with the unemployed. Zalalem's future was a weight on his mind.

Melesse had one problem, and he'd told Zelalem about it our first day. He needed a new wife.

"In the Gumuz culture," Zelalem explained, as we floated down river, "men give each other their sisters. That is how they get a wife. If you have a sister and you know a man with a sister, then you make an exchange."

Each man then had a wife. But if one of the sisters died, the bond between the men was broken, and the other wife was free to leave her husband. That is what had happened to Melesse. His sister (who was also his friend's wife) had died. Melesse's wife had then left him. They had one child, a boy of seven, who was staying now with Melesse's father. Melesse needed to find another wife, one who could be a mother to his son, and a helper on his farm. The search for a new Gumuz wife wasn't going well, since he had no more sisters to offer in the "exchange game."

"He could marry an Oromo woman," Zelalem said. "He says his brother did this. But I think maybe his Orominya is not that good, so the Oromo girls don't want to go with him."

Zelalem thought that one reason Melesse had joined our adventure was to look for a wife. "Maybe he will find one somewhere here."

It was hard for Nevada, Kate, and me to understand why a woman wouldn't want to marry Melesse. He was a handsome, strapping man with broad shoulders and a narrow waist that would have turned Scarlett O'Hara green with envy. He wore a bright blue boiler suit and a red webbed belt, which highlighted his good physique, although he was neither vain nor proud. He seemed a good, kindhearted man. We wanted to help him find his new wife.

WE FLOATED PAST SEVERAL SETTLEMENTS, WHERE SMALL CLUSTERS OF thatched-roofed houses were tucked in behind the fields of tall sorghum. A soft breeze blew over the Nile, and swallows skimmed overhead.

Nevada asked Speaks to stop at the next village we saw. We were curious about how the settlements here differed from those of the highlands. Speaks nodded, and when we saw an elderly man standing next to a sorghum field, we stopped.

"*Nehgay! Nehgay!*" he called to us.

He held his hands up in disbelief, then reached out to help us when he saw we were coming ashore.

"His name is Danyo Doye," said Zelalem, "and he cannot believe you are here. He heard about the British expedition, but he missed them and did not think he would ever see this."

Melesse asked if there was a village close by, and if it would be okay if we visited.

"Yes, yes," Danyo said.

A little girl—his youngest daughter—stood at his side, and he sent her to fetch his good shirt. Since the village, Botume, was some distance downriver, we suggested he come with us on our rafts. Danyo quickly climbed on board, patting the boat's rubber tube, and inspecting the floor. He approved.

We floated along to Botume—although we would never have known the village was there without Danyo's help. The houses were hidden behind the crops and not visible from the river. He knew the shoreline, though, and pointed to a place for us to stop. As we jumped ashore, several men came running out of the sorghum fields, Kalashnikovs and spears in hand, looks of alarm on their faces.

"*Nehgay!*" Melesse shouted. "*Salaam! Salaam!*"

Danyo was laughing. He spoke to the wild-eyed men, who dropped their weapons to their sides, and then sauntered up the riverbank smiling proudly as if to say, "Look what I found."

"They were afraid you were coming to attack," Melesse told Zelalem. "Now they can see you are here in peace, and that you are friends of Danyo's."

Danyo led the way into the village. Unlike the Amhara villages, where each home had a separate fenced yard, the houses here were clustered around a large center courtyard shaded by a big fig tree. People were going about their daily chores: One woman was pounding grains with a heavy wooden stick in a tall, wooden mortar, another was making clay storage pots; and several others were tending babies. A little boy held a toy bow and arrows, and ran to his mother as soon as he saw us. Most of the women wore T-shirts and cotton sarongs, and had decorative scars on their cheeks and upper arms. Their ears and noses were pierced, and they wore copper-and-beaded earrings, and little ivory or bone sticks through their septums.

We were equally exotic to them. At first they stared in simple disbelief, then they moved forward and surrounded us, touching our skin and petting and pulling at our hair.

"They think your hair is something you are wearing," Zelalem explained.

I had mine in pigtails, so I pulled out the rubber band to show them that the hair actually did grow from my head.

"Ayyy!" they cried in disbelief. Then they gave me an extra petting.

"Your hair is like a colobus monkey's," one woman told the fair-haired Nevada through Melesse and Zelalem. "Or maybe a lion's."

"Yours is like a baboon's," they told me. "And your eyes," they said, peering intently at mine, "are like a cat's." Then they laughed, putting their hands over their mouths to giggle.

Our skin was equal cause for consternation. They turned my arm over and studied the pale underside, then ran their fingers along it.

"Can this be skin?" they asked each other.

"Watch out," one man cautioned the honey-colored Zelalem. "You are beginning to fade like them."

They felt our smooth hands, too, and murmured among themselves.

"They can tell you do not grind corn," Zelalem said.

They weren't really sure that Kate, Nevada, and I were women, until we let them peek down our blouses. And they couldn't get over Bruce's hairy chest. "He is like an animal," they said.

We had noticed a small group of women next to one of the homes, and partly hidden behind a screen of woven palm strips. One older woman held the upper body of a younger one, whose face was tight with pain.

"She is giving birth," Zelalem said.

"Is she having any trouble?" Kate asked. "Would they like me to look?"

"They say, 'Yes, if you can help, you can look.'"

Kate walked behind the screen and returned a few minutes later. The woman had given birth before, but this baby had not yet crowned. "She's in the first stages. It'll be awhile yet, but she's doing okay." She'd been circumcized (a common custom in sub-Saharan Africa), Kate could see the scars, but these would not cause her any trouble in this delivery.

A woman in a patterned sarong tied prettily around her neck then appeared with an armload of corn.

"It is for our journey," Zelalem said.

We each took several cobs and thanked them, and Danyo guided us back to the Nile. Everyone followed, even the frightened little boy with the bow and arrows. One of the men spoke up, and Melesse passed his words to Zelalem.

"They say that Danyo is now the highest man in the village because he traveled on this boat and brought us to their village."

We gave them soap, razor blades, and some more empty plastic bottles. What they most wanted, we did not have: malaria medicine. Even here, among people who had lived with the disease for centuries and probably had some resistance to it, the new strains were taking their toll.

WE MADE ONE MORE STOP ON THE BLUE NILE THAT AFTERNOON. A group of men and women were busy planting a crop on the bank right next to the water. They had short, wooden hand hoes, capped with a metal blade, and they dug energetically into the soil, planting beans. They were working as a group for one man who had hired them all, they said, and they would share the crop.

I recalled hearing that some of the farming people of Kenya sing toe-tapping songs when they plant their crops, and somewhat idly I asked through our interpreters if these people had any such songs. They all stopped working and looked at one another. Then one man spoke with Melesse.

"He says, 'Yes, they sing, but they cannot now because they do not have their instruments. If you want, they will get these.'"

"Sure," Nevada and I said.

They dropped their hoes and ran off to their village, then returned with elaborate, fanciful horns made from gourds and bamboo and lashed together with leather. Some of the horns were a foot in length, others extended from their mouths to the ground. The women brought a big drum, and necklaces and anklets made of round seed pods. They fastened the anklets on their feet, while the men and boys placed their horns in the Nile, wetting them. Some scooped up mouthfuls of water and sprayed these over their instruments as well.

A tall, muscular man stepped toward the front of the group and raised his horn in the air, like a band conductor. Then the men and boys puffed out their cheeks like Dizzy Gillespie and blasted the air with the call of trumpets, trombones, bugles, and saxes. The women sashayed along the riverbank, their anklets and necklaces ringing like little bells. They waved long, thin sticks at the men and danced toward them and back again. And the men blew on their horns and jumped and leaped in the air until they were wet and lathered in sweat.

This was more than just music to plant beans by, and I asked Melesse what it meant. "It is a song," he replied through Zelalem—and one with a universal theme. "My girl has big breasts and a big behind; she is the shapeliest and most beautiful of all." It was a popular Gumuz tune, because Melesse told us later, the band played it three times.

The women invited Nevada and I into their line, and we danced back and forth with them. The horns blew loud and strong, and there was no other sound to be heard along the Blue Nile.

THE HEADMAN OF THAT VILLAGE, WHO CAME TO GREET US IN A worn but spotless gray suit and black shoes, and who carried an open umbrella, invited us to camp there that night. (Zelalem said that the "cadre leader," as he called the headman, "must have clothes like this, because he must sometimes go to government meetings in Debre Markos.") "He wants us so much to stay," said Zelalem. I would have done so on the spot. The singing and dancing would continue into the night, and we were lucky to be so celebrated and entertained.

Speaks paced the beach, presumably looking for a place to pitch our camp, but there was no question about his body language: we weren't staying. "Well, they've planted their crops everywhere, and I just don't feel right about putting our tents on their young beans," he said, although the headman had assured him that it was not a problem; the beans would survive.

Instead, we bid the band and headman goodbye and floated downriver another mile to another sandbank, where young bean plants were also beginning to sprout. We pitched our tents on top of these.

nineteen

〜〜〜

IN THE MORNING, NEVADA AND I HAD A QUICK HUDDLE. NEITHER of us was happy with Speaks's decision to pull us away from the dancers and village.

"Those are exactly the kinds of scenes I need," she said, "and I'm not getting them. It's great seeing people in mid-day, but the light is terrible then. It couldn't be worse." She had always wanted to camp close to the villages, but there hadn't been any along the upper part of the river. That had changed; there seemed to be villages every few miles. By camping close to these, we could visit the people at dusk and dawn, when the light was beautiful, and the people weren't away in their fields.

I agreed wholeheartedly. The previous evenings' villagers had been joyous and welcoming, and had dropped their work to dance and sing for us.

Nevada then called to Mick, thinking he would join us in pressing Speaks once again on this issue. He listened, but disagreed.

"There were too many people there last night," he said, concurring with Speaks's assessment.

Our journalistic trio had been getting along fine up to that point, but now our alliance began to unravel. Mick wouldn't support us. It seemed a fault line was opening between the rest of the group, and Nevada and me.

Nevertheless, Nevada and I brought up the matter with Speaks and managed to get him to agree to let us linger if we happened to chance on a similar scene farther down the river. It was irritating to have to ask for his permission for such things—or to be denied the chance to fully experience an unexpected, spontaneous celebration. I'd seldom encountered such difficulties when gathering material for a story, and I began to feel the bratty child within me stir.

I put my feelings aside as best as I could and once again rode on Speaks's boat that morning. Zelalem and Melesse rode with us and I asked Melesse about the Gumuz songs and music we had heard. Would we find other villagers who played so beautifully?

"He says, 'Yes, we can find them,'" Zelalem translated. "We can ask some other people. They will know a village with good musicians."

Several miles downstream, we saw more people on shore who waved and called to us. Speaks rowed over to them, and Melesse asked them where we might find more "*musicana dancen*," music and dancing.

The men conferred briefly. "They are from the village of Kwale," Zelalem translated. "They have a nice, big drum. Some men will carry it to the next village at Meten, and they will sing for us there." Meten was about an hour away by foot.

A man with his hair in short braids and several copper-and-aluminum studs in his ears offered to show us the way. He said his name was Ashegur Bugabaw, and he climbed on board our raft, and sat down between Zelalem and me. "He says he likes our car," Zelalem said, as Speaks rowed downstream. "Melesse has told him it is a boat. And he likes listening to us talk, to hear this foreign language."

I asked if he had any stories or proverbs about the Nile. "No, he doesn't have," Zelalem translated. "He says once the river washed away a corn crop near here. But they don't think about the river."

The villagers the previous night had drawn blank looks, too, when I asked if they had a song about the river. The farther away we got from the highland Orthodox Christians, the more the Blue Nile seemed to be only a river; it provided good soil and water for these Gumuz, and that was enough. To them, it was not the Abay or Gihon, it held no special spirit. It was simply the Dal, the Big River.

Ashegur was not as curious about our pale skins as the people had been the day before, until I referred to myself as "a ferenji." Then he jerked his head back, studied me closely, and pulled off my hat: straight hair, the tell-tale sign of a ferenji. "Aaaah!," he said, nearly fainting with amazement.

Zelalem and Melesse were choking with laughter. "He didn't know you were a ferenji," Zelalem said. "He has never seen ferenjocch before, and he didn't know he was sitting next to one. He cannot believe this. He thought you are looking like this—white—because you and all of us are just people from Addis."

Ashegur than gave me the full-tilt eyes-hair-skin inspection, but did so politely. "He is so happy to see you," Zelalem said. "He likes this hair."

At Meten, we tied up the boats to rocks along a steep, grassy bank and followed Ashegur through a sorghum field to a village that was arranged much like the first one we'd visited: about fifteen round huts set in a circle around a central courtyard, with a shady fig tree in the middle. Runners from Ashegur's village had already alerted the people here about our imminent arrival, and they'd placed long wooden benches and stools beneath the tree. Their were many exclamations and close examinations of our skin and hair, and once again, we three women had to prove our womanhood. None of us ever objected to this treatment, since we all were staring equally hard at our hosts and hostesses.

We loved studying the women, as much as they loved looking at us. Several of them had round, decorative scars on their cheeks, and wore jewelry cleverly fashioned from bits of Western flotsam--the blue caps of ball point pens, gun-shell casings, burned out flashlight bulbs, metal watch bands, zippers and safety pins. They'd strung these treasures together with colored glass beads on leather cords to wear as necklaces. Their arms shone with brass, copper and aluminum bracelets, and the lobes of their ears were bright with more beads, metals and bone. When they saw we were interested in their jewelry, they held up their bracelets and necklaces for a closer look, and we showed them ours.

All the musical instruments—the horns--at Meten were stashed on the roof of one of the huts. They were bundled together in a row on top of the thatch, and held in place by a long bar. A couple of the men and boys began taking them down, and readying them for the coming concert by spraying water from their mouths over them. One of the men explained that the water gave the horns (which he called duwa) a rich, full sound—just as wetting the reed of a clarinet improves its tone.

The men with the drum from Kwale then appeared. The drum was big, about three feet long and a good 18 inches in circumference, and they carried it between them on a long pole, like an antelope they'd speared in the forest. Other Kwale men arrived, too, holding their duwas.

"This is going to be a big jam session," I said to Nevada.

"Well, I wish it was a different time of day," she said, looking at the sun which was nearly overhead. "At least I've got the shade from this tree to help me." Otherwise, the hot sun would cause too much glare for her photos, and make the peoples' features dark and indistinguishable.

Once again, the music started up suddenly. Two men this time raised their arms and horns overhead. They stood back-to-back, each facing a semi-circle of men and boys with varying styles of long and short horns. At some unseen cue, they simultaneously dropped their arms, and the duwa blaring began. It was hot and the men blew their instruments as if they were highlanders summoning all the Abay's saints, kings, jinns, and spirits. They jumped in the air, swooped low toward the ground, and rocked from side to side, like rockers trying out for American Bandstand. Sweat poured down their faces and backs, and some stripped off their shirts, or stepped aside to take long drinks from a gourd. Their cheeks bulged, their eyes popped, and the music never stopped. Nevada crouched in the middle, her camera racing on motor-drive.

As before, the women had strapped on seed-bell anklets and necklaces, and danced—ching, ching, ching—back and forth in a skipping motion. They tilted their chins in the air, and waved their sticks at the men.

"This is a competition," Zelalem explained, after discussing the dance and two groups of musicians with Melesse. "The men from Kwale are playing their duwas against the men from Meten to see who has the best band." But it was a friendly competition, Zelalem added, and both sides would win. "They do it just to make everyone happy."

There weren't lyrics as such—the horns "sang" the songs. The tunes they were playing were old, going back to the time of their grandfathers. One celebrated their bravery as "people of the forest" who came to the river to settle; one teased the village of Meten for supposedly having only one glass of beer on hand to serve its guests; and one told about the beauty of the girls in the two villages, their firm bosoms, their tight behinds.

The duwa competition lasted well over an hour. The two band

leaders called an end to it when they could blow no more. We joined the other villagers in applauding. Then the men and women gathered in a circle around the big drum. They had placed it on its side, putting small blocks of wood under either end, so that it was raised about three inches off the ground. A tall young man squatted behind it. He reached his arms toward either end and beat out a slow, steady rhythm. One man began singing, his voice rising above the drum, and then the men and women joined together in the chorus: Ovanda, Ovanda. It was a long song, and ended with an act Madonna could have choreographed: A man took a young woman with a baby strapped to her back in his arms, straddled her, and rocked her toward him, up and down, up and down. Then the party broke up.

Later, Melesse translated this last song for us through Zelalem. Mick had taped it while he was filming, and he played it back for them. The song was bawdy in a frat-boy sort of way, as that last act had suggested.

"It is about a hero of the Gumuz, a man named Ovanda," Zelalem began. Then, as Melesse translated the words, Zelalem began laughing. "It's a little hard for me to explain," he said. He looked embarrassed. "What do you call this motion?," he asked me, poking a stick into the ground.

"Poke?," I said, beginning to guess why Zelalem was blushing.

"It's okay to use it?" He asked.

"It's a fine word."

"Okay. The song is something like this: 'Ovanda is a strong man and he comes from the forest. Ovanda is a hero. He crossed the river to poke a girl, and the people saw him. Ovanda is a hero. He has some love medicine, and he pokes all the girls. Ovanda is a hero. That is Ovanda's job, poking the girls. Ovanda is a hero."

"Well, 'sleeps with' or 'seduces' the girls might be a better translation," Mick and I suggested.

The Ovanda song had a melody and rhythm that reminded me of a recording of Congolese singers performing the Latin mass. It had been a lovely moment, standing beneath the big tree in Meten village, watching the Gumuz people link arms and sway to their drum and music. I'd even felt a little misty-eyed. Now I was laughing.

THAT NIGHT WE CAMPED ON A SANDY BLUFF—AND ON TOP OF ANOTHER bean crop, which were everywhere we'd discovered and impossible to avoid. Thick bushes crowded the beach behind us, and somewhere behind them, apparently not too far away, was a Gumuz village. It didn't take long for an admiring, curious group of people to appear. Many of the men were dressed in long, green robes, with colorful turbans; their faces had large, ornamental scars, and their front teeth were filed to sharp points, like a crocodile's. The women were equally stylish in printed sarongs tied around their necks, beaded necklaces, and brass bracelets. Both men and women carried long pipes made from leather and clay. They leaned on their walking sticks and spears, smoking their pipes and studying us.

Speaks went about his tasks as if the people were invisible, or made shoving motions with his hands to indicate that they should step back. He had not expected to find people on this beach; it was deserted when we landed. Only later, after the villagers arrived, did we spot the trail through the bushes that led to their homes.

Before night fell, the people quietly left. They'd come back in the morning, we knew, and Nevada was excited. "I know I'm going to get some good shots tomorrow," she said.

After dinner, as we sat on our chairs on our blue tarp, Bruce suddenly stood up. He had something to say about us as a group, he announced. He had noticed the "National Geographic people," as he referred to Nevada, Mick, and myself, talking amongst themselves— whispering, even—that morning. If we had something to say, he said, we should speak up and talk directly. He felt it was impolite to the others, and especially to our trip leader, Mike Speaks, who was working hard to guide us safely down this river and among these unknown people. Bruce went on awhile in a rambling kind of way, and then asked if anyone else had something to say.

I did. I let it be known that I was angry about being pulled away from the previous night's dancing. I didn't understand what there was to be afraid of—no one had attacked us or acted in a hostile manner anywhere on the river. The villagers were friendly and as we had all seen exceedingly honest. I said all the things I'd wanted Nevada to say at the beginning of our journey about this being a National Geographic expedition. My loyalty, I concluded, was to the magazine which had sent me here to get a story, and I was going to get it.

You could feel the fault line between myself and most of the rest of the group widen to an abyss.

The others took turns speaking, nearly all in defense of Speaks and his decisions. They talked about the fears and worries they'd felt on this journey and how he'd helped alleviate them. Then Nevada tried to find a Buddhist-path through the schrapnel bomb I'd dropped, and we all went to bed out of sorts.

We had a little more than one week left together. The different versions of our trip—what it was about and the events we'd experienced together—convinced me of one thing: We were all traveling down the Nile in our own Private Ethiopias.

Before the journey, we had each imagined that our biggest problems on the Blue Nile would come from the shiftas, crocodiles, malaria, and rapids. But the real difficulties we faced were the ones people encounter everyday, everywhere: trying to get along with each other.

THE VILLAGERS CAME BACK FIRST THING THE NEXT MORNING, AND Nevada had a fine time taking their pictures. They were a colorful lot, with delicate features and oval faces, and they seemed greatly amused by all our actions. They would watch us for awhile, then turn to each other, say something, and simply burst into laughter.

We had packed most of our gear, when I noticed that Ephrem had gathered our garbage from the night before in front of him. He had a small pile of plastic bags, empty beer bottles, a couple of tin cans, and an old cabbage. Some of the villagers stood around him, while he held forth in Amharic, making a big speech. His audience didn't speak the language, but they listened politely, as if he was saying something important. Zelalem, of course, understood every word, and he was nearly doubled over with laughter. Zelalem had once told me that Ephrem was a comic and a wit, saying things throughout the day that made Zelalem laugh. The jokes were always double and triple entendres in Amharic, very hard to translate, and therefore I could not easily appreciate them.

Ephrem seemed to be in good comic form that morning. He stood before the Gumuz people as if he was impersonating an ambassador. He gestured toward the largesse at his feet and talked with the intonation of a government official. I couldn't catch it all, but I got the gist of it when he mentioned "these fine gifts from the National Geographic and Mountain Travel-Sobek."

I caught my breath. Last night's encounter session had torn the curtain on how we ferenjocch felt about one another. And now Ephrem's routine lifted another one, revealing how our Ethiopian guides thought of us: as tightwads who handed out mostly junk and garbage to the impoverished but generous people we were traveling among.

I'd thought we'd been inching up the charity scale with the gifts of soap, razor blades and the occasional birr. Somehow, though, we had to be well-short of the mark for a scene like this to take place.

At lunch, I pulled Zelalem aside and asked him what we were doing wrong; how would Conrad have managed the gifts?

"Well, Conrad, the people always loved him so much," Zelalem began. "He invited them to stay with us. He had one tarp for them if they want to sleep by our camp, because he knows seeing the ferenjocch is special for them. And he gave them soaps, razor blades."

"We're doing that now," I said.

"Yes, but…," Zelalem shrugged. He didn't like to be critical. "Maybe a little more?… And it's good maybe to give the headman some birr, something small, fifteen or twenty. Then they can buy araki [the local hard liquor] and have a party to celebrate seeing us."

It would be a way for us to pay our respects to the local officials and for them to commemorate our visit. As Zelalem outlined it, the token gift-exchange wasn't all that different from what Cheesman had done on his survey treks along the Blue Nile, seventy-plus years ago. He had been a representative of a foreign country and government, and had stopped at various points along the way to greet the officials of the lands he passed through, and to present them with small gifts. We, too, were representatives of our countries and institutions—or at least the local people perceived us like this—and we needed to behave accordingly.

We had no reverse on our cars, as Zelalem had told Abush many days ago. We could not go back upstream to make up for our faulty behavior.

From this point on, however, I would ask Zelalem to tell me what things we should give out and how much.

WE SAW VERY FEW PEOPLE THAT DAY AND DID NOT VISIT ANY VILLAGES. We were entering a stretch of Gumuz country, Melesse told us, where few people lived, and eventually would once again travel through a completely uninhabited region. The lack of people was surprising because the river valley was broad and obviously held rich soil. Tall green grasses grew thickly on both banks, and the Nile purled between them with a slow, steady current. The river's pace had slowed considerably over the last few days to a two-to-three mile rate, and the boatmen now had to row to make up the difference. The river was no longer doing their work.

The wooded hills closest to the river were lush and green. The country looked untouched, pristine, but that was an illusion. Another group of people, the Limo, lived in the mountains beyond the hills and when the grass began to turn gold, they would move here, setting fires as they traveled.

"It's good for the land," Melesse said. The burning kept the forest open, making it easier for people to travel through, and encouraged the growth of new grass. They needed good grass like this for their thatched roofs.

When Nevada had studied anthropological maps of the lower Blue Nile, where we were now traveling, she had seen the names of several tribes in addition to the Gumuz. The Mande, Berta, Limo were all mentioned as river-dwellers. And they were, Melesse told us, but not at this time of year.

"Now, they live in the mountains," he said, pointing to the distant ranges. "They come here later, when the river is low, and when they can pan for gold."

That was another gift the Blue Nile gave the lowlanders, but not the people of the highlands: hard cash. In the past, though, most of the gold made its way into the highlands anyway, as taxes and tribute.

"The old governments always took from the Gumuz people," Melesse said through Zelalem. "But the new one is helping."

It had built schools, clinics, and mills for grinding their grains. In fact, Melesse added, that was one reason why no one lived here anymore in these rich Nile bottomlands.

"They used to live here, but they moved about four years ago because there is a school now in another area," Melesse continued. "The parents want their children to go to school. If they finish high school, they can get a government job."

He had himself finished grade four; his older brother had completed grade nine and now had a government job with the EPRDF.

I was still surprised that all the people would have moved away, leaving their good farm land behind. Zelalem was not.

"Of course, they want to move to a bigger town and where there is a school. A farmer's life is hard. It is better if their children have an office job."

The new government was bringing other changes, the most immediately obvious one being the custom of wearing clothes. In the not-so-distant past, Zelalem and Melesse said, the Gumuz went about naked. The men might wear a small loin cloth, and the women a grass skirt, but that was all. They covered their bodies instead with elaborate raised scars. We'd seen some of these on their cheeks and arms, but not the complete chest and breast patterns for which they were renowned.

"The government tells them now they must wear clothes," Zelalem said. "They cannot go to school without clothes."

It wasn't the usual practice to sit in an office in the buff either, and since that was now the career of choice, they were eager to wear clothing.

Our camp that night was along a stretch of the river called the "Western Cataracts." These were several short whitewhite runs, like wet staircases. The river had narrowed again and regained its speedy eight mile-per-hour flow. And once again the shores were a tumble of pink quartzes and black gneisses, with mountains rising up steeply behind them.

Nevada pulled out her telephone after dinner and suggested we call Conrad. We were about six days from Bumbadi, our take-out point, and she thought it would be fun to let him know that the trip had been a success. I dialed his number, and his partner, Cynthia Moss, answered.

"You're calling from the Nile and you're okay?," she repeated, as incredulous as all our family and friends were when we telephoned.

"Yes, and we want to tell Conrad that we're all thinking about him and that we've had a good trip. Is he there?"

"No. He's had to go back to the hospital for more treatments," Cynthia said. "He's doing fine."

I said we were sorry to hear that and we hoped he returned home soon. Cynthia was adamant: Conrad was fine, there was just something more his physicians wanted to do for him. She would tell him about our phone call. "He's going to be so happy to hear about this. He really wanted to lead this trip."

We wished each other well and said good-bye.

Despite Cynthia's assurances, none of us liked hearing that Conrad was in the hospital again. It didn't sound like good news.

twenty

THE ROCK DOVES WOKE US JUST BEFORE DAWN WITH THEIR
cooing, as they often did. Then the forest behind us erupted in
birdcalls—trills, squawks, whistles, and bells all sounding at once. Some
colobus monkeys hooted across the river, and we saw a small group feeding in the tops of the trees, their long black-and-white tails hanging
down like braided curtain pulls. We were once again in the forest and
among the animals.

There was never as much wildlife about, however, as a naturalist
might expect to find in such a remote area. Several Gumuz people had
told us that we would see big herds of hippopotamus at different points
along the river; we never did. We saw small groups of five or six, and a
couple of times saw mothers with their small black-and-pink babies,
but nothing that approached the huge herds early explorers on this part
of the Blue Nile had seen. There were elephants along the river at
the turn of the 20th century, and even in Cheesman's day. We did not
see any, and the villagers only shrugged when we asked. Even the

crocodiles were not as plentiful as we'd expected—we'd counted a total of 135 by our 16th day on the river—and they were not as big as the behemoths that had attacked some other rafters and kayakers. None of this was surprising given the numbers of automatic weapons that the villagers now had. Many of them told us they used their guns to kill the crocodiles, hippos, leopards, and lions. The game along the Blue Nile seemed to have been very nearly hunted out.

All the men with Kalashnikovs we'd met so far were members of their militias. They carried identity cards with their photographs as a kind of license. But Melese and Zelalem told me that morning, as we set out on the river once again, it was easy for any man to get such a weapon, especially here, close to Sudan, if he had the money. The Sudanese Peoples Liberation Army, which had long been trying to free southern Sudan from the government in Khartoum, had bases scattered throughout the Blue Nile Basin—and weapons from that war could easily be smuggled across the long Ethiopian-Sudan border. And there were other weapons left over from the Derg. When that government collapsed, many of its soldiers sold their weapons and fled.

"If you have 2,000 birr [$160.00], you can buy one," Zelalem said.

A man could make that kind of money if his crops were good, and if he had good cattle. He could sell them and buy a gun.

"Many people have them," Zelalem said. "They just don't show them."

The river turned south that morning, making another big meander before turning slightly north and west. We were losing altitude again—the rapids were a sign of that—and were at about 2,000 feet, and traveling at five miles an hour once more.

"This river really has a heartbeat, a pulse to it," said Speaks, giving short, steady forward strokes on the oars. "It slows down, gets a new burst of speed, and ticks right along."

The river ran through a narrow canyon lined in places with broad beaches shaded by the largest fig trees we'd seen. There were thickets of bamboo in these forests, too, and sweet flowering vines strung from tree to tree like party decorations. On a few previous days, we'd been unlucky and hadn't come across the usual freshwater streams and waterfalls; once we'd had to scoop rainwater from a rocky basin we'd found onshore for our drinking water. Now, though, we were once more in a land of plummeting waterfalls and silver streams. We took turns sitting for long stretches at the base of one pretty fall, lingering as if we might never find such a gushing bounty of clear water again.

By the next day, the river regained its width, and in no time we were in the midst of sorghum fields. Curiously there were no people about. We floated a mile, two miles, the boatmen rowing, their oars slapping the slow water, while Melesse and Mike Borcik shouted our, *"Nehgay! Nehgay!—Salaam! Salaam!"—* "Hey, everybody we're on your river."

No one appeared.

Then Melese pointed to a sorghum field a short ways downstream. He'd seen some children flee into it. We rowed along and tied up beneath a fig tree close to where the kids had disappeared.

Speaks broke out our lunch and we sat back, waiting.

Five minutes later, a small group of men accompanied by two young women and two little dogs burst out of the field. The men, of course, had Kalashnikovs. They came to a sudden stop when they saw us, then put their guns down and smiled.

"Nehgay! Nehgay!" they said, exchanging greetings with Melesse.

The children had run all the way to the village, they said, shouting in alarm to their parents, "Come quick, come quick! There is something big flying down the river."

They thought our boats looked like giant geese flapping downstream—

the rafts' long oars stroking the water in circles reminded them of a bird's wings.

Our visitors sat down on the riverbank above us, and we handed them some granola bars and a bag of kolo, the mix of toasted nuts and grains that Ethiopians love. One of the older men had seen the British here, but they had only motored by and waved, and since then they had never seen another ferenji on the river. Sometimes, though, they saw ferenjocch at their big market, a day's walk from here. The proximity of the market, we decided, explained why this group was so well dressed: they had good T-shirts, lots of copper and bronze jewelry, glass and shell beads, and everyone was wearing a pair of plastic shoes. One young woman wore hers beneath a red skirt; above the skirt, she was bare-breasted and "wore" the traditional scars. Circles, diamonds, and chevrons in raised flesh ran across her neckline, looped around her breasts, and covered her stomach. An equally fanciful pattern waltzed over her back. She was pretty and, we teased Melesse, would probably make a good wife.

"She could," he told Zelalem. "But it would be hard to arrange, because she lives too far from his home."

We gave them a generous supply of soap and razor blades, and an empty glass jar with a screw-on lid. "That is good for them," Zelalem said.

The Nile plowed on. It coursed its way between some small rocky islets that formed small ripples, cascades, and trains of whirlpools. Melesse laughed as the boats spun in big circles, and told Zelalem that he wished we could travel like this on the river for another month.

Zelalem liked to tease Melesse about his hunt for a new wife.

"I told him that he should raise some white teff [the best tasting and most expensive type of this millet]," Zelalem told me. "Then he could get a Gojami wife." (Gojami women are considered extremely beautiful and desirable wives, in part because they are not circumcised.) "But he says,

'No. She would cost too much, as much as one cow, so I don't want her.'"

Zelalem then offered to introduce Melesse to some girls from Addis. "Sure," said Melesse, "and then after we've been married one week, she'll take my ox and cows, and all my things and go back to Addis. Do you think I'm such a fool?"

No, the kind of wife Melesse needed, he later told us at breakfast one morning was "a good one from the Gumuz. A city wife wouldn't be any good for my farm. She couldn't follow behind my plow breaking up the clods of earth." He wanted a good, strong country gal.

The Nile made a big curve to the north and, after a few miles, another curve to the south, and we found ourselves at the broad mouth of the Didessa river—the old military stomping grounds of Zelalem and Melesse, although that camp was far from this confluence. The Didessa looked about as big as the Nile—or its mouth did anyway—and where they met, the two rivers easily flooded an area 600 feet across. We made camp that night on a bluff above the two rivers, looking north over the broad Blue Nile. Its green valley ran to the far horizon with only little bumps of hills breaking the plain.

It was the first time in weeks that we did not hear the Nile at night. Instead, we listened to the rain. It poured, pounded, and drummed against our tents, and drowned out the river. By daybreak, everything inside and outside our tents was sodden and sandy. I'd tried to stash my pathetic convict's uniform in a dry spot, but even it was damp. There was nothing to do, but put it on and wait for the sun.

Beyond the Didessa, the river flowed west and north again, turning now toward Khartoum. It cut through more sandstone and quartzite hills, some with big granite outcroppings at their summits. On the shores, we spotted baobab trees with their distinctive, swollen trunks and palms—good floral indicators of the lowland tropics we were now in. And we saw our first local boats. Two parties were crossing the river in dugout canoes on their way to a market upstream, and they stopped to greet us. Like the people we'd met the day before, they were well dressed and had plastic shoes and wristwatches. We were on the reentry path to Western Civilization.

In one of those modern ironies, though, the appearance of familiar cultural icons didn't mean we had reached a safe haven. If anything, the people we met along this last stretch of the Blue Nile were even more distrusting of our sudden appearance. Many of them had radios, and they knew the news of the world, especially the news of the Ethiopian-Eritrean war. They followed the war closely, since many Gumuz men were at the front. And there were other wars, too, close at hand: To the southwest, the Sudanese Peoples Liberation Army (SPLA) was battling to free southern Sudan; to the southeast, the Oromo Liberation Front was stirring up rebellion among pastoral Ethiopians.

Nevertheless, I was caught off guard by our reception in the next big village we visited, Abay Goma. We'd camped a 20-minute walk away from this town, but were soon met by a young man who spoke good Amharic, and who offered to show us the way.

"It's a nice village with a school—up to the third grade," he told Zelalem.

Nevada and I didn't wait. We grabbed cameras and notebooks, and followed Zelalem and the local man to his village. Mick trailed along behind. The trail wound through some sorghum and cottonfields, and along a pasture. We met two women who'd been panning for gold; they held their wooden gold pans at their side and showed us the results of their afternoon's labor: a single flake of bright gold.

The village sat on a slight rise and was dramatically pretty in the afternoon light, with a tower of pink-and-blue-and-gold thunderheads climbing the sky behind it. Nevada and Mick gasped and turned their lenses on the village's fine thatched homes, well-fed cattle, and handsome men and women. I followed Zelalem and the guide to meet the head-man. The homes were spread out here, and the headman's was a large, circular affair, surrounded by a low wooden fence.

"His name is Menshur Tatchew," Zelalem said as the guide introduced us. Menshur also spoke Amharic. He was about 30, and was dressed Western-style in gray trousers, a striped red shirt, and white plastic san-dals—and had two large scars like Mercedes-Benz logos carved on each cheek. He shook my hand limply, but did not smile. A scowl instead settled on his face.

"He is suspicious," Zelalem said. "He wants to know if we have per-mission to be here."

Zelalem said we did, but the permits were on our boats. We would bring them in the morning, or he could send someone with us now to look at them.

Menshur continued to scowl. By now a large party of men, includ-ing 22 armed militiamen, had gathered around us. A discussion ensued. They weren't sure we were tourists. They suggested a range of possibil-ities: invading Italians; Eritreans sneaking into the north to attack Ethiopia; Oromos joining up with the Oromo Liberation Front to do the same; or traders smuggling weapons to the SPLA. For a moment, I thought they would arrest us.

Zelalem, though, simply shook his head and said again, we were none of the above. "They are tourists who are traveling down the Blue Nile and have come to visit your town. And I am an Ethiopian, not an Eritrean. We have the permits, but they are on our boats."

Again Zelalem suggested that someone come with us to our camp to look at these. Menshur seemed to be on the verge of agreeing to this idea when a wild-eyed man in an olive green jacket stepped forward, gesturing wildly.

"How do you know they are who they say they are?" he demanded. "Why should you trust what they say? Maybe it's a trick. You'll go to their boats and they'll kill you there!"

Others joined in, shouting their opinions and demanding some proof that we were harmless.

Zelalem placed his palms together and faced our accusers. He made a slight bow, and repeated that we were only tourists and that it was impossible to travel up the Nile; they knew how rough a river it was, especially at this time of year.

"We are who we say we are," he repeated. "Our papers are in order; how else could we have traveled beneath the Abay and Gumare Bridges and be here? The soldiers would have shot us if we did not have their permission."

The temper of the crowd cooled as he spoke; even the wild-eyed man began to calm down. "I gave them a reasonable answer," he told me later, "and they understood this."

The reasonable answer still required proof, however. All 22 militiamen, the headman, and the chairman (an even higher personage), and various other officials and interested parties returned with us to our camp to inspect our documents. If Speaks was irritated when we showed up with this armed entourage, he didn't show it. He produced the permits, the headman and chairman wrote down our names and the numbers on the documents, and then everyone smiled and shook hands.

"Come back and see us in the morning," the officials said. "Our village and country is peaceful; enjoy it."

Some of the militiamen turned out to be friends of Melesse; they had trained together, and they sat around the fire drinking tea and enjoying our ferenjocch show.

Nevada and I were up before dawn. At last we had a village to visit early in the day. She wandered off, as she liked to do, getting pictures of villagers going about their tasks, while Zelalem and I visited several homes, as well as the one-room school and its sole teacher. He was an Oromo man who could not believe that anyone would take the trouble to visit a town like this.

"But you can travel anywhere," he said, a look of consternation on his face. "Why would you come here?"

Another man, Atenefew Kono, invited us to join his family for coffee, and asked much the same question. "Because it's good to travel and see distant lands, and because this is part of the world that Americans have seldom read about or seen pictures of," I said. "We'll share everything we've seen here with our friends in America." Atenefew nodded.

"He says this is okay, because you are Americans and Americans have never attacked Ethiopia," Zelalem translated. "And he says he'd like to travel to America for the same reason you are here."

Zelalem responded that the government controlled that kind of travel, but our host disagreed.

"He says the government has no control over him. He is a Gumuz," Zelalem translated, adding "and very proud."

Atenefew and several other Gumuz we talked to were equally proud of the school in their village. Their sons and daughters were enrolled; some had graduated and moved to another town to continue their education. "We must have our children educated," said one village elder, "so that the Gumuz can have what the Amhara and Oromo people have: roads, schools, clinics, office buildings. We would like these things here."

We'd been sitting in a round mud home, where the women still ground their grains with grinding stones chiseled from rock. The only light came from the fire on the cooking hearth and through the chinks in the wall and single doorway. But I didn't discount the peoples' dreams or their ability to attain them. They had a school, the first most of them had ever seen; the office buildings could not be that far behind. I felt the fire of ambition in Atenefew's home.

Before we left, the village's headman, Menteshur arranged a small musical performance for us—drums, a stringed instrument called a *krar*, and several phallic-looking horns made of clay and leather. First, they played a song of peace for us, marching around Menteshur's compound in a stately fashion. The next pieces, although not as raucous as the duwa bands, were charged toe-tappers, and a couple danced for us, the man leaning in toward the bare-breasted woman to lightly brush his shoulder against hers.

At the end, taking a cue from Ephrem, I asked Zelalem to tell them how much we'd enjoyed the music and our visit; that as visitors from National Geographic and America, we appreciated the way they had opened their village and homes to us. Zelalem then presented Menteshur with the small gift of birr. He nodded gravely, and put his right hand on his heart. For once, we'd done it right.

Then everyone, including the 22 militiamen, walked us back to our boats and called out "*Melkam gouzo*—Good travels," as we pulled away.

It was early afternoon by the time we left Abay Goma and we traveled only a short distance, about eight miles that day. The river had widened once more and its flow had slowed considerably. The next day, the boatmen decided they would lash the rafts together and mount the motor. We'd feel more like Cleopatra then, traveling by barge down the Blue Nile.

We camped on a sandy beach, strewn with large boulders. No people came to visit. Bruce had torn his raft on some sharp rocks, and the boatmen set about repairing this while the rest of us pitched the tents and helped Zelalem cut up some vegetables for a spaghetti dinner. Nevada had promised to telephone Maurizio in Addis that evening. He was to be leaving soon with a convoy of vehicles to meet us at the take-out, and they needed to touch bases once more.

The satellite telephone was much like a cell phone. Everyone in our group could hear the caller's end of the conversation, and just from the tone of Nevada's voice, I knew something bad had happened.

"When?" She asked.

There was a long pause.

"I see. Okay," and she sighed.

I guessed instantly: It was something to do with Conrad. As I asked her what had happened. She hesitated.

"Conrad has died."

My knees began trembling, but then I looked at Zelalem. He had put his knife down and turned away. He did not look at us but left the camp and walked toward his tent, sobbing.

"*Abbatye, abbatye, abbatye*...my father, my father, my father...my life and my light...I am lost...."

No one could console him.

FOR ALMOST A MONTH, I'D GONE TO SLEEP EVERY NIGHT LISTENING TO the sound of the Blue Nile. Some nights it had the deep-throated roar of the ocean, others the gentle lap of a lake's waters breaking onshore, and on others it rushed along like the determined river it was, cutting beneath the gravel banks where we slept. We often heard the sand and boulders give way, slide into the Nile's dark waters and join them on their journey to Khartoum.

But this night the river sounded like nothing but sadness, a never-ending stream of tears.

twenty-one

~~~

THE MORNING BROKE COLD AND CLOUDY; A GRAY DRIZZLE fell over the gray Nile. We were in a somber mood; we packed quietly. The boatmen steadied the rafts on the river, tied them together in a triangle, and mounted the motor on the trailing boat.

While they worked, we noticed a group of men assemble on the opposite shore. At first, there were only a few, and we assumed they'd come to watch our show, and simply waved to them. Within a few minutes, however, more had gathered, and each one, we now saw, had a Kalashnikov.

They began shouting to us in Gumuz, and one man wearing a dark suit jacket and white Muslim's cap waved a white flag.

"Melesse says they want us to stop there and show them our permits," Zelalem translated.

We boarded our raft-barge, Mike Borcik tested the motor, and we crossed the river with all the grace of a wallowing rubber dingy.

There were at least two dozen men apparently, since they were armed, from a local militia. Some were dressed in khaki uniforms, others in coats and jackets. Several wore turbans and had big tribal scars on their cheeks; all of them looked unhappy. They held their Kalashnikovs at the ready and clambered down to us the moment we landed.

Mike Speaks pulled out our sheaf of documents. He, Zelalem, and Melesse greeted the men. They were, as surmised, militiamen. Some of them spoke Amharic, and they formed a circle around Zelalem while Speaks knelt down at his side. Nevada and I stood nearby, watching.

One man wearing a soiled white turban took the permits. He frowned as he thumbed through them, and Zelalem pointed to certain ones. They stood together to read these. It wasn't going well. The man smacked the papers with his hand and gestured as if swatting a fly away. Zelalem's voice rose, a hint of anger in it. They scowled at one another. Then Zelalem tried again. He sounded exasperated. The other fellow, nursing his Kalashnikov in both arms, now turned his back and waved the papers away.

"They want us to go to their police station," Zelalem said.

It was a six-hour walk away. A cold, pelting rain had begun to fall, and the thought of a long walk to some distant police station made us look as unhappy as our hosts. Bruce was sick, lying on top of our barge and shivering from the cold and a fever. How would we get him there?

The men wanted to disarm Melesse, too. He wouldn't let them.

"Wherever my gun goes, I go," he said, holding it now with both hands.

Zelalem turned to the man who had flagged us down and again went over our papers and permits. The turbaned fellow intervened, and again they exchanged harsh words.

Later Zelalem told me that particular man only wanted to see one permit—the one from the governor of this region of Beni-Shangur. We didn't have it. "He didn't care about any of the letters from Addis," Zelalem said. "Not even the one from the army."

It was like the armed troop that had visited us in the highlands. They had also dismissed our papers from the central government, and had insisted instead on seeing one from their region's ruler. Since we did not have that document, they too had tried to make us "visit" their police station. It was as if the old, feudal days had never ended.

Zelalem kept hammering away at the man with the flag. He used the same arguments he'd used in the Abay Goma village. We weren't traveling up the Nile; we weren't taking weapons to any rebels; he was not an Eritrean. What proof did we have, this man finally asked, that other soldiers or militiamen had let us pass?

I turned to my notebook to find the headman's name from Abay Goma. And Ephrem had written down the names of all twenty-two militiamen at that village. He'd done it as a game, and now his idle amusement saved us a long, cold walk in the rain.

"Okay," said the flagwaver, "since you know his name, he must have said you could pass. We will let you go." The man with the turban nodded his agreement, but he did not look overjoyed about the decision.

Everyone else did. Suddenly the men were shaking our hands and asking about our country and our travels. They noticed Nevada's cameras and asked if she would take their photo. In the next instant, all the militiamen were jockeying with one another for the best camera angle and fiercest pose. One young fellow who had only a transistor radio, and no firearm, held it up as if he were taking aim at the enemy.

No question about it, these Gumuz militiamen were ready to defend Mother Ethiopia.

When we boarded our barge and pushed back on the river, they ran along the banks, waving good-bye.

For the next four days, we motored down the Nile. It had widened to a small sea in places, but still had enough power to form big, sucking whirlpools that sent our barge spinning. There were small islands, too, some dotted with trees and ferns like Japanese gardens. And always there were hills and mountains about. None of us had expected this. We'd thought that by now, this close to Sudan, the river would be fat and lazy, and we'd be hot and sweaty in the swampy lowlands. Instead, the terrain remained fairly mountainous, the river still had rapids, and the weather was cold and rainy.

Whenever we stopped for the night, Nevada and I would head for the hills and any villages. We'd discovered that the trails leading through the tall grass weren't necessarily only those left by hippos; they were often paths to someone's home. As soon as we spotted one, we were off, like two kids playing hooky.

Zelalem always came with us. We hiked through the grass and bushes, calling out, "Nehgay! Nehgay!…Salaam! Salaam!…and *Koyaes! Koyaes!*" an Arabic greeting Bruce taught us. This close to Sudan we could easily run into people who spoke nothing but Arabic.

Most of the people we met were Gumuz, and they were generally welcoming, inviting us into their homes for coffee or letting us just sit with them by their fires while we asked about their lives and Nevada took pictures. Some told us that they had once lived in Sudan but had fled about ten years ago, when invaders chased them from their homes. They traveled here, and the government gave them some land and seeds for crops. Now they had new houses, and a new life, and the government had promised to build a clinic in a nearby village. Their lives were good again.

One village headman's life was so improved that he now had two wives. "He is very busy, like Ovanda," quipped Zelalem, referring to the great Gumuz hero.

In another village we met an elderly woman who had never traveled farther than a big market town a day's walk away. She had lived her whole life here next to the river. There had been wars, famines, and droughts. She'd lost three of her children, and now had five grandchildren, several of whom lived nearby. She cradled one in her arms as she told us about the ebb and flow of her life along the Blue Nile.

Most of the Gumuz we met said they were Orthodox Christian (and therefore, they implied, Ethiopians), although in the past they practiced an animistic religion. Their animism had provided the highland Ethiopians with simply another reason to enslave them. One Ethiopian emperor had once decreed that no one who was Orthodox Christian could be a slave. When they learned of this, several Gumuz leaders sent a message to the king, begging him to make them Christians. He refused their entreaties. If they were Christians, who would be his slaves?

Other Gumuz we met were recent converts to a Protestant religion, the Ethiopian Makane Yesus Evangelical Lutheran Church, which was supported by missionaries in Norway. Our entire group had hiked several miles inland one day to visit the main mission along the river. It was headed by a soulful-eyed man, Stale Storaas, who had spent four years among the Gumuz, building a clinic and helping them adjust to the new government's many edicts.

"The Gumuz are under tremendous pressure to change," Stale told us. "They must now wear clothes, go to school, get jobs that pay cash— and this in a culture that does not like to see one person get ahead of another. We're trying to help them retain the best of their traditional values, to move into this new life as painlessly as possible." That was his chief goal, rather than changing their religious beliefs.

In the last few months, the government had enacted the biggest change of all: It had banned the Gumuz's custom of sister-exchange marriages. "Now, we can marry for love," said Stale's Gumuz assistant, Machochin, who spoke excellent English. He drew out the word—"luuuvh"—as if it held possibilities he had never dreamed of before.

So many of the Gumuz's social bonds were based on this marriage custom, Stale said it was hard to predict what the repercussions of suddenly ending it would be. The government's edict did mean that Melesse might have a better chance at a Gumuz wife after all—although we thought that "'love" wouldn't rank very high on his list of wifely traits.

Stale had told us that we would see more Amharas as we approached the border. "It's crowded in the highlands, and people are moving here to start new lives," he said. "They're bringing in more changes, new businesses, new ways of thinking. The life you see now along the Blue Nile won't last."

He was right. In the bigger towns, we met numerous Amharas. Some were traders who'd come to buy gold. They would transport it on their donkeys to the highland jewelry merchants whose workers would hammer it into finery. Others had opened little kiosks, selling soaps, safety pins, lanterns, and aluminum bowls. One enterprising couple had started a small coffee- and teahouse. There were refugees in these larger villages from the days of the Derg, and some from the Sudan. There were Muslims, and Oromos, and people from the hill tribes—the Limo, Birte, and Mande. There were even a few Tigreans from the far north. People from every province were washing up along the distant shores of the Blue Nile, adding new layers of life, new social strata, and customs.

Every day now, we saw boats on the Blue Nile. There were small dugout canoes, shaped from single tree trunks, and smart ones like sleek skiffs, and there was one large dory that the people used as a ferry boat to get from shore to shore. People used the ferry to travel to the big Thursday market at Tamare, which we also visited. All the new trappings were on sale here: plastic shoes, wristwatches, soaps, and T-shirts. The traders had brought these goods in on their donkeys, they said. You could reach Tamare here even faster by car, they added, since there was a road a half-day's hike away.

A road—that was "the" road in our minds, the one Maurizio would be driving down to meet us. He could have been on it at that very minute, for all we knew.

We spent two more nights on the Blue Nile, one camped outside Tamare, the other—our last—alone on an empty shore. Nevada had asked Speaks specifically to find a spot with a village, but we'd ended up by ourselves instead. She and I did find a trail, and we set off on it with Zelalem, but it led only to crops, and although we called, "Salaam! Salaam!" no one came to greet us.

"I think maybe there was someone there," Zelalem told me as we walked back to camp. "But maybe they think we're with the SPLA, so they won't come see us."

The magic of our tarik had worn off. We were traders or arms merchants or rebels—something big and dangerous that had come down the Blue Nile, but no longer possessed of magical wings.

THE BLUE NILE CHANGED, TOO, THE NEXT MORNING. WE WOKE UP to a pretty dawn with steamy mists and fogs rising off the water, and draping the mountains. We packed and pushed the barge onto the river for the last time. Not far downstream, the water slackened its pace. We all felt it. We were not yet at the border, and still about 50 miles from the Roseires Dam, but already it had caught and trapped the Nile. The river's frisky spirit was gone. There were no rumbling stretches of white water; there were no demons or kings in its depths. We began to call the river Lake Abay.

We motored on. We had only a few miles to travel that morning, and soon were down to a mere mile. But even Lake Abay had a last trick: A sudden patch of big boulders appeared in the middle of the river.

"Holy moly!" shouted Mike Speaks. Borcik slowed the motor, while Speaks climbed up on his center platform and guided Borcik through this last, unexpected stony obstacle course. Below the rocks, we hit a final little run of rapids and several huge whirlpools.

"This Abay," Speaks said. "I tell you, it is one river of surprises."

The way ahead appeared calm and open—just a wide stretch of water between two green banks dotted with big baobab trees and boulders. We'd passed several groups of people. Some had waved, some ran off (apparently fearing we were with the SPLA), while others had just stood and stared. And then there was no one, not a soul on shore. It was as if the world had fled at our approach.

Speaks began to get nervous.

"Well, we should be seeing that road and Mau right along here," he said, scanning ahead with his binoculars.

We watched the shore carefully for a break in the crops or bushes that might suggest a road. And then, suddenly, there was Mau, right on the riverbank.

"Hey," he called to us. "You made it."

We had.

twenty-two

~~~

IT HAD TAKEN MAU AND HIS CARAVAN OF FIVE LAND CRUISERS three-and-a-half days of hard driving from Addis to meet us at Bumbadi. One vehicle hadn't made it; it was stuck in the mud some distance from the border town. Mau spotted a man from a government agency driving a small pickup truck into the town, and he begged the man to help us. We had a lot of gear and people to haul out, and the fellow had kindly agreed.

"We got stuck a million times," Mau said about their overland version of our journey to Bumbadi. "The story is mud, mud, mud; bridges washed out—everything you can imagine."

We unloaded the rafts, and the boatmen deflated and dismantled them. Then we—and several of the townspeople, whom Mau hired—carried everything into the town center, where we began loading the vehicles.

Bumbadi seemed to exist because of the border. It was a ramshackle town of peeling, whitewashed buildings and dirt streets. Two big fig trees in the central court provided some shade. Aside from the border, there was no other apparent reason for the town to be larger or better equipped—with a couple of fly-blown restaurants and small government offices providing gainful employment—than any other village we had passed in recent days. The local Bumbadians didn't seem to know quite what to make of us. A crowd quickly gathered—a mix of Sudanese, Arabs, Gumuz, Amharas and Tigreans. There were women dressed in long, colorful robes with bright veils that blew in the breeze, and children who stood in a row against a building and never took their eyes off of us, and numerous soldiers and militiamen milling about. They studied us intently and shook their heads at the idea of our long journey.

"This is such a nice travel you have made," a Tigrean gold trader told me. "It is something famous for Ethiopia. But I think it was hard."

"No, not too hard," I replied. Then I looked down at my convict's uniform. It was by now nearly the color of the Blue Nile, and hung on me like my brother's old hand-me-downs. All of us had suffered with a minor complaint at some point—a stomach bug, foot rot, a fever—and at other times we'd been hot and tired, or cold and tired. And yet, these were small problems. We were 560 miles from our starting point at Lake Tana, and I at least was thinner and certainly dirtier than at the beginning, but we were well.

Mike Speaks and Mike Borcik decided to put most of the river bags with our personal gear onto the borrowed pickup truck. Nevada and I weren't going back to Addis with the rest of the group. We were traveling with Mau and his assistant, Ermes Kifle, to Mount Gishe and the source of the Blue Nile, so we loaded our stuff in Mau's car. Speaks stopped by to see if we had everything. We did, we told him; we were ready to go. Then he looked at Nevada.

"Nevada. Put your seat belt on," he said, giving her one last command.

For once, Nevada almost lost her Buddhist-cool. Her mouth opened as if she was about to finally send the Captain and his orders packing.

But she didn't. Her back stiffened slightly, and she turned instead to Mau and asked idly. "You were saying that the roads were muddy?" She did not put on her seat belt.

Speaks, I decided, couldn't help himself. He'd told us early on that he never would change, and true to his word, he didn't. He could never stop giving Nevada orders, and he could never find a way to trust the Ethiopians.

It's said that you can't choose your family, and so it was with our "team." We hadn't chosen each other for travel mates; the fates had tossed us together. We'd tried to get along as best we could, but I was relieved that we were parting, that we weren't traveling together for life.

As Mau had promised, there was lots of mud on the track leading to the main highway. We had to camp on the road that night. Our permit troubles finally caught up with us there. The police came in search of us, and once again we were handed an invitation to headquarters. And once again, we evaded it, but only because Mau and one of the other drivers went in our place to sort things out. It seemed that our old friend, the turbaned, scowling fellow in the last militia group, had reported us—not only were we missing a permit, he'd also seen us taking photographs at two o'clock in the morning. Indeed, one night Bruce had risen every hour or so to photograph the moon in the night sky. That was all, but someone had seen him do it. We had been spied on.

Like Zelalem, Mau was a good diplomat, and somehow—mostly by swearing on his grandmother's grave that he would stick his hand in a fire if we'd done something wrong—we were given a final reprieve.

We hit the main highway and made good time. At the town of Injibara, where buses, trucks, donkeys and goats jostled together on the road, our paths separated. All the vehicles, except Mau's, took the highway to Addis Ababa. For the boatmen, and Mick and Kate, the trip was over. They were checking their hotel reservations, their airline tickets. Their thoughts were of home.

We said good-bye, exchanging hugs and handshakes. Melesse left us here, too. He'd received good wages and a fat tip for his time with us, and had enough money to add a cow and bull to his farm. "With that, he can get a wife," Zelalem said, even if Melesse didn't have a sister to exchange, and even if he wasn't in love. Some good, clod-busting Gumuz woman would see that he was a man of worth, and marry him.

Nevada and I also said goodbye to Ephrem and Zelalem. Zelalem would help look after Conrad's equipment, and begin making plans to send his nephew Hailu to a boarding school in Addis. I would call him, I said, when I returned to the city.

Then we were off.

Mau popped a tape of Ethiopian music in his recorder. A famous singer, Muhammad, serenaded us with love songs the Ethiopians have sung for more than one hundred years. I laid back and shut my eyes, and let the haunting, undulating rhythms carry me away.

FOR THE NEXT THREE WEEKS, NEVADA AND I MADE SHORT JOURNEYS to other regions of the Blue Nile. At the source, priests who rule over the holy springs told us women were not allowed. What would happen to us if we violated the order and touched the water?

"You will die," said a priest.

Oh.

Instead, we sent Mau and his assistant, Ermes Kifle, inside the sacred enclosure to spy on the springs for us, and we followed another guide to the second most holy spot at the source where even women are allowed. Here, a wooden pipe funneled water from the spring into a small, natural pool. I held my hands beneath the pipe and let the cold, clear waters spill through my fingers and sprinkle on the pebbles in the pool. These were the waters that begat the Blue Nile. They circled the pool, seeming to gather strength and momentum, and then flowed into a tiny channel, making a first cut in the earth on their way to the sea.

I washed my face and hands, and poured some of the water on my hair. Our guide nodded his approval. "Now you'll return to the Abay," he said, as if it were already a fait accompli.

Ermes found us there. "Oh, I am sorry you cannot go inside," he said. A young man of 25, he had a square-face and chiseled jaw, and he set about describing what he had seen. "It is really incredible. It looks just like a small thing, a pool only five or ten centimeters deep [about two to four inches], but the priests said, 'Take care! Stay on the path! The water is deep there.' They said it is more than 100 meters deep [about 30 feet], and if you fall in, you may die." There were actually several small pools, each one a part of the source, and all edged with grasses and mosses.

I wondered if our local guide, Melku Alemaw, or the holy instructor Marigeta Birhane Tsige (who led us to the summit of Mount Gishe) had ever heard of James Bruce, the Scot who journeyed here more than three hundred years ago. The emperor had given him the font of the Blue Nile as a gift, I said. But neither of the two Ethiopians had ever heard of the tall, red-haired ferenji or his claim on their holy waters. They dismissed the notion. Besides, in their opinion there was a far more important person associated with the springs. His name was Saint Zarabruck, and he too had come to the source some three hundred years ago. It was he who had given the springs their name, Gishe Abay. Saint Zarabruck had performed so many miracles that even today people came from all over Ethiopia to pray to him and hear the priests relate the tales of his good deeds. The saint had been born blind, Marigeta Birhane told us, but at age seven, he found an *enku*, a pearl more precious than gold, and he swallowed it. "His eyes opened and he became strong," the priest told us, "and the Holy Spirit, which was inside the pearl, entered him." After that, he glowed from within like a candle on the church altar. He prayed ceaselessly and did countless good works, and because of that the angels caused 12 white wings to sprout from his body, 6 on each side from his shoulders to his feet.

"But that created a lot of rumors," the priest continued, "so the government arrested him and put him in prison." Just before going to jail, Zarabruck dropped his prayer books into the springs of the Blue Nile and asked the Abay to protect them. "He was held many years, and had no light or contact with anyone. Once in a while, they fed him a little injera. And then one day a light like a rainbow came into his cell, and when the government people saw this, they set him free." Zarabruck returned to the springs and said to the water, "Gishe-Abay…Abay, toss up my books." And the books shot up from the depths of the water. "Even though they had been in the water for five years," the priest said, "the books were still coated with the same dust" they'd had on them when Zarabruck dropped them in the water. "They were not spoiled in any way."

Zarabruck's books had been lost over the years, but the priests living by the springs had collected the story of his life and miracles in *The Book of Zarabruck*. That was the book from which they read when people came to be blessed at the source of the Blue Nile at Gishe Abay.

Even the silt from the spring was holy. Priests dried it on the altar in Saint Michael's Church of Gishe Abay and sprinkled the resulting gray powder into the containers of holy water that worshipers brought. Then, making the sign of the cross over the assembly, they anointed each person's head and body with the silty liquid. The pilgrims were now protected, they were healed, their weapons would shoot straight, their cows would give good milk, they would bear a child, their male member would once more stand erect, they would lose their hunchbacks, the curses of the buda would be erased, the bombs of the foreigners would lose their power.

We asked the priests if we could give a gift—a sacrifice—to the source of the Abay, and after some discussion, it was agreed that in two days' time, we would offer a fat sheep. In the meantime, we would take a short pony trek along the Little Blue Nile. Melku, our local guide and a district officer, had promised to introduce us to Ehmama Gojam, a prophetess who lived in a forest along the Gilgel Abay, as the Ethiopians call this river.

It took us most of the day to reach her home in the woods. Like the Big Abay, the Little Blue Nile grew in size and volume as numerous tributary streams and rivers rushed into its channel. It ran through the green Gojam highlands, cascading through valleys and mountains bright with purple lupine and yellow daisies. Everywhere there were farms with crops shooting up green and strong, and sleek cows, horses and sheep grazing in the meadows. No wonder Menelik had asked Castanio, the Italian engineer, to build a bridge to Gojam—it was a rich land as the Rases of old well knew.

It was a land, too, of magicians—of priests with tricks up their sleeves and farmers who knew sleight of hand. The day before, our priest-guide, Marigeta Birhane showed us how he could boil water without fire. The bubbling brew (which he held in a glass as it boiled and fizzed, something like Alka Seltzer) would make a shy person confident, he told us, or the dull witted, smart. He could also whip up a concoction that would cure someone with a snake bite; even if the bitten person did not come to see him in person, another could drink the medicine, while the priest read from his prayer book, and the other one would be healed.

As we rode through the countryside, Melku pointed out the homes of other men with powers. There was one who could turn leaves into money, he said, although regrettably, the change did not last. And there was the house of another, who could command a rope to behave like a snake.

But none of these people had the power of Ehmama, the Mother of Gojam, as Melku called her. She could foresee the future. She had come to the Gilgel Abay almost 40 years ago, in the time of Haile Selassie, Melku said. It had been her practice to follow the priests when they carried the tabot (the replica of the Ark) on processions through the countryside. One day, as the procession wound its way along the Little Blue Nile, the angels spoke to her. "They told her to stop and live in those woods," Ermes translated for us. "And she has lived there ever since. She lives only on fruits and leaves, and whatever the monkeys bring her. She refuses any gifts and will not even eat injera." Because of her dedication to the Holy Spirit, she had been given the gift of prophecy. Melku regarded her as his spiritual advisor and often made this journey to hear her pronouncements. He would ask her to talk to us.

The trail led between fine crops of sorghum and tef, and thick stands of eucalyptus. Then we left the main road, and led the ponies down a hill to a forest of acacia and olive trees.

"She lives in there," Melku said, pointing with his chin. He called a greeting to her.

Nevada, Mau, and I hung back a short distance, not wanting to surprise her with our white skins. We saw some movement in the woods, and then the short, bent figure of a woman, dressed in a cotton robe so old and worn it looked like leather. Leaves and sticks poked from her gray hair, which was wrapped like a turban around her head. She grasped a sturdy walking stick in each hand and came slowly toward Melku. Then she spotted the three of us and stopped.

Melku stepped forward. We ferenjocch were friends of his, he said, adding that the two foreign women had made a long journey along the Abay. We had come to seek her wisdom now, just as we had sought the wisdom of the Nile.

Ehmama Gojam turned her stooped body toward us, but would not look at us directly. She cast small glances up the hill, then shook her head.

"She says she can't talk to us," Mau translated, "because she says, 'I am black and you are white. How can we talk?'"

Mau showed her how. He greeted her in Amharic and begged her to stay, saying we had made a long trek to meet her.

Ehmama Gojam stopped and looked at him.

"She says she is not a person from the earth, but she has come here from the sky," Mau translated.

She started back toward her forest home again, but stopped once more, and gave Nevada and me a long look. Then she spoke in a sing-song voice, the words rising and falling with the cadence of a bird's song.

"I don't believe it," Mau said. "She says she knows you had trouble with the government in Beni-Shangur. You are to stay away from there now."

She came close to me and looked me in the eye. "She wants to know your father's name," Mau translated.

"Lyall…Lyall Morell," I said.

The old prophetess sniffed, and then spoke at length again.

Mau gave a low whistle. "She says she knows we bought a sheep to make a sacrifice at Gishe Abay tomorrow. She says we are not to do it. She says, 'The blood that's running from that sheep you bought will come against you. It will cause you nothing but trouble.'"

She stood silently for a moment, swaying slightly as if she were as light as a leaf and waiting for the next breeze to blow her back to her sky home. And again she spoke.

"What you were looking for on the Blue Nile, you did not find," she pronounced. She said nothing more to us, but turned and started back toward the woods.

"I think she's finished," said Mau.

We watched her make her way slowly into the shrubs. Then she stopped once more, seemed to hesitate, and walked back up the hill to us, very deliberately this time. She had a message to deliver, she told Mau.

"She wants to know when you are leaving Ethiopia," he translated.

"In about a week," we said.

"She says you should not leave then. You must wait until the beginning of Timkat, the next Ethiopian month. That's about three weeks away. You can't get home until the first of Timkat, she says."

Nevada and I looked at each other.

"Well, it's a nice idea," I said. "But I can't do it."

"Neither can I," said Nevada. "I've got lots to do at home."

Ehmama Gojam didn't wait to hear about our schedules. She'd made her final pronouncement, and now left us without another look or word.

It had clouded up during our visit, and as soon as she departed a blast of thunder shook the ground, and lightening lit the distant peak of Mount Gishe. The skies opened and we rode the long distance back to our little mud-room hotel in a hard, cold rain.

"You know, every drop of this water is going to the Blue Nile," said Mau as we sat drenched and shivering on our wet ponies.

THE NEXT DAY, WE RETURNED TO SAINT MICHAEL'S CHURCH AT GISHE Abay. A big funeral service was under way for a nun and priest who had recently died. Men came in blowing trumpets and leading riderless horses to honor the dead, and women wept and tore at their faces until they bled.

Afterwards, Mau talked to the priests about the sacrifice we had planned. Our sheep was tethered outside the church, and Mau offered to share its meat with all those who'd come to the service.

Instantly, a huge debate erupted. Priests in colorful vestments began shaking their fingers at one another, and then at us and Mau. Their voices grew hot and angry. Some turned away in disgust. Mau pleaded. The oldest priest shook his head, then turned on his heel.

There would be no sacrifice.

"Everyone is quarreling over our sheep," Mau said. "Can you believe it? I can't even give it away!"

Melku was with us. He said two words: "Ehmama Gojam."

EHMAMA GOJAM SURFACED AT EVERY TURN. WE WANTED TO VISIT villages at the mouth of the Little Blue Nile, and to trek to the main river through the cattle country of the Borana herders. Every plan went awry; something always delayed us. One week turned to two, and two weeks crept ever so slightly toward three.

It was almost the beginning of Timkat, and we had not yet found a way to give the Blue Nile an offering.

Nevada and I traveled separately for awhile. I went off to Kenya to visit friends, while she stayed in Bahir Dar to fly over the Little Blue Nile for aerial shots of the river's mouth, where it poured into Lake Tana. Nevada exclaimed over the beauty of this stretch of the river, which she, Ermes and Mau also visited by boat.

"You would not believe the bird life," she said when we met again in Addis. "And the way the people live there! The waters of the Little Blue

Nile have flooded their homes; there is standing water inside their houses. But they're not the least bit upset. They say they love the Abay—they call it Gihon—and they say even when it comes into their homes like that, they never leave. It protects them, and they have refused every attempt the government has made to move them."

Nevada wished I'd been there with them.

I did, too. "So, I'll get Ermes and go back," I said.

"I'm coming, too," Nevada said.

We left the next day. We'd be gone only a few days, and I could still catch a plane home before the first of Timkat. I booked a seat on it.

All went well at the village at the mouth of the Little Blue Nile, although the river had dropped since Nevada's first visit. No longer was water sloshing through peoples' homes; now it lapped a few feet from their front doors. No one seemed to mind.

"Look at all that Gihon gives us," said Watadnu Getenet Abba, a farmer of about forty. Like many people of Gojam, he had a long, oval face and thin, aquiline nose, and he used his chin like a pointer, aiming it now at the river, now at the village's fat cows.

"We always have food and a good life because of Gihon," he said.

Watadnu Getenet sat with a group of men under a row of eucalyptus trees, talking to us through Ermes and a government official, Chernet Tilahun, who had joined us on our visit. After we had visited awhile, Chernet asked if they would help us give a gift to the Abay. The men looked at each other. It might be possible, said one. A few nodded in agreement. But a few hesitated.

"You know," Chernet explained to us. "It's not the season for making sacrifices to Gihon. Some of them are a little worried that an offering now may cause trouble. But the others have said, 'Let us try.'"

For our offering, we bought three chickens—one red, one white, one brown—a fat sheep, a sack of coffee and a bottle of *araki* (grain alcohol). A mother and daughter put on clean, white dresses embroidered with elaborate crosses, and prepared the coffee. After roasting the beans, they first wafted its fragrance toward the river and the spirit of Gihon, and then to us and the other villagers. The first sip of coffee was given to Gihon, too, as was the first shot of araki. A turbaned man tossed this to the river, and his friends called out, "Now, careful there. Don't give him too much. Save some for us." Then a round of drinks was served to everyone.

Three men stepped forward to offer the chickens. They stood in a row along the bank and sliced the chickens' throats, and held them over the water so that they bled into Gihon's belly. They placed the carcasses on the water and watched for a moment. The carcasses floated. Another group of men cut the sheep's throat, again bleeding the animal into the water. They removed its intestines and placed the steaming mass on the river. These, too, did not sink, but floated off downstream toward the Little Blue Nile's junction with Lake Tana.

The villagers smiled and relaxed.

"That's a good sign," said Watadnu Getenet. "Gihon is surprised by this unexpected offering, and he is happy. He will give you his blessing."

The chicken and sheep meat was salted and rubbed with spices and grilled over an open fire, and then, like Gihon, everyone feasted until we could eat no more.

OUR FLIGHT THE NEXT AFTERNOON TO ADDIS FROM BAHIR DAR WAS delayed, rescheduled, then delayed again.

"Ehmama Gojam," Ermes said, while we fretted over our plans.

I was lucky, or so I thought. The plane had finally arrived, and I reached Addis with just enough time to catch my rescheduled flight home. Nevada stayed for two more days to take aerial shots of the Big Abay, something that had taken several weeks to arrange. She would fly home on the day Ehmama Gojam had pronounced, the first of Timkat. I left the day before.

And everything was fine, until I hit San Francisco. I was only an hour's flight from home now, and close to Michael, our home, our pets. The plane was delayed, rescheduled—then canceled. I had to check into an airport hotel. Ermes, of course, was no longer with me, but I could hear his voice, "Ehmama Gojam."

Nevada left Ethiopia on the first of Timkat, and I finally arrived home that same day.

I'd brought a little vial of Blue Nile water home with me and I set that on our kitchen counter. An Ethiopian would drink it or bathe in it, but I kept it bottled like a genie. I did not want to break the spell the Abay had cast over me.

I cannot end this book without relating the last tale we heard about the orphan Abush, the Original Budget Traveler.

Mau told us that he had bumped into Abush at the Second Portuguese Bridge after Abush had called to Zelalem and me from across the river, begging us to drive our "cars" back to pick him up. We'd last seen him in the care of a soldier.

Mau and his men were preparing to trek back to the highland town of Mota, where they'd left their vehicles. It was already dark when Abush approached him. Could he join Mau's caravan, Abush wondered.

"The poor kid," said Mau. "He looked like he was having a rough time, so I gave him an extra paddle to carry for us."

Abush walked all night carrying the paddle to Mota. Once, he stumbled and fell "face first" on the trail, said Mau. "But he just picked himself right up and kept walking. He didn't even cry." That sounded like our plucky, dog-bitten little friend all right.

When they reached Mota, Mau gave him ten birr (about 80 cents). It wasn't enough to buy a shoeshine box, but it would take a traveler on a budget a fair distance in the land of the Blue Nile.

Beyond that, we could only guess at Abush's destiny.

acknowledgments

MY JOURNEYS ON AND ALONG ETHIOPIA'S BLUE NILE RIVER were made possible by many people and institutions, some but not all of whom are mentioned in this book. Thanks must first go to my editors, Oliver Payne and Robert Poole, at *National Geographic* for proposing the trip to me, supporting me on the river expedition and treks, and publishing my article about these adventures.

In Ethiopia, I would like to thank the commissioner for the Ethiopian Tourism Commission, Yusuf Abdullahi Sukkar, who helped our party travel safely in his country despite the-then border troubles with Eritrea; Maurizio Melloni of Wonz-Dar Expeditions, who first gauged the length of our trip by tracing the river's course on a map with a piece of dental floss, and then worked tirelessly to obtain the many necessary permits; and Red Jackal Tour Operator Yohannes Assefa and his drivers who ferried supplies to us along the way.

In the National Geographic offices, I am also indebted to Elsa Abraham, who helped translate the Amharic poetry I collected, and our expedition's Ethiopian government permits, and to Karen Font and Valerie Mattingley for their assistance with research materials. Valerie did a masterful job locating a copy of Major Cheesman's unpublished autobiography and other biographical materials about this rather self-effacing great geographer. Many heartfelt thanks, too, to my editor Kevin Mulroy, for asking me to write this book, and to Johnna Rizzo for assisting with the manuscript.

I want to especially thank Rahel Fikre Selassie for reading the entire manuscript on very short notice, and offering insights into Ethiopian customs and the Amharic language. Special thanks are also due to Jon Kalb and John Kappelman at the University of Texas, Austin for their explanations of the geology of the Blue Nile gorge.

I wish also to thank my research assistants, Mwangi Njagi and Richard Shackleford, for ferreting out numerous out-of-print volumes and articles about Ethiopia and previous Blue Nile journeys.

Many thanks as well to my agent, Michael Hamilburg, for once again offering me his sage advice and great support during all the phases of writing this book.

And I give my very deepest thanks to my husband, Michael McRae, who, although he has never traveled to Ethiopia, understands my affection for the country and its people, and who was there—as he always is—as friend and helpful critic.

Lastly, although they may never see my book, I would like to thank all of the people I met along the Blue Nile for their generosity and many acts of kindness. They opened their homes and shared their lives, music, stories and poetry with me. Most of all, they made me feel part again of a country I once loved and lost. For all of this, I am forever grateful.